"Danbo Wang has written a timely and courageous work centering non-Western voices in the spiritual formation conversation. . . . Her findings challenge educators and ministry leaders to examine cultural assumptions embedded in formation practices. This book should be required reading for anyone serious about intercultural theological education and spiritual formation for the global church."

—**Jamie N. Sanchez**, Chair, Doctoral Department, Talbot School of Theology, Biola University

"Wang has provided a superb model for assessing the cross-cultural impact of a spiritual formation program at a North American seminary. . . . How encouraging to see the ways that Chinese students reexamine assumptions from their upbringing and become more dependent on God!"

—**Kenneth Nehrbass**, author of *Advanced Missiology*

"By engaging in cross-cultural dialogue, Wang deepens awareness of Confucian values within spiritual formation and contributes meaningfully to ongoing conversations about faith, culture, and formation in a global context."

—**Eunice Hong**, Director of Research and Assistant Professor of Ministry, Wheaton College

"*In Cross-Cultural Spiritual Formation*, Danbo Wang offers a compelling qualitative study of transformative learning at the intersection of Confucian culture and Western Christian spiritual formation. . . . This book is a valuable resource for spiritually and culturally sensitive educators, ministers, and mentors in seminaries and churches."

—**Soo-Young Lee**, Director of the PhD in Educational Studies Program, Grace Mission University

Cross-Cultural Spiritual Formation

Cross-Cultural Spiritual Formation

Chinese Seminary Students' Transformation at a North American Seminary

Danbo Wang

Foreword by Leanne M. Dzubinski

WIPF & STOCK · Eugene, Oregon

CROSS-CULTURAL SPIRITUAL FORMATION
Chinese Seminary Students' Transformation at a North American Seminary

Copyright © 2026 Danbo Wang. All rights reserved. Except for brief quotations in critical publications or reviews, no part of this book may be reproduced in any manner without prior written permission from the publisher. Write: Permissions, Wipf and Stock Publishers, 199 W. 8th Ave., Suite 3, Eugene, OR 97401.

Wipf & Stock
An Imprint of Wipf and Stock Publishers
199 W. 8th Ave., Suite 3
Eugene, OR 97401

www.wipfandstock.com

PAPERBACK ISBN: 979-8-3852-6619-7
HARDCOVER ISBN: 979-8-3852-6620-3
EBOOK ISBN: 979-8-3852-6621-0

VERSION NUMBER 04/09/26

Unless otherwise noted, all Scripture quotations are taken from the *New American Standard Bible*® (NASB), © 1960, 1962, 1963, 1968, 1971, 1972, 1973, 1975, 1977, 1995, by The Lockman Foundation. Used by permission.

Contents

List of Tables | vii
Foreword by Leanne M. Dzubinski | ix
Acknowledgments | xi

1 Introduction | 1
2 Literature Review | 8
3 Methods and Procedures | 58
4 The Impact of Spiritual Formation on Chinese Students | 69
5 Transformation Through the Program | 107
6 Mechanisms and Applications of the Program | 144
7 Discussion | 177
8 Conclusions and Implications | 225

Appendix: Interview Protocol | 237
Bibliography | 239

List of Tables

Table 1. Phases Participants Experienced in Transformative Learning | 187

This table presents the ten phases of transformative learning identified by Mezirow alongside corresponding themes that emerged from the study data. It illustrates how participants experienced disorienting dilemmas, engaged in critical reflection and reassessment of assumptions, and underwent perspective transformation within the spiritual formation program.

Table 2. Cultural Clashes Between Western Spiritual Formation and Chinese Confucian Upbringing | 191

This table summarizes major cultural tensions experienced by Chinese students as they engaged in Western spiritual formation practices. It highlights the contrasts between Western emphases on self-awareness, emotional honesty, and personal reflection and Chinese values shaped by Confucian traditions, including filial piety, hierarchy, communal harmony, and moral performance.

Table 3. Participants' Transformed Views of Self | 217

This table outlines the significant shifts in participants' self-understanding before and after the program. Many participants moved from shame-based, performance-driven identities toward a deeper sense of being loved, accepted, and valued by God, resulting in healthier emotional and spiritual self-perception.

Table 4. Participants' Transformed Relationships with God | 219

This table illustrates key changes in participants' relationships with God following their engagement in the program. As participants learned to slow down and rest in God's presence, they increasingly described a shift from performance-oriented striving toward grace-based relating, marked by greater intimacy with God and a more secure identity as his beloved children.

Table 5. Participants' Transformed Relationships with Others | 220

This table summarizes changes in participants' relational patterns through the program. While many participants continued to struggle with shame, fear of confrontation, and emotional inhibition, the spiritual formation process supported growth toward healthier communication, greater honesty, and more authentic relational engagement.

Foreword

SPIRITUAL FORMATION AS A practice within evangelical Christianity has gained attention and traction in recent years. However, the practice of spiritual formation is not new. The Church has focused on spiritual formation of believers since the early days of Christianity. The disciplines of the medieval monastic movements—both men's and women's traditions—offer a rich heritage for contemporary readers. So do the disciplines of the Protestant Reformation and the Wesleyan Holiness movements. While each has a different emphasis, the goal is always to help Christians grow in Christlikeness.

This book draws from the rich heritage of spiritual formation literature across the millennia and across different Christian traditions. What is new and particularly helpful in this work is the empirical approach to the research. It goes beyond the theological and philosophical literature on spiritual formation by investigating the lived experiences of Confucian-background Chinese believers participating in a Western seminary program. Given the divergent cultural backgrounds of the two sides—the Western seminary's approach to spiritual formation and the Eastern culture of Chinese seminary students—the potential for misunderstanding and lack of effectiveness is heightened. However, despite the many potential areas of incongruence, the study shows that, carried out in a thoughtful and understanding manner, such a program can and did have a transformative impact on students. Even with the apparent cultural mismatch, the capacity for spiritual growth is present. And that is good news for us all. After all, for Western Christians, there is also a huge cultural gap between the ancient writings and the present-day culture.

All of us can benefit from an intercultural understanding of the spiritual formation process.

The book you hold in your hands is a much-needed piece of empirical research in the area of spiritual formation. Dr. Wang's diligent and careful work is not only helpful for spiritual formation programs working with Confucian-background believers. It sheds light on the entire formation process and will benefit all who are engaged in this important work.

Leanne M. Dzubinski, PhD
January 2026
Santa Barbara, CA

Acknowledgments

THIS WORK IS, ABOVE all, a testimony to God's will, guidance, and love. I give all glory to my heavenly Father, who created me, sustained me, and called me to complete this work. I am deeply grateful for his presence, provision, and gentle reminders throughout the entire process that, apart from him, I can do nothing.

I am profoundly thankful for the many people who have made invaluable contributions to this research. My heartfelt thanks go first to my dear husband, whose companionship, encouragement, and unwavering support sustained me through every circumstance. I am also deeply grateful for my beloved daughter, who journeyed with me through this season during her years of growth. You are God's masterpiece and a precious gift and blessing to me.

I wish to express my sincere appreciation to Dr. Leanne Dzubinski, my dissertation chair, whose kindness, patience, wisdom, and guidance shaped this work from beginning to end. I am also grateful to Dr. Steve Porter and Dr. Jamie Sanchez, members of my committee, for their thoughtful feedback, generous investment of time, and valuable recommendations. I extend my appreciation to the faculty of the Cook School of Intercultural Studies—now part of the Talbot School of Theology at Biola University—including Dr. Douglas Hayward, Dr. Rich Starcher, and Dr. Tom Sappington, whose teaching, mentorship, and care contributed significantly to my formation and to the development of this research.

I am further indebted to Dr. John Coe, Dr. Judy TenElshof, and Dr. Betsy Barber. Your love, acceptance, and profound ministry through teaching and training have forever changed my life. I thank God for the ways he uses you to form the souls and lives of so many.

Special thanks are also due to those who supported me in various ways throughout this journey. I am grateful for my spiritual directors—Penny Hansen, Melissa Romero, and Larry Warner—who walked alongside me, helping me discern God's will and become more attentive to his presence. I am thankful to the participants who generously shared their stories with honesty and vulnerability; I learned deeply from each of you. I also extend my sincere gratitude to family members, close friends, and many sisters from my former Bible study group and church community, whose love, encouragement, and generosity supported this work.

Above all, I give thanks and glory to our faithful and loving triune God.

1

Introduction

According to Poston and Wong, more than forty million ethnic Chinese were living outside mainland China, Taiwan, Hong Kong, and Macau, dispersed across more than 149 countries.[1] By 2018, that number was estimated to exceed fifty million, while mainland China itself had a population of over 1.4 billion.[2] Within this expansive global Chinese community, many have encountered Christianity. As increasing numbers of Chinese people move abroad to live and study, more are exposed to the gospel and come to faith in Christ. Some remain in their host countries, while others return home carrying their newly embraced faith with them. Alongside the growth of Christian communities among Chinese believers, there is a corresponding need to give focused attention to the spiritual formation of Chinese churches and believers.

One significant issue in this task is the enduring tension between Christianity and traditional Chinese culture. Since Western missionaries first arrived in China in the sixteenth century, they have grappled with the dominant philosophical system of Confucianism.[3] Some missionaries, such as the Jesuits, approached Chinese civilization with notable sympathy and adaptability.[4] Others, particularly early nineteenth-century missionaries, viewed Confucianism as fundamentally incompatible

1. Poston and Wong, "Chinese Diaspora."
2. Worldometers, "China Population (2018)."
3. Xu, "Dilemma of Accommodation."
4. Xu, "Dilemma of Accommodation."

with Christian belief and sought to reshape Chinese thought according to Western theological and cultural norms.[5] Still others attempted to integrate particular elements of Confucian ethics, especially filial piety, into a Christian framework, emphasizing possible points of harmony between the two traditions.[6]

Chinese Christians themselves have likewise confronted the dissonance between Christianity and their indigenous culture.[7] Because Confucianism has shaped Chinese life for more than two millennia, Chinese emigrants who left China beginning in the nineteenth century carried its values and social patterns with them to their host countries. Consequently, in the twenty-first century, many diaspora Chinese Christians continue to experience tension between their faith and their cultural identity. Both missionaries and Chinese believers have struggled either to transplant "one fundamental element of Western culture onto an alien cultural soil" or to accommodate Confucianism within Christianity.[8] As a result, Chinese Christians, both within and beyond mainland China, often experience spiritual stagnation or burnout under the continued influence of Confucian values.[9] In short, many Chinese believers find it difficult to embody Christian doctrines within daily life still shaped by Confucian patterns of thought and practice.

In fact, many Christians, regardless of nationality or ethnicity, experience a gap between their religious creeds and their practical application.[10] Since the early 1990s, several North American seminaries have sought to address this gap by incorporating spiritual formation programs into their theological curricula.[11] This development has not only fostered the spiritual growth of seminary students but has also equipped them with skills essential for effective ministry and leadership.[12] Given that Chinese students come from a distinct cultural background, this study explores how participation in a Christian spiritual formation program

5. Xu, "Dilemma of Accommodation."

6. Xu, "Dilemma of Accommodation."

7. Xu, "Dilemma of Accommodation."

8. Xu, "Dilemma of Accommodation," 38.

9. MacEwen, "Contextualized Spiritual Formation Strategy."

10. Sheard, "Role of Spiritual Formation."

11. Sheard, "Role of Spiritual Formation."

12. Freeburg, "Nurturing Spiritual Formation"; Keely, "Spiritual Formation for Ordained Ministry," 202–10; Sheard, "Role of Spiritual Formation."

at a North American seminary has shaped the lives of Chinese students influenced by Confucianism.

WHAT PIQUED MY INTEREST IN THE PROBLEM

My interest in this topic emerged from my experience as a Chinese Christian receiving Western theological education. After accepting Jesus as my Savior, I sought earnestly to live as a faithful Christian through regular church attendance, participation in prayer meetings, engagement with Scripture, and leadership in a Bible study group. Yet my inability to live as Jesus lived, to love God and neighbor as commanded by the Lord and taught by the church, often left me frustrated and, at times, discouraged. I struggled to understand why I could not experience the freedom Jesus promised his followers: "You will know the truth, and the truth will make you free" (John 8:32). I also observed similar struggles among many other Chinese Christians.

Shaped by deeply ingrained habits of mind, many Chinese believers labor to please God primarily through personal effort. In my own experience, I longed for a deeper relationship with God, one that went beyond the external performance of faith. Desiring to understand the truth of God more fully, I pursued formal theological training. Within the context of seminary education, I devoted myself almost entirely to study, often neglecting physical and emotional limits, a pattern shaped largely by internalized, performance-oriented expectations. Within a few months, I experienced significant physical and emotional exhaustion, reflecting a mindset influenced in part by Confucian values.

Over time, however, participation in a Christian spiritual formation program became a turning point. Through coursework in spiritual theology, spiritual direction, community groups, and practices of spiritual discipline, I became increasingly aware of God's presence and learned to "walk by the Spirit" (Gal 5:16). This process contributed to a reorientation of my understanding of Christian life and growth, fostering inner healing and renewal. I came to experience more fully what Scripture describes as "the spring of the water of life" (Rev 21:6) and the freedom of life as God's child.

These experiences, shared by many Chinese students in similar educational contexts, motivated this study. As a Chinese Christian engaged in North American theological education, I became interested in how Western Christian spiritual formation programs influence students whose outlook has been shaped by Confucianism. Scholars such as Richard Nisbett have argued that Eastern and Western worldviews differ significantly.[13] How, then, might these cultural differences shape the process of Christian spiritual formation? This study explores how participation in a Western Christian spiritual formation program has influenced the lives of Chinese students.

PROBLEM STATEMENT

Since the 1990s, spiritual formation has been increasingly incorporated into North American evangelical theological education to help seminary students grow in the life of Christ. However, it remains unknown how this development has influenced the lives of Chinese Christians or how effectively it has supported their spiritual growth. In particular, it remains unclear how Chinese students at North American seminaries, shaped by Confucian cultural values, perceive the impact of a Christian spiritual formation program on their lives.

PURPOSE STATEMENT

The purpose of this grounded theory study is to understand the impact of a Christian spiritual formation program at a North American seminary on the lives of Chinese students who have been influenced by Confucianism.

RESEARCH QUESTIONS

The main research question guiding this study is "How do Chinese students who have been influenced by Confucianism describe the impact of a Christian spiritual formation program at a North American seminary?" Sub-questions include,

1. How do participants describe the impact of the spiritual formation program on their relationship with themselves?
2. How do participants describe the impact of the spiritual formation program on their relationship with God?

13. Nisbett, *Geography of Thought*.

3. How do participants describe the impact of the spiritual formation program on their relationships with others?
4. What additional impact of the spiritual formation program do participants describe?

DEFINITIONS

Christian Spiritual Formation

There are many perspectives on spiritual formation. For this study, the following definition is used:

> Christian spiritual formation can be understood as the transforming work of the Spirit in every aspect of the life of the believer. This understanding leads to two interesting consequences. First, formation is seen to involve the whole of a person's life—embodied thinking, feeling, acting, and being in relationship. Second, as Paul asserts in . . . 2 Corinthians, because of the nature of the Spirit, formation results in freedom.[14]

Moral Temptation

In this study, I use Coe's definition:

> The attempt of the hidden heart (not conscious) to try to perfect oneself in the power of the self, the attempt to use service, ministry, obedience, spiritual formation, the spiritual disciplines, spiritual experiences—being good—to relieve the burden of spiritual failure, lack of love, and the guilt and shame that results, to try to relieve the burden that Christ alone can relieve.[15]

Soul Care

Soul care encompasses "the nourishment, healing, and flourishing of the whole person with an emphasis on that person as a participant in the

14. McGrath, *Psychology of Christian Character Formation*, 5.
15. Coe, "Resisting the Temptation," 1.

body of Christ. We focus on the nurturing care and progressive sanctification of a soul."[16]

Spiritual Discipline

For this study, I use the following definition:

> A spiritual discipline is (1) a repeated bodily-spirit-Spirit activity, (2) the doing of which is in our power, (3) which forms a habit over time and repetition, (4) that opens our heart to the work of the Holy Spirit, (5) who transforms us spiritually—that is, in cooperation with our spirit, fills us with His presence and, by so doing, in union, conforms us more and more to the image of Christ.[17]

Transformative Learning Theory

Transformative learning theory has developed since Mezirow first proposed it.[18] For this study, I use Mezirow's definition:

> The process by which we transform our taken-for-granted frames of reference (meaning perspectives, habits of mind, mind-sets) to make them more inclusive, discriminating, open, emotionally capable of change, and reflective so that they may generate beliefs and opinions that will prove more true or justified to guide action.[19]

SCOPE

This research explored how the Christian spiritual formation program at a North American seminary has impacted the lives of Chinese students who participated in the program. The participants were eighteen diaspora Chinese, each with at least one Chinese parent. Half were male and half female. They were selected from the program's student and alumni directory. All participants had successfully completed the requirements

16. Barber and Baker, "Soul Care," 270.
17. Coe, "Spiritual Disciplines," 1.
18. Mezirow, "Perspective Transformation."
19. Mezirow, *Learning as Transformation*, 8.

for either an MA or an MDiv in spiritual formation between 2010 and 2019. Their ages ranged from twenty-five to fifty-five years old.

LIMITATIONS

This study has several limitations. It focused specifically on the impact of a Western Christian spiritual formation program on Chinese students. Although some findings may be transferable to other Asian cultures that share significant Confucian influence, they cannot be generalized to all cultural contexts. In addition, because all participants studied and lived in the United States, the findings may not be applicable to seminaries in other countries. Furthermore, since the participants were drawn from a single program at one seminary, the results are context-specific and may not be transferable to other institutional settings or program designs.

SIGNIFICANCE STATEMENT

Although significant research has examined how spiritual formation influences North American and Asian Christians, relatively little attention has been given to its impact on Chinese Christians. This study therefore adds an important new dimension to the literature on spiritual formation and transformative learning theory by exploring its particular influence on Chinese Christians.

Practically, the study offers valuable insights for spiritual formation ministers and transformative-learning educators. It may help Chinese church leaders better understand their own paths of spiritual growth and open their hearts to greater honesty before God, themselves, and others. In doing so, they may more fully cooperate with the Holy Spirit to be transformed by Jesus Christ and to reflect God's glory in the world. This study may also equip church leaders to guide others toward greater authenticity and Christlikeness. Finally, it can assist Chinese seminary teachers and missionaries in identifying key components for teaching and supporting their students' spiritual growth.

2

Literature Review

IN THIS CHAPTER, I introduce Confucianism and its influence on the lives of Chinese people. I also examine the definition and history of spiritual formation, its incorporation into North American theological education, the outcomes of spiritual formation in North American seminaries, concerns that have been raised about spiritual formation, and various responses to those concerns. Although a handful of studies have explored spiritual formation in Western and some Asian contexts, few have examined its effect within a Chinese context. In other words, Chinese students' perspectives on spiritual formation in North American seminaries remain largely unexplored.

The framework of this literature review is based on sensitizing concepts, which, as Charmaz defines them, refer to "those background ideas that inform the overall research problem."[1] Sensitizing concepts are especially useful when researchers "know about their topic and the literature about it."[2] They offer "initial but tentative ideas to pursue and questions to raise about their topics."[3] In the following section, I employ sensitizing concepts to shape the conceptual framework for this study.

1. Charmaz, "Grounded Theory," 515.
2. Charmaz, *Constructing Grounded Theory*, 31.
3. Charmaz, *Constructing Grounded Theory*, 30.

INFLUENCE OF CONFUCIANISM

In this section, I introduce Confucianism, its historical development, and its influence on the lives of Chinese people. I also discuss the spiritual dimension of Confucianism, which originated in China and permeates nearly every aspect of Chinese culture. Understanding Confucianism provides essential context for comprehending how spiritual formation practiced in the West interacts with Confucian principles.

Confucianism has had a profound and enduring influence on Chinese civilization. Although it arose in China, its impact has extended far beyond Chinese borders. Through emigration, immigration, and cultural exchange, Confucian thought has spread throughout East Asia, shaping the societies of Korea, Japan, Malaysia, the Philippines, Singapore, Indonesia, and Vietnam.[4] As Berthrong and Berthrong observe, "Confucianism touched the lives of all the peoples in East Asia" and shaped virtually every area of life, including "art, morality, religion, family life, science, philosophy, government, and the economy."[5] The influence of Confucianism can best be understood by examining its historical development.

The History of Confucianism

In this section, I present the origins of Confucianism and explain how it became the dominant ideology in China.

The Origins of Confucianism

Confucianism was first articulated by Confucius and later developed into the dominant ideology of China for more than two millennia. Although associated with Confucius, its intellectual roots extend far earlier. Prior to his birth in 551 BC, China already possessed more than a thousand years of civilization.[6] Thong and Fu note that, long before Confucius, Chinese dynasties were "culturally sophisticated and technologically advanced for their day.'"[7] This ancient cultural and political heritage formed

4. Goldin, *Confucianism*; Onsman, "Recognizing the Ordinances."
5. Berthrong and Berthrong, *Confucianism*, 1.
6. Goldin, *Confucianism*.
7. Thong and Fu, *Finding God*, 19.

the foundation on which Confucius built his ethical and philosophical teachings.[8]

Early records indicate that several dynasties ruled China for centuries before the time of Confucius. One of the earliest, the Shang Dynasty, reigned for more than six hundred years.[9] The subsequent Zhou Dynasty governed from roughly 1122 to 249 BC.[10] As the Zhou weakened due to attacks from surrounding tribes, regional lords struggled for dominance, ushering in an era of instability known as the Warring States Period.[11] During this time, the Hundred Schools of Thought, including Daoism, Mohism, Legalism, and Confucianism, emerged.[12]

Among these schools, Confucianism developed later and ultimately exerted the most profound and enduring influence on Chinese society. Confucius (551–479 BC), a scholar who lived during the late Spring and Autumn Period, sought to restore harmony and order within a deeply fragmented and tumultuous society. To this end, he emphasized moral education and sustained self-cultivation, urging individuals to become *junzi* ("noble-minded") persons.[13] He further taught that rulers should embody moral virtue themselves, so that their subjects would follow them willingly and be guided not by coercion but by moral example.

Many of Confucius's teachings are preserved in the books he compiled and in the *Analects*, which his followers assembled from his sayings.[14] To promote his ideas, Confucius organized and edited what later became known as the Five Classics, collections of sayings, stories, and legends that predated his lifetime.[15] Among these works, *The Classic of Changes* (*Yijing*) explores transcendental phenomena, including divination, and seeks to help people "pursue an exhaustive understanding of the universe in order to do God's will."[16] *The Classic of History* (*Shangshu*) records the ancient past of China, including the sayings and deeds of the legendary emperors Yao (尧) and Shun (舜), who reigned during what

8. Küng and Ching, *Christianity and Chinese Religions*; Thong and Fu, *Finding God*.
9. Confucius, *Analects* (Hinton).
10. Thong and Fu, *Finding God*.
11. Confucius, *Analects* (Hinton).
12. Confucius, *Analects* (Hinton).
13. Confucius, *Analects*, 129 (Hinton).
14. Confucius, *Analects* (Hinton); Goldin, *Confucianism*.
15. Thong and Fu, *Finding God*.
16. Thong and Fu, *Finding God*, 20.

later tradition called "China's Golden Age," before 2200 BC.[17] Confucius hoped that the people of his own era would emulate these virtuous rulers.

To achieve this vision, he compiled the *Record of Rites* (*Liji*), which emphasizes "the moral principles that underpin the development of rites, royal regulations, rituals, objects and sacrifices, education, music, [and] the behavior of scholars."[18] For Confucius, these ethical and social norms provided the means by which subjects would follow their rulers through moral example and proper conduct. In addition, the turmoil of his age is reflected in the *Spring and Autumn Annals* (*Chunqiu*), which chronicles the history of Confucius's home state of Lu from 722 to 479 BC.[19] The fifth work, the *Classic of Poetry* (*Shijing*), collects poetry from the Zhou Dynasty to the sixth century BC. Together, these Five Classics represent Confucius's enduring contribution to the moral and intellectual foundations of Chinese civilization.

These writings reveal that Confucius sought to revive "what was already the truth,"[20] building upon the foundations of ancient Chinese culture. As Berthrong and Berthrong note, Confucius did not see himself as the "founder of a new movement" but "believed fervently that his role was to restore the way of the ancient sages," who served as "historical models of what true culture should be about."[21]

As such, Confucius's ideas were not widely welcomed by the rulers of his day. He traveled among various states, offering counsel that was largely ignored, urging rulers to "return to the ways of the ancient sage kings."[22] He hoped that by following "the ways of the ancients, then there would be the creation of peace and harmony."[23] However, the era in which Confucius lived differed markedly from the earlier Golden Age of antiquity. By the late Spring and Autumn Period, moral order was widely perceived to be in decline, and society was increasingly marked by turmoil, conflict, and instability.[24]

17. Thong and Fu, *Finding God*, 20.
18. Thong and Fu, *Finding God*, 21.
19. Thong and Fu, *Finding God*, 21.
20. Berthrong and Berthrong, *Confucianism*, 11.
21. Berthrong and Berthrong, *Confucianism*, 11.
22. Taylor, *Religious Dimensions*, 9.
23. Taylor, *Religious Dimensions*, 11.
24. Confucius, *Analects* (Hinton).

The Development of Confucianism

In the following dynasties, Confucianism developed and gradually became the dominant ideology of Chinese imperial society. Many rulers and emperors found its concepts of hierarchical relationships and power structures particularly useful for governance. During the Han Dynasty, the scholar Dong Zhongshu (179–74 BC) synthesized elements of Daoism and Legalism and integrated *Yi Jing*'s "yin-yang theory into Confucianism"[25] to meet the "social need for a unity of ideology that would serve the authority of the emperor."[26] Seeking to "create a static and fixed order of social relationships,"[27] Dong justified "a normative hierarchical ordering"[28] in which yang dominates yin. In this kind of social relationships, "*he* as an imposed unity may require the other party to disregard its own distinctive differences and force it into some uniform pattern of order."[29]

According to Dong's system, which posited two opposing yet complementary principles in nature, rulers, fathers, and husbands represented yang, the bright and active side of heaven, while subjects, sons, and wives embodied yin, the dark and passive side of heaven.[30] This worldview assumed that these relationships were established by heaven and possessed an unchanging moral order: yang is always superior and authoritative, while yin is always inferior and submissive.[31] On this basis, Dong Zhongshu codified the hierarchical structure of Chinese imperial society and affirmed the controlling power of rulers, fathers, and husbands through the sacralization of political and social order.[32]

Through his reinterpretation of Confucianism, Dong extended Confucius's teachings on human relationships and social structure: rulers are superior to subjects, fathers to sons, elder brothers to younger brothers, and husbands to wives. In each pair, the former is categorized as yang and the latter as yin.[33] Within this hierarchical framework, superiors possess

25. Wang, "Dong Zhongshu's Transformation," 209.
26. Wang, "Dong Zhongshu's Transformation," 216.
27. Wang, "Dong Zhongshu's Transformation," 214.
28. Wang, "Dong Zhongshu's Transformation," 216.
29. Wang, "Dong Zhongshu's Transformation," 214.
30. Wang, "Dong Zhongshu's Transformation."
31. Wang, "Dong Zhongshu's Transformation."
32. Wang, "Dong Zhongshu's Transformation."
33. Wang, "Dong Zhongshu's Transformation."

the right and power to rule, while inferiors bear the duty to respect and obey.[34]

During the Song Dynasty, Confucianism developed into what later became known as Neo-Confucianism. Zhu Xi (1130–1200), the leading representative of Neo-Confucian thought, emphasized maintaining the Mandate of Heaven, which justified the authority of emperors, and the annihilation of human desires as the pathway to self-cultivation.[35] His doctrines proved favorable to imperial governance and were therefore adopted as the official philosophy of feudalistic despotism during the Southern Song Dynasty.[36] As a result, the commentaries Zhu Xi compiled for the Five Classics became the official textbooks for the imperial examinations in subsequent dynasties. Neo-Confucianism remained the dominant ideology of Chinese society for more than a thousand years,[37] and its influence extended beyond China to Japan and Korea, where it was likewise embraced by ruling elites.[38]

In the modern era, Confucianism continues to play an important role in Chinese society, even though some view it as irrelevant or obsolete. Critics have described it as "a backward-looking ideology, sterile textual studies, a society of hierarchical relationship excluding reciprocity, the permanent dominance of parents over children and of men over women, and a social order interested only in the past and not in the future."[39] Yet Confucianism has been deeply ingrained in Chinese and broader East Asian thought and value systems for millennia. Its influence "permeates the social and family structures,"[40] shaping nearly every dimension of human activity, spiritual, psychological, and physical. Consequently, contemporary Chinese society cannot ignore the continuing significance of Confucianism in the lives and moral imaginations of its people.

34. Wang, "Dong Zhongshu's Transformation."
35. Lee, "Neo-Confucianism."
36. Lee, "Neo-Confucianism."
37. Ames, "Zhu Xi."
38. Lee, "Neo-Confucianism"; Levi, "Confucianism."
39. Küng and Ching, *Christianity and Chinese Religions*, 90.
40. Yep et al., *Following Jesus*, 22.

The Spiritual Dimensions of Confucianism

Based on its historical origins and development, Confucianism possesses distinct spiritual dimensions that are closely related to the spiritual formation of the Chinese people. These dimensions appear in its teachings on the authority of heaven, its foundations in the *Yi Jing* (Book of Changes), which includes divination and astrology, its implicit understanding of faith, and its emphasis on a sense of shame. Although Confucius's teachings, as embodied in the Five Classics and the *Analects*, are often regarded as philosophical and ethical, they also carry profound religious implications. Because Confucianism integrates the metaphysical cosmology of the *Yi Jing* and stresses the supreme authority of heaven, it cannot be reduced merely to philosophy or ethics; it also bears unmistakable spiritual significance.[41]

As R. L. Taylor observes, Confucius's teachings had their "religious genesis in an already-established religious dynamic at the very heart of the early political order."[42] The following sections explore these spiritual dimensions of Confucianism in greater depth, focusing on its teachings concerning (1) the authority of heaven, (2) the integration of the *Yi Jing*, and (3) the cultivation of the sense of shame.

The Authority of Heaven

Confucianism places strong emphasis on the authority of heaven. As R. L. Taylor explains,

> Heaven for the Confucian tradition is not thought of, as some have argued, as an abstract philosophical absolute devoid of religious meaning. In the Classical Confucian tradition Heaven functions as a religious authority or absolute often theistic in its portrayal. In the later Neo-Confucian tradition, Heaven, or the Principles of Heaven, *Tian-li*, also functions as a religious authority or absolute frequently monistic in its structure.[43]

This reverence for heaven is deeply embedded in the Chinese language itself, as reflected in numerous idioms expressing awe, fear, and submission toward this transcendent authority:

41. Goldin, *Confucianism*, 75; Wu, "Service to Heaven."
42. Taylor, *Religious Dimensions*, 7.
43. Taylor, *Religious Dimensions*, 2.

对天发誓 (to swear by heaven)

乐天知命 (to accept heaven's will and be content with one's fate)

天经地义 (to regard something as morally right according to heaven's order)

天理不容 (an offense intolerable to heaven)

泄漏天机 (to reveal heaven's secrets)

顺天应时 (to follow heaven's mandate and the proper timing of events)

真命天子 (the son of heaven; the legitimate ruler chosen by heaven)

在天之灵 (the spirit of the deceased in heaven)

天命有归 (heaven's mandate ultimately belongs to someone)

天命不韬 (the mandate of heaven is not to be deceived)

弥天大罪 (a crime so great it offends heaven)

怨天尤人 (to complain against heaven and blame others)

丧尽天良 (to be utterly devoid of the conscience given by heaven)

伤天害理 (to commit acts offensive to heaven and moral principle)

仰不愧天 (to feel no shame before heaven)

天理昭昭 (heaven's justice is clear and cannot be hidden)

谋事在人成事在天 (man proposes; heaven disposes)

人不为己天诛地灭 (if one does not act for oneself, heaven and earth destroy him)

These expressions reflect a worldview in which heaven is regarded as a supreme moral and cosmic power governing human destiny and social order.

Heaven, in fact, stands at the apex of the Confucian cosmological hierarchy and possesses ultimate authority to appoint rulers and legitimate their power. As Goldin observes, "In Bronze Age politics, even the highest king, the Son of Heaven, is conceived as a lord to all other human beings but only a vicegerent of Heaven above."[44] Thus, in traditional Chinese political thought, the ruler's authority was understood to derive from heaven's mandate, and heaven's will was believed to determine both the rise and fall of dynasties. For many Chinese people, heaven's decrees govern not only the stability of the national order but also the course of individual destiny,[45] sustaining a cosmic hierarchy grounded in moral and metaphysical order.

The Book of Yi Jing

The spirituality of Confucianism is further evident in its foundational connection to the *Yi Jing* (Book of Changes). This classic introduces and explains "a system of sixty-four six-line figures used for oracular divination."[46] Confucius studied the *Yi Jing* intensively and composed commentaries on it, placing it above all other classics.[47] He regarded the *Book of Changes* as a guide for nearly every aspect of life, a text through which divine patterns could illuminate moral and practical decisions.[48] In this way, Confucianism offered not merely an ethical framework but a spiritually informed worldview, shaping a way of life attuned to the moral and cosmic order.

Moreover, Confucius personally affirmed belief in heaven and destiny.[49] Although the *Analects* contain relatively few explicit discussions of spirituality, possibly because Confucius assumed such matters were not easily grasped by ordinary people, he nonetheless participated fully in the religious practices of his time.[50] In the *Analects* 3:12, he remarked, "If I do not personally offer the sacrifice, it is the same as not having sacrificed at all."[51] Confucius offered sacrifices to both his ancestors and "other spiritual beings" and sensed the presence of their spirits.[52] In this sense, spirituality forms the backdrop of Confucius's moral teachings. His vision of self-cultivation was grounded not only in ethics and social

44. Goldin, *Confucianism*, 27.
45. Zhang, "Confucius' Transformation."
46. Ritchlin, "Oneness of the Way," 22.
47. Wilhelm and Baynes, *I Ching*.
48. McGreal and Roth, "I Ching."
49. Confucius, *Analects* (Hinton).
50. Beck, *Confucius and Socrates*.
51. Confucius, *Analects of Confucius* (Muller), 3.12.
52. Beck, *Confucius and Socrates*, para. 3.

harmony but also in reverence for heaven and the unseen order that governs all existence, a legacy that continues to influence the spiritual consciousness of Chinese culture.

Emphasis on Shame

Another spiritual dimension of Confucianism is its emphasis on the sense of shame, which has profoundly shaped the inner life of many Chinese people. As Thompson describes, shame is "ubiquitous, seeping into every nook and cranny of life."[53] It is "pernicious, infesting not just our thoughts but our sensations, images, feelings and, of course, ultimately our behavior. It just doesn't seem to go away."[54] Many assume shame to be merely "some abstract emotional or cognitive phenomena."[55] However, as Thompson further argues, it functions as an "emotional weapon that evil uses to (1) corrupt our relationships with God and each other, and (2) disintegrate any and all gifts of vocational vision and creativity."[56]

Within this framework, the Confucian emphasis on shame has profoundly shaped Chinese moral consciousness. Historically, shame functioned as a moral regulator, promoting social harmony and self-restraint; yet it also carried an embedded spiritual burden that could distort one's sense of worth before others and before the transcendent. In this way, what Confucianism upheld as moral virtue often became, for many, a site of inner struggle, revealing the complex and ambivalent intersection between cultural ethics and interior formation.

Augsburger observes that shame manifests in two forms: one positive and one negative.[57] The positive face suggests that shame may help individuals "develop proper self-regulatory behavior"[58] and reflects a deep human desire to maintain or restore caring and harmonious relationships.[59] In this sense, shame can serve a constructive role in moral formation and communal sensitivity.

53. Thompson, *Soul of Shame*, 10.
54. Thompson, *Soul of Shame*, 10.
55. Thompson, *Soul of Shame*, 10.
56. Thompson, *Soul of Shame*, 13.
57. Augsburger, *Pastoral Counseling Across Cultures.*
58. Thompson, *Soul of Shame*, 16.
59. Jamieson, *Face of Forgiveness.*

The negative face of shame, however, is "a painful experience of the disintegration of one's world."[60] When shame becomes excessive or distorted, it often leads to "disintegrated communities with little creative capacity for goodness and beauty."[61] Thus, while an awareness of shame can expose human brokenness and evoke a longing for reconciliation with God and others, its misuse or internalization as self-condemnation can instead drive people further away from divine grace and relational wholeness.

Theologically, shame is rooted in original sin. After the fall, humanity's separation from God produced an inherent awareness of brokenness and vulnerability.[62] The image of God (*imago Dei*) was distorted by the human desire to be like God (*sicut Deus*).[63] The resulting void in the human heart, which was created to be filled by the Holy Spirit, renders human beings instinctively aware of their inadequacy.[64] This sense of inadequacy, often experienced as shame, alienates humanity from both God and others. It exposes the illusion that human beings are "independent, limitless and self-creating" and reveals, instead, their true condition as finite, dependent, and vulnerable creatures.[65]

Shame manifests itself in multiple ways. As Thompson notes, the experience of shame often results in "judging, hiding, reinforcement, and isolation."[66] One of the "hallmarks of shame," he explains, is "its employment of judgment, . . . the spirit of condemnation or condescension with which we analyze or critique something, whether ourselves or someone or something else."[67] Another common expression of shame is the impulse to hide.[68] Out of fear of rejection, people often labor to conceal their true selves until the burden of concealment becomes unbearable. Yet this very act of hiding "ironically simultaneously reinforces the very shame we are attempting to avoid,"[69] because it prevents the self from being revealed

60. Augsburger, *Pastoral Counseling Across Cultures*, 116.
61. Thompson, *Soul of Shame*, 16.
62. Jamieson, *Face of Forgiveness.*
63. Jamieson, *Face of Forgiveness.*
64. Jamieson, *Face of Forgiveness.*
65. Jamieson, *Face of Forgiveness.*
66. Thompson, *Soul of Shame*, 33.
67. Thompson, *Soul of Shame*, 28.
68. Thompson, *Soul of Shame.*
69. Thompson, *Soul of Shame*, 31.

and healed. Ultimately, shame leads to "isolation and disconnection,"[70] the "natural consequences of hiding and resisting reengagement."[71]

In this sense, shame operates not merely as a psychological response but as a deeply spiritual condition that reveals humanity's alienation from God and its longing for restoration in divine grace. While shame is a universal human experience, each culture "has its own particular way of manifesting shame."[72] Cultural traditions differ in the intensity with which they cultivate shame, depending on their inherited moral norms and social expectations.[73] In the Chinese context, this dynamic has been profoundly shaped by Confucianism, which for millennia has employed shame as a moral instrument for governance and self-regulation. As Confucius taught,

> Leading the common people with administrative regulations and keeping them in order with penal punishments, they will try to avoid troubles (mian 免) but will have no sense of shame (chi 耻). Leading them with virtue (de 德) and keeping them in order with ritual propriety, they will have a sense of shame and will constrain (ge 格) themselves.[74]

Confucius's insight into the moral power of shame, particularly its capacity to cultivate self-restraint and social harmony, was adopted by Chinese rulers for centuries as a guiding principle. As the dominant ideological force in Chinese society, Confucianism instilled a strong sense of shame in people striving to achieve the Confucian ideal of moral self-perfection.

From these observations, it becomes clear that Confucianism is more than a philosophical or cultural phenomenon. As Berthrong and Berthrong argue, "Although known in the West mostly as a philosophic movement, . . . Confucianism is better understood as a compelling assemblage of interlocking forms of life for generations of men and women in East Asia that encompassed all the possible domains of human concern."[75] In other words, Confucianism represents a holistic outlook that governs a person's spirit, soul, and body. It possesses unmistakable spiritual dimensions and

70. Thompson, *Soul of Shame*, 32.
71. Thompson, *Soul of Shame*, 32.
72. Thompson, *Soul of Shame*, 16.
73. Jamieson, *Face of Forgiveness*.
74. Confucius, *Understanding the Analects*, 95–96.
75. Berthrong and Berthrong, *Confucianism*, 1.

functions as a means through which people pursue their innate longing for transcendence and for relationship with God.

Pocock, Rheenen, and McConnell make a similar point: "Religion, although molded and shaped by culture, is more than a cultural phenomenon. The search for God and the need for relationship with him—the inner essence of religion, its spiritual core—are embedded within the human psyche."[76] In light of this understanding, Confucianism may rightly be regarded as a religion, one that has provided moral structure, spiritual aspiration, and existential meaning for generations of East Asian peoples.[77]

Confucianism's Influence on Chinese Culture

As previously discussed, Confucianism has exerted a profound and enduring influence on Chinese culture. For thousands of years, it has served as the dominant ideological system in China, shaping moral values, social relationships, and the everyday behavior of the vast majority of the Chinese people.[78] More than a set of abstract teachings, Confucianism provided a comprehensive way of life that permeated the collective consciousness of Chinese society.

To understand more fully how Confucianism has impacted Chinese culture, it is first necessary to clarify what is meant by culture. Although numerous definitions have been proposed, Clyde Kluckhohn's anthropological formulation remains among the most widely accepted.[79] As McCombe, Vogt, and Kluckhohn summarize,

> Culture consists in patterned ways of thinking, feeling and reacting, acquired and transmitted mainly by symbols, constituting the distinctive achievements of human groups, including their embodiment in artifacts; the essential core of culture consists of traditional (i.e., historically derived and selected) ideas and especially their attached values.[80]

76. Pocock et al., *Changing Face*, 83.

77. Pocock et al., *Changing Face.*

78. Berthrong and Berthrong, *Confucianism*; McDonald, "Confucian Foundations to Leadership."

79. Anderson et al., *Handbook*; Clark and Clark, *Choosing to Lead*; Hofstede, *Culture's Consequences* (2001).

80. McCombe et al., *Navaho Means People*, 86.

Similarly, Hofstede defines culture as "the collective programming of the mind which distinguishes the members of one human group from another. It is the software behind how we operate."[81] Livermore extends this idea by comparing culture to an iceberg.[82] On the visible surface, culture is expressed through artifacts, including "foods, eating habits, gestures, music, economic practices, dress, use of physical space (e.g., office setup), order of worship, art, and so on."[83] Yet, as Livermore notes, what lies beneath the surface is even more significant. These are the "invisible yet powerful elements" such as "unconscious, taken for granted beliefs, perceptions, and feelings," that ultimately shape how people think, feel, and live.[84] In this light, Confucianism can be understood as the deep moral and philosophical foundation beneath the visible patterns of Chinese culture, including its values, rituals, and social norms, forming the unseen structure that guides the Chinese way of life.

Hofstede and Hofstede proposed cultural dimensions theory to analyze differences among national cultures.[85] These dimensions include power distance, collectivism versus individualism, femininity versus masculinity, and Confucian dynamism.[86] In the following discussion, Confucianism's influence on Chinese culture will be examined in relation to these four dimensions.

High Power Distance

Power distance refers to "the degree to which less powerful members of a society or organization expect and accept the unequal distribution of power among members."[87] Chinese culture exhibits a high level of power distance, a characteristic deeply rooted in Confucian social ethics.[88] Wright describes one of the defining traits of the Chinese people

81. Hofstede, *Culture's Consequences* (1984), 21.
82. Livermore, *Cultural Intelligence.*
83. Livermore, *Cultural Intelligence*, 81.
84. Livermore, *Cultural Intelligence*, 85.
85. Hofstede and Hofstede, *Cultures and Organizations.*
86. Hofstede and Hofstede, *Cultures and Organizations.*
87. Jackson, *Introducing Language and Intercultural Communication*, 382.
88. Jackson, *Introducing Language and Intercultural Communication.*

as "submissiveness to authority—parents, elders, and superiors."[89] This enduring disposition is a direct outgrowth of Confucian teaching.[90]

Confucianism articulates a distinct concept of relationships and power structures, emphasizing "hierarchy and patriarchy."[91] In teaching filial piety, Confucius instructed that children should "never disobey" their parents.[92] He further taught that those in higher positions should exercise benevolence toward their subordinates, while those in lower positions should show respect and obedience to their superiors.[93] This hierarchical social ethic profoundly shaped Chinese culture, producing a general acceptance of unequal power distribution. As Hofstede observes, Chinese people accept "an unequal distribution of power and thus do not try to bring about a more equal distribution."[94] Throughout Chinese history, social respect has been conferred according to the hierarchy of "age, seniority, rank, maleness, and family background," patterns sustained largely through the enduring influence of Confucianism.[95]

Masculine Culture

Chinese culture also demonstrates strong masculine tendencies, derived from Confucianism's emphasis on male authority within both family and society.[96] Under the "principle of the Three Obediences," women could not find their "identity as a person."[97] As the lowest members in the hierarchical structure of feudal society, women were expected to obey their fathers before marriage, their husbands after marriage, and their sons after their husbands' deaths.

Reagan writes, "For the most part, the role of the woman in traditional China was limited to the duties and obligations of being a wife and a mother, and her education was oriented toward these goals."[98]

89. Wright and Twitchett, *Confucian Personalities*, 8.

90. Cha et al., *Growing Healthy Asian American Churches*; Wright and Twitchett, *Confucian Personalities*.

91. Cha et al., *Growing Healthy Asian American Churches*, 61.

92. Confucius, *Analects* (Hinton).

93. Zhao, *Father and Son in Confucianism*.

94. Hu et al., *Encountering the Chinese*, xxvi.

95. Hu et al., *Encountering the Chinese*, xxvi.

96. Cha et al., *Growing Healthy Asian American Churches*.

97. Yep et al., *Following Jesus*.

98. Reagan, *Non-Western Educational Traditions*, 145.

Consequently, Chinese women have historically been excluded from "leadership roles," and their voices have often been silenced or disregarded.[99] Confucian ideology has exerted a far-reaching influence on the attitudes and behaviors of both Chinese men and women, shaping gender expectations and reinforcing patriarchal norms that continue to echo within Chinese society.

Collectivism

Chinese collectivism is also deeply rooted in Confucianism. According to Ralston et al., "Collectivism consists of benevolence, tradition and conformity."[100] Further research identifies "three unique-to-China subdimensions"[101] of collectivism that mirror the central values of Confucian thought: "societal harmony, virtuous interpersonal behavior, and personal and interpersonal harmony."[102] For the governance of rulers and the maintenance of social harmony, Confucianism teaches that individual desires should yield to the welfare of the collective.[103] Consequently, Chinese people "have been culturally conditioned to suppress their own personal needs and think in terms of collective responsibility—first, to their families, then community, clan, and nation at large."[104]

In this collectivist culture, the individual is "defined by his or her relationship to the group"[105] and the well-being of the community is prioritized over personal interests. As Sugikawa and Wong explain, "In a society that is based on the collective identity of community or family, hierarchy gives the individual his or her identity."[106] Moreover, personal achievement is viewed as "a way for the individual to bring honor to the collective."[107] Thus, under Confucian influence, self-expression is tempered by social obligation, and honor is sought not for individual acclaim but for the sake of the family and community.

99. Cha and May, "Gender Relations," 168.
100. Ralston et al., "Doing Business," 420.
101. Ralston et al., "Doing Business," 420.
102. Ralston et al., "Doing Business," 420.
103. Liu, "May One."
104. China Mike, "Understanding the Chinese Mind," para. 3.
105. China Mike, "Understanding the Chinese Mind," para. 3.
106. Sugikawa and Wong, "Grace-Filled Households," 32.
107. Sugikawa and Wong, "Grace-Filled Households," 32.

Confucian Dynamism

Chinese culture is also characterized by what Hofstede later identified as Confucian dynamism, which he "adopted as a fifth dimension."[108] Rooted in Confucian values, this dimension encompasses traits such as "persistence, personal stability, traditions, frugality, respect for elders, status-oriented relationships, a long-term orientation to time, hard work, a sense of shame and collective face-saving."[109] These characteristics reflect Confucianism's emphasis on moral endurance, respect for hierarchy, and the pursuit of long-term goals grounded in ethical self-discipline. In this sense, Confucian dynamism captures the enduring vitality of Confucian ideals in shaping Chinese attitudes toward time, achievement, and moral responsibility.

According to Confucian teaching, self-cultivation is the primary means by which people attain moral excellence and embody the ideals of virtue and harmony. Chinese society has long encouraged the emulation of the ancient "sages," who were revered as paradigms of moral integrity and noble character.[110] As Goldin summarizes, the Confucian principles of self-cultivation include the following:

(i) Human beings are born with the capacity to develop morally.

(ii) Moral development begins with moral self-cultivation, that is, reflection on one's own behavior and concerted improvement where it is found lacking.

(iii) By perfecting oneself in this manner, one also contributes to the project of perfecting the world.

(iv) There were people in the past who perfected themselves, and then presided over an unsurpassably harmonious society—these people are called "sages."[111]

Confucianism employs the models of the "noble men" and "little people" as moral contrasts to inspire continuous self-improvement and the pursuit of righteousness.[112] Within this collective system, individuality is neither encouraged nor celebrated; instead, people are expected to

108. Hofstede, *Culture's Consequences* (2001), 71.

109. Jackson, *Introducing Language and Intercultural Communication*, 289.

110. Goldin, *Confucianism*, 5.

111. Goldin, *Confucianism*, 5.

112. Confucius, *Analects* (Hinton).

align themselves with the moral patterns embodied by the ancient sages, who were idealized as righteous, noble, and exemplary.

Furthermore, Confucius emphasized the use of shame as a means of moral discipline and social order. Because shame can be intensified by culture norms, Confucianism has often contributed to its amplification within Chinese society. While intended as a moral restraint, shame has also functioned as an instrument of governance, compelling conformity and obedience. As a result, the long-standing influence of Confucianism, marked by perseverance, hierarchy, restraint, and moral self-cultivation, remains deeply embedded in the Chinese cultural ethos.

Influence of Confucianism on Chinese Christian Spirituality

While Confucianism has fostered certain positive moral and relational values, numerous studies over the past three decades have also identified its lingering and often problematic effects on Christians shaped by Confucian cultural frameworks.[113] As Shin and Silzer observe,

> The similarity of Confucian values with some biblical values, particularly values in the Hebrew culture, easily leads to the misunderstanding that God's grace is based on fulfilling the social obligations of one's role in life and quietly following the wishes of authority figures, instead of being based on what God has done for us through the death of his Son on the cross for our sins.[114]

In his research on Chinese American church dynamics, Quen found that many American-born Asian millennials were leaving the Bay Area Chinese Bible Church due to concerns related to community life, preaching, church leadership, the lack of life-stage transition ministries, and an overemphasis on Chinese cultural identity.[115] He further observed that many Chinese Christians raised in honor-shame family systems had internalized patterns of "performance-based parenting," which significantly shaped both their expression of faith and their sense of belonging within the church.[116] Similarly, Ro identified persistent challenges in Chinese congregations, including leadership burnout, emotional suppression,

113. Cha and May, "Gender Relations"; Quen, "Reaching and Retaining"; Shin and Silzer, *Tapestry of Grace*.

114. Shin and Silzer, *Tapestry of Grace*, xii–xiv.

115. Quen, "Reaching and Retaining."

116. Quen, "Reaching and Retaining," 79.

and authoritarian family patterns, which he traced in part to enduring Confucian social expectations.[117]

Sugikawa and Wong offer a penetrating diagnosis of the distortions that can arise when churches privilege Asian cultural values over biblical grace:

> Churches that have tried to build on a foundation of Asian cultural values rather than on a foundation of grace have found that their desire for order through hierarchy can evolve into tyranny, that the emphasis on the collective can smother individuals, that performance orientation can become meritocracy, that humility can become self-hatred, and that tradition can become a source of legalism.[118]

Taken together, these findings reveal how Confucian cultural residues, particularly hierarchy, collectivism, and performance-based worth, can subtly shape Christian belief and practice in ways that obscure the message of grace and freedom in Christ.

In this section, I examine several challenges that Chinese Christians continue to face as a result of Confucianism's enduring influence. Although believers from other cultural backgrounds may encounter similar struggles, these challenges are often more pronounced among Christians shaped by Confucian traditions and values.

Hierarchical Structure

Ching observes that, under the continuing influence of Confucianism, some Chinese churches maintain a hierarchical structure in which the young are expected to obey the old and women to submit to men, often leaving the voices of both women and younger members suppressed and their dissatisfaction unexpressed.[119] Sugikawa and Wong similarly report that the hierarchical and collectivist patterns emphasized by Confucianism can lead believers to define their identity primarily through the community rather than in Christ, while simultaneously fostering unhealthy relationships between congregants and church leaders.[120] In such

117. Ro, "Globalization's Impact."

118. Sugikawa and Wong, "Grace-Filled Households," 34.

119. Ching, "Helping English Pastors."

120. Sugikawa and Wong, "Grace-Filled Households."

contexts, pastors and elders, who are frequently regarded as unquestionable authority figures, may adopt directive or authoritarian leadership styles.[121]

Jiang also notes that many Chinese churches struggle with forms of despotism resulting from Confucian hierarchical influence.[122] In such settings, church leaders sometimes exercise near-absolute authority and demand uncritical obedience from the congregation, a posture that stands in tension with biblical models of servant leadership.[123] This hierarchical dynamic not only distorts ecclesial relationships but also constrains spiritual growth, replacing the grace-based community envisioned in the New Testament with one rooted in cultural obligation and fear of disapproval.

Gender Roles

Another significant challenge for many Chinese Christians concerns gender roles, which have been deeply shaped by Confucianism's unequal assumptions about men and women.[124] Cha and May observe that in many Asian churches, understandings of gender roles are shaped more by cultural tradition than by biblical teaching on complementarity.[125] As a result, women often struggle to discern their identity and vocation within the life of the church.[126]

Because Confucianism has traditionally elevated male authority and restricted female participation, women in many Chinese congregations continue to be excluded from leadership roles, and their voices often go unheard.[127] This imbalance not only limits the expression of women's spiritual gifts but also impoverishes the life of the church as a whole. Addressing gender inequality is therefore essential to the health and growth of Chinese Christian communities, enabling both women and men to live out their God-given identities and callings beyond the constraints of Confucian cultural influence.

121. Shin and Silzer, *Tapestry of Grace.*
122. Jiang, "Crisis of Despotism."
123. Jiang, "Crisis of Despotism."
124. Yep et al., *Following Jesus.*
125. Cha and May, "Gender Relations," 178.
126. Yep et al., *Following Jesus.*
127. Cha and May, "Gender Relations," 168.

Sense of Shame

Because of Confucianism's pervasive influence, many Chinese believers, including church leaders, carry a strong sense of shame into their spiritual lives and often conceal their weaknesses and vulnerabilities.[128] For the sake of harmony, many Chinese Christians also avoid conflicts that might appear shameful, preferring instead to hide or cover their failures.[129] This culturally reinforced tendency to conceal imperfection inhibits authentic community and spiritual transparency. As Kang's study notes, "many people feel inadequate to serve in church that seemed [*sic*] to demand excellence in all aspects."[130]

Performance Orientation

Closely related to this sense of shame is the performance orientation evident among many Chinese Christians. Rooted in Confucian teachings on self-cultivation and compounded by misunderstandings of God's grace, this mindset equates spiritual maturity with flawless performance.[131] The tension between the "desire to do things perfectly" and the inevitable inability to attain perfection places many believers under significant psychological and spiritual pressure.[132]

Ro reports that in some urban Chinese churches, pastors experience "overload and burnout" as a result of excessive ministry demands and insufficient emotional support.[133] Similarly, Quen found that church leaders often suffer exhaustion as they attempt to fulfill multiple roles while lacking opportunities for deep, nurturing relationships.[134] This culture of overwork and self-reliance reflects Confucian ideals of diligence and responsibility, yet it can obscure the gospel's invitation to rest in divine grace.

128. Ching, "Helping English Pastors."
129. Lee, "Healthy Leaders, Healthy Households."
130. Kang, "Truth-Embodying Households," 40.
131. Sugikawa and Wong, "Grace-Filled Households."
132. Tokunaga, "Pressure, Perfectionism and Performance," 26.
133. Ro, "Globalization's Impact," 123.
134. Quen, "Reaching and Retaining"

Emotional Concerns

The Confucian tendency to suppress emotion also shapes relational and spiritual life within many Chinese congregations. Emotional expression is often viewed as disruptive or shameful, making it difficult to cultivate trust and vulnerability among church members or within ministry teams.[135] While many Chinese churches place strong emphasis on biblical teaching and doctrinal truth, they frequently give insufficient attention to the emotional dimensions of spiritual formation.[136] As Ro observes, "the focus on truth and not emotions" significantly influences leadership styles, church structures, and the overall spiritual ethos of numerous Chinese churches.[137]

Moreover, societal pressure to project success and happiness discourages believers from expressing pain, grief, or disappointment.[138] Out of fear of bringing shame upon themselves or others, many Chinese Christians communicate indirectly and avoid confrontation, thereby suppressing their true feelings.[139] As a result, unresolved emotions often remain hidden and unprocessed, leading to inner bitterness and relational distance.[140] Over time, this pattern of emotional restraint undermines both personal spiritual growth and the authenticity of communal life within the church.

Unhealthy Parenting

Another significant challenge for many Chinese Christians concerns strained relationships between parents and children.[141] Ro observes that "a common emotion that young people have towards their parents is anger and even hatred."[142] Because early attachment patterns are closely correlated with later perceptions of God and relationships with him,[143] Chinese parenting styles can significantly shape how children come

135. Lee, "Healthy Leaders, Healthy Households."
136. Ro, "Globalization's Impact."
137. Ro, "Globalization's Impact," 132.
138. Lee, "Healthy Leaders, Healthy Households."
139. Jao, "Relating to Others."
140. Jao, "Relating to Others."
141. Ro, "Globalization's Impact."
142. Ro, "Globalization's Impact," 151.
143. TenElshof and Furrow, "Secure Attachment."

to understand God's character.[144] As a result, some Chinese Christians envision God as strict, difficult to please, distant, judgmental, easily angered, and ready to punish.[145] Such perceptions, shaped by cultural and familial experience, often hinder both emotional well-being and spiritual growth.[146]

Ro found that the primary sources of resentment or bitterness among many Chinese children include parents' "strict parenting, a lack of love, forcing [their children] to study and perform, and yelling at them when they underachieve."[147] He further notes that "many young people also see a bad relationship between the parents, who are constantly fighting and arguing."[148] With the continuing effects of globalization, many young Chinese now have greater exposure to Western cultures and values.[149] As they come to recognize that the physical punishment or verbal reproach they experienced was abusive, and in some cases traumatic, they "become angry and realize what they went through is wrong."[150] This growing "awareness of emotional and physical abuse in China has created a generation of young people longing for healing and comfort from their past hurts."[151] Likewise, many Chinese Christians around the world share this deep need for restoration and inner healing.[152]

Ro further reports that some Chinese believers find healing through "strict discipleship disciplines and Reformed theology of the cross."[153] He clarifies, however, that "neither Reformed theology nor strict discipleship disciplines have a monopoly on healing people from past abuse in China,"[154] emphasizing instead that these practices "were just very instrumental in helping people . . . in their spiritual journey."[155] One of the most significant factors in recovery, he notes, is the experience of belonging to a community of grace, namely, being with others who do not judge or

144. Sugikawa and Wong, "Grace-Filled Households."
145. Sugikawa and Wong, "Grace-Filled Households."
146. Ro, "Globalization's Impact."
147. Ro, "Globalization's Impact," 151.
148. Ro, "Globalization's Impact," 151.
149. Ro, "Globalization's Impact."
150. Ro, "Globalization's Impact," 151.
151. Ro, "Globalization's Impact," 151.
152. Yang, *Chinese Christians in America.*
153. Ro, "Globalization's Impact," 155.
154. Ro, "Globalization's Impact," 155.
155. Ro, "Globalization's Impact," 155.

attempt to fix them.[156] When churches become safe spaces where people can "slowly open up their hearts," genuine healing and spiritual growth become possible.[157]

In this way, addressing the lingering effects of Confucian-influenced parenting is essential to the holistic formation of Chinese Christians. Churches that nurture emotional safety and spiritual authenticity can help believers encounter the true image of God, one marked not by fear or performance but by grace, love, and relational trust.

SPIRITUAL FORMATION IN WESTERN CONTEXT

In this section, I introduce the concept of spiritual formation and examine how it is practiced within Western Christian contexts.

Definition of Spiritual Formation

The term spiritual formation has often been used interchangeably with related expressions, such as spiritual theology, transformation, sanctification, Christian spirituality, and discipleship,[158] each highlighting different aspects of the believer's growth in Christlikeness. Scorgie explains that the word *spiritual* is the adjectival form of *spirituality*, a term that first appears in the New Testament when "the apostle Paul used *pneumatikoi* (literally, spiritual persons) to describe people who keep in step with the *pneuma* (Spirit) of God."[159] Hence, spiritual formation refers to the shaping of persons who progressively "walk by the Spirit" (Gal 5:16).

Because spiritual formation is ultimately the work of the triune God in the life of the believer,[160] Howard emphasizes that it nevertheless highlights the "human side" of this divine process.[161] Christians participate in God's transforming work through practices such as "spiritual disciplines, nourishing relationships, formative strategies, [and] spiritual warfare," among other means.[162]

156. Ro, "Globalization's Impact."
157. Ro, "Globalization's Impact," 155.
158. Coe, "Resisting the Temptation"; Porter, "Sanctification."
159. Scorgie, "Overview of Christian Spirituality," 27.
160. Averbeck, "Spirit, Community, and Mission," 28.
161. Howard, "Advancing the Discussion," 13.
162. Howard, "Advancing the Discussion," 13.

Scorgie further asserts that Christian spiritual formation encompasses the whole of a believer's life and involves "living all of *life*—not just some esoteric portion of it—before God, through Christ, in the transforming and empowering presence of the Holy Spirit."[163] Its essence, he writes, "is ultimately about being attentive to the Holy Spirit's voice, open to his transforming impulses, and empowered by his indwelling presence."[164] Likewise, Averbeck defines Christian spiritual formation as the promotion of "Christ-like spirituality in the lives of genuine Christians."[165]

For the purpose of this study, spiritual formation is defined as

> the transforming work of the Spirit in every aspect of the life of the believer. This understanding leads to two interesting consequences. First, formation is seen to involve the *whole* of a person's life—embodied thinking, feeling, acting and being in relationship. Second, as Paul asserts in . . . 2 Corinthians, because of the nature of the Spirit, formation results in freedom.[166]

The History of Christian Spiritual Formation

The practice of spiritual formation has varied across generations, cultures, and denominational traditions. As Hall observes, "The history of God's kingdom and God's church is in many ways the history of the Holy Spirit."[167] Throughout history, the Spirit has guided believers to cooperate with God's work through spiritual disciplines and has empowered them to follow Jesus along the path of self-denial.[168] Hall also reminds us that "all spiritual formation is time-bound, historical, and specifically contextual."[169] He explains,

> The spiritual formation of a Roman Catholic historical theologian is significantly different from that of a Baptist or a Pentecostal, a Presbyterian or a Methodist. Yet there are also vital

163. Scorgie, "Overview of Christian Spirituality," 27.

164. Scorgie, "Overview of Christian Spirituality," 27.

165. Scorgie, "Overview of Christian Spirituality," 28.

166. McGrath, *Psychology of Christian Character Formation*, 5.

167. Hall, "Historical Theology and Spiritual Formation," 210.

168. Sittser and Peterson, *Water from a Deep Well*; Smith, "Generation to Generation"; Willard, *Divine Conspiracy*.

169. Hall, "Historical Theology and Spiritual Formation," 211.

> commonalities and overlap. Christian historical theologians, for instance, share and affirm key theological commitments and essential spiritual disciplines: the Trinity, the Incarnation, the Atonement, the resurrection of Christ from the dead, the assurance of Christ's return to judge the living and the dead, the importance of baptism, the practice of communion or the Eucharist, and of course prayer in its many forms and manifestations.[170]

Similarly, Coe observes that "every generation of the church faces the unique challenge to understand the process of transformation and cooperate anew with the Spirit."[171] This historical awareness underscores that while the forms of spiritual formation vary across traditions, the Spirit's transforming work remains constant throughout the history of the church. Moreover, because churches are inherently "intergenerational,"[172] the spiritual heritage of past generations provides rich resources for contemporary Christians who seek to cooperate with the Holy Spirit in their own spiritual formation.[173]

For example, during the so-called "Dark Ages" of Western Europe, monastic communities structured around rhythms of prayer, Scripture meditation through *lectio divina*, and manual labor became among the most stabilizing and spiritually formative forces within an otherwise volatile society.[174]

During the Reformation, the reformers urged believers to practice not only the traditional disciplines of the monastery, such as "solitude, fasting, celibacy and meditation," but also to embrace everyday practices like hospitality and service as means of discipleship.[175] In this way, Christians today can draw from the essence of these historic practices, adapting the spiritual wisdom of past generations to contemporary contexts as they cooperate with the Holy Spirit in the work of transformation.

Contemporary evangelical approaches to spiritual formation have developed their own distinct emphases. Building upon the deep spiritual heritage of the Christian tradition, evangelicals affirm the importance

170. Hall, "Historical Theology and Spiritual Formation," 211.

171. Coe, "Call and Task," 138.

172. Smith, "Generation to Generation," 183.

173. Sittser and Peterson, *Water from a Deep Well*; Smith, "Generation to Generation."

174. Sittser and Peterson, *Water from a Deep Well*, 106.

175. Sittser and Peterson, *Water from a Deep Well*, 206–7.

of "church attendance, liturgical practice, sacramental observance and creedal assent,"[176] while also emphasizing the holistic transformation of believers' lives. The central conviction of evangelical spirituality, articulated most clearly by Jonathan Edwards, is that only God's grace can transform sinners into saints.[177]

Although understandings of evangelical spirituality differ among traditions, they share the common goal of becoming like Jesus. As Hindmarsh observes, "Evangelicalism is, above all, a *form of spirituality*."[178] He further explains that "it was precisely a focus on 'lived experience' that united evangelicals in a common mission from the outset of the movement."[179] Jonathan Edwards, while affirming the primacy of divine initiative in transformation, emphasized the "consistent practice of faith, which manifests itself in holiness of life, delight in God and love for neighbor."[180] This emphasis is significant because, despite differences in individual experiences of conversion, evangelicals recognize a shared set of spiritual practices that nurture growth in Christlikeness. Through disciplines such as prayer, worship, study, and service, believers participate in the ongoing work of the Holy Spirit and are increasingly conformed to the image of Jesus.

This brief historical overview has outlined the spiritual resources that North American Christianity sought to recover through a renewed emphasis on spiritual formation in the late twentieth century. In the following section, I examine how the concept and practice of spiritual formation have been incorporated into the life and curricula of North American seminaries.

Spiritual Formation in North American Seminaries

Spiritual formation did not become an integral part of Western evangelical theological education until the 1960s.[181] Since the early eighteenth century, North American seminaries have provided theological education

176. Sittser and Peterson, *Water from a Deep Well*, 231.

177. Edwards and Houston, *Religious Affections*; Sittser and Peterson, *Water from a Deep Well*.

178. Hindmarsh, "Contours of Evangelical Spirituality," 197.

179. Hindmarsh, "Contours of Evangelical Spirituality," 197.

180. Sittser and Peterson, *Water from a Deep Well*, 247.

181. Howard, "Advancing the Discussion."

for future pastors and ministers.[182] By the late twentieth century, however, widespread dissatisfaction had arisen regarding the effectiveness of seminary training.[183] Many students complained that seminaries relied on outdated instructional models and that they felt unprepared for ministry upon graduation.[184] Churches, closely linked to these institutions, voiced similar concerns about the inadequacy of theological education for practical ministry.[185]

Scholars have argued that these challenges stem from a gradual shift in the focus of theological education. Liefeld and Cannel observed that seminary training had become increasingly compartmentalized, privileging the cognitive and academic dimensions of learning over the spiritual and formational.[186] By contrast, the early church regarded spiritual and character formation as central to pastoral preparation.[187] The primary qualification for ordination was not intellectual mastery but "the desire for God."[188] Over time, however, under the influence of the Enlightenment and American educational systems, "the study of theology has become a science supporting the profession of the ministry."[189]

In response to these concerns, many theological institutions began to reform their approach to ministerial training by incorporating spiritual formation into the curriculum. Howard notes that "interest in spiritual formation spread from Roman Catholic training to Protestant circles after 1960."[190] Since then, an increasing number of seminaries have recognized the importance of integrating spiritual formation as a core component of theological education.[191]

Liefeld and Cannell further observed that many contemporary seminary students and ministers "come from dysfunctional families"[192] and often lack "strong church links."[193] For this reason, they argued that

182. Sheard, "Role of Spiritual Formation."
183. Sheard, "Role of Spiritual Formation."
184. Sheard, "Role of Spiritual Formation."
185. Sheard, "Role of Spiritual Formation."
186. Liefeld and Cannel, "Spiritual Formation."
187. Liefeld and Cannel, "Spiritual Formation," 239.
188. Liefeld and Cannel, "Spiritual Formation," 240.
189. Liefeld and Cannel, "Spiritual Formation," 240.
190. Howard, "Advancing the Discussion," 12.
191. Liefeld and Cannel, "Spiritual Formation."
192. Liefeld and Cannel, "Spiritual Formation," 247.
193. Liefeld and Cannel, "Spiritual Formation," 247.

seminaries must assume greater responsibility for fostering students' spiritual development.[194] Such formation, they maintained, should not consist merely of additional lectures but should instead provide opportunities for students to "witness what God is already doing in their lives and in the lives of others."[195] They stressed,

> It would be tragic if the members of a theological faculty who have been immersed in Bible and theology, informed by church history, trained in the mysteries of the mind and spirit and experienced in pastoral ministries and cross-cultural encounters could not together guide the students for whom they are responsible through a holistic process of spiritual formation.[196]

From their perspective, theology and spirituality are inseparable, and intellectual study must be integrated with spiritual transformation.[197] The renewed emphasis on spiritual formation in theological education thus reflects a rediscovery of this ancient unity, seeking to restore the balance between knowing God and being formed by God.

Addressing the challenges identified in theological education, Coe outlined what he termed the "seven deadly disconnects" in seminary training and proposed a transformation model for student formation.[198] According to Coe, these disconnects occur between the following:

1. word and Spirit;
2. knowing God and knowing the self;
3. theological knowledge, ministerial skills, and the intentional goal of transformation;
4. theology and its integrative role as queen to all the creation disciplines;
5. theology and praxis;
6. ministry, the Spirit's power of gifting, and the example of gifted people; and
7. seminary education, intentional training in discerning God's calling, and nurturing the wisdom to obey.[199]

194. Liefeld and Cannel, "Spiritual Formation."
195. Liefeld and Cannel, "Spiritual Formation," 248–49.
196. Liefeld and Cannel, "Spiritual Formation," 247.
197. Liefeld and Cannel, "Spiritual Formation."
198. Coe, "Seven Deadly Disconnects," 1.
199. Coe, "Seven Deadly Disconnects."

In light of these concerns, Coe proposed a "Transformation Model for the sake of spiritual formation in the seminary and church."[200] This model seeks to bridge the gaps between academic instruction and the transformative work of the Holy Spirit in students' lives, thereby integrating knowledge, practice, and spiritual maturity within theological education.[201]

Research has shown that seminary students face a variety of challenges, including academic and financial pressure, limited community support, and difficulty sustaining spiritual discipline and growth. As a result, they require multidimensional forms of support.[202] In this context, Christian spiritual formation refers to the process by which the heart, mind, will, and character are transformed so that believers live out the reality of their union with God through the redemptive work of Christ.[203]

In response to these realities, many North American seminaries have intentionally reformed their curricula by integrating spiritual formation into theological education.[204] This integration seeks to foster holistic growth by attending not only to intellectual development but also to spiritual maturity and emotional well-being. Through such reform, seminaries aim to cultivate leaders whose theology is inseparable from their spirituality and whose ministry flows from a deeply formed life in Christ.

The Outcomes of Spiritual Formation in North American Seminaries

Recent research on evangelical seminaries that have incorporated spiritual formation, either as a curricular requirement or as elective coursework,[205] demonstrates that this practice has become a fundamental and transformative component of theological education.[206] Four primary outcomes of integrating spiritual formation into Christian leadership training have been identified. The following section examines these four key outcomes.

200. Coe, "Seven Deadly Disconnects," 1.

201. Coe, "Seven Deadly Disconnects."

202. Freeburg, "Nurturing Spiritual Formation"; Keely, "Spiritual Formation"; Miller, "Keeping the Faith"; Sheard, "Role of Spiritual Formation."

203. Coe, "Spiritual Theology."

204. Freeburg, "Nurturing Spiritual Formation"; Keely, "Spiritual Formation"; Miller, "Keeping the Faith"; Sheard, "Role of Spiritual Formation."

205. Liefeld and Cannel, "Spiritual Formation."

206. Keely, "Spiritual Formation"; Sheard, "Role of Spiritual Formation."

Equipping Church Leaders as Spiritual Guides

Spiritual formation programs have played a vital role in preparing church leaders to serve as spiritual guides. In his study of twelve graduates from the MDiv program at George Fox Evangelical Seminary, Sheard found that spiritual formation significantly equipped graduates to lead their congregations in discernment of God's will.[207] Through the practice of spiritual disciplines, students deepened their relationship with God and became more firmly rooted in that relationship.[208]

This outcome is significant because, as Keely observes, a church leader's personal life of prayer and intimacy with God enables him or her to be "a model of being in the world that is anchored in God."[209] In developing a course on spiritual formation for students "in an ecumenical seminary grounded in the Reformed tradition," Keely affirmed that such formation provides both practices and community that allow students to "live without pretense" and to keep their attention focused on God.[210] This posture of authenticity and attentiveness not only nurtures personal transformation but also equips leaders to guide others toward deeper communion with God.

Spiritual formation courses enabled students to know God not merely at an intellectual level but through lived experience, integrating knowledge of the mind with formation of the heart.[211] Students were encouraged to sustain a spiritual rhythm amid the demands of academic study and everyday life beyond the classroom.[212] Miller observed that "hands-on devotional practices," such as *lectio divina* and the Ignatian exercises, effectively prepared students for the stresses of future ministry.[213]

Similarly, in Keely's research, participants reported that the required senior-level spiritual formation course in the MDiv program was crucial in preparing them for ordained ministry.[214] They noted that spiritual formation offered both academic and experiential resources that enriched

207. Sheard, "Role of Spiritual Formation."
208. Sheard, "Role of Spiritual Formation."
209. Keely, "Spiritual Formation," 202.
210. Keely, "Spiritual Formation," 202.
211. Keely, "Spiritual Formation."
212. Keely, "Spiritual Formation."
213. Miller, "Keeping the Faith," 98.
214. Keely, "Spiritual Formation."

their service within the church.[215] These effects also proved enduring, as many graduates remained actively engaged in their spiritual journeys and continued to practice the disciplines learned in seminary, thereby sustaining an intimate relationship with God.[216]

Taken together, these studies demonstrate that spiritual formation equips seminary students to serve as spiritual guides, whose ministry flows from deep and sustained communion with God.

Redeemed Understandings of Self, Vocation, and Pastoral Identity

Spiritual formation programs also contribute to the redemption of seminarians' understandings of self, vocation, and pastoral identity. Research over the past several decades has shown that burnout and inadequate practices of self-care are widespread in Christian ministry.[217] Many seminarians tend to define themselves primarily by their ministry roles, often overextending themselves under the weight of academic and vocational expectations.[218]

In his action research at Northern Baptist Seminary, Freeburg gathered seven full-time students into small groups "for a period of two hours, once a week, for seven weeks" with the aim of nurturing their spiritual formation.[219] He found that the process of "intentionally engaging in disclosure and being known," supported by spiritual practices and communal relationships, enabled students to rediscover their true identity in Jesus Christ.[220]

Similarly, Sheard observed that graduates who experienced intentional spiritual formation were empowered to follow God's leading in ministry "regardless of what [was] happening in the world around them."[221] Through formation, they deepened their understanding of themselves as children of God, learning to embrace freedom, vulnerability, and authenticity. As they shared their weaknesses and sufferings, they

215. Keely, "Spiritual Formation."
216. Keely, "Spiritual Formation"; Sheard, "Role of Spiritual Formation."
217. Miller, "Keeping the Faith."
218. Freeburg, "Nurturing Spiritual Formation."
219. Freeburg, "Nurturing Spiritual Formation," 64.
220. Freeburg, "Nurturing Spiritual Formation," 111.
221. Freeburg, "Nurturing Spiritual Formation," 119.

modeled for their congregations what it means to walk faithfully along the spiritual journey.

Redeemed Relationships

Spiritual formation programs also foster redeemed relationships through intentional practices of community and accountability. Freeburg noted that his spiritual formation project enabled students not only to grow spiritually but also to relate to others more deeply through participation in small cohort groups.[222] Such programs commonly include mentoring, spiritual direction, and opportunities for honest storytelling and mutual prayer. These communal practices deepen relational trust and cultivate a supportive environment that encourages both spiritual and emotional wholeness.

A recent study found that participation in cohort groups creates "a pause in academia for spiritual application," opening space for "authentic relationships . . . necessary to develop students into healthier, higher-functioning pastors and leaders after graduation."[223] This communal experience also offers healing for relational brokenness by cultivating "an environment of social support, intimacy, and disclosure."[224] Through shared vulnerability and intercessory prayer, students learn that formation occurs most deeply within community, where grace can be both received and extended.

Nurturing the Spiritual Lives of Others

Research further demonstrates that spiritual formation programs equip students to nurture the spiritual lives of others.[225] Sheard found that students who studied in seminaries incorporating spiritual formation were empowered to assist others in their spiritual growth.[226] Their own experience of formation not only strengthened their relationship with God

222. Freeburg, "Nurturing Spiritual Formation."
223. Miller, "Keeping the Faith," 104.
224. Freeburg, "Nurturing Spiritual Formation," 110.
225. Miller, "Keeping the Faith," 104.
226. Sheard, "Role of Spiritual Formation."

but also prepared them to guide others faithfully along their spiritual journeys.[227]

As a result of their personal transformation, students became far less prone to burnout or spiritual stagnation in ministry.[228] Instead, their deepened awareness of "different paths of spiritual growth" enabled them to recognize the diversity of God's work in others.[229] They also learned to accept themselves as unique and to appreciate the uniqueness of other people. Through this process, students developed deeper relational connections with both individuals and the wider church community. Spiritual formation, therefore, does more than shape private devotion; it cultivates ministers who are able to nurture spiritual vitality in others and to foster communities that reflect the transforming presence of Christ.

These studies demonstrate that seminaries integrating spiritual formation into their curricula have effectively equipped students to serve God and the church faithfully as ministerial leaders.[230] Through such integration, seminaries empower students to live in accordance with God's calling. Spiritual formation not only nurtures the development of students' inner spiritual lives but also prepares them to guide others in the ongoing process of becoming Christlike.

Faculty's Role in Spiritual Formation

Studies have also examined the crucial role of faculty in facilitating seminary students' spiritual formation. In recent years, theological education has undergone significant shifts in its goals and emphases, increasingly recognizing that spiritual formation must be intentionally integrated not only into curriculum design but also into classroom practice.[231]

In his proposal for a spiritual formation program within theological education, Coe emphasized the faculty's central responsibility in guiding students toward holistic learning through both course design and

227. Sheard, "Role of Spiritual Formation."

228. Sheard, "Role of Spiritual Formation."

229. Sheard, "Role of Spiritual Formation," 123.

230. Freeburg, "Nurturing Spiritual Formation"; Keely, "Spiritual Formation"; Miller, "Keeping the Faith"; Sheard, "Role of Spiritual Formation."

231. Freeburg, "Nurturing Spiritual Formation"; Keely, "Spiritual Formation"; MacEwen, "Impact"; Miller, "Keeping the Faith"; Pennington, "Dynamics"; Sheard, "Role of Spiritual Formation."

classroom engagement.[232] He explained that curricula should "address the heart and the knowledge of self," as well as the knowledge of God, if genuine transformation is to occur.[233] Professors, he argued, must help students recognize that their seminary experience should be grounded in both Scripture and the Spirit.[234] To this end, Coe urged seminaries "to intentionally build a depth understanding and training of the life of prayer and growth into the curriculum."[235]

When designing such curricula, Coe noted that faculty should provide both instruction and opportunities for students "to open themselves to the reality of their sin and need for application of the Cross and Spirit to their heart."[236] Faculty can guide students through "course lecture, classroom experience and assigned prayer projects and reflection papers,"[237] treating all class activities as potential spiritual disciplines. In this way, coursework becomes a means of "training-in-righteousness, and in fostering . . . identity in Christ" for both teachers and students.[238]

Similarly, Holm argued that faculty serve as co-laborers with God in shaping students' spiritual identity.[239] Because of their unique influence, professors model formation not only through their teaching but also through their character and way of life.[240] Holm asserts, "The heart of teaching lies in the identity and integrity of the teacher. Teachers must teach from their true selves, from their deepest identity."[241] Yet, as Coe observed, faculty themselves often struggle to remain grounded in their own spiritual identities.[242] For this reason, he insisted that professors must first be formed in the life of prayer if they are to guide students faithfully along the same journey.[243] In this way, spiritually grounded faculty participate in the transformative work of the Holy Spirit, helping students

232. Coe, "Seven Deadly Disconnects."
233. Coe, "Seven Deadly Disconnects," 4.
234. Coe, "Seven Deadly Disconnects."
235. Coe, "Seven Deadly Disconnects," 2.
236. Coe, "Seven Deadly Disconnects," 3.
237. Coe, "Seven Deadly Disconnects," 4.
238. Coe, "Seven Deadly Disconnects," 95.
239. Holm, "Identity Formation Through Classroom," 47.
240. Holm, "Identity Formation Through Classroom."
241. Holm, "Identity Formation Through Classroom," 50.
242. Coe, "Seven Deadly Disconnects."
243. Coe, "Seven Deadly Disconnects."

open their hearts to the truth of themselves and of God through the intentional integration of spiritual formation into theological education.[244]

Moreover, Coe strongly suggested that evangelical seminaries should "develop departments of Spiritual-Theology and hire or train 'Spiritual Theologians' who seriously study both the Scriptures and the phenomena of the Spirit in human affairs."[245] From his perspective, spiritual theology can effectively facilitate the sanctification of both students and faculty by integrating theological reflection with lived spiritual experience.[246] He further proposed that seminaries employ faculty members with a diversity of spiritual gifts beyond those of teaching, preaching, and administration, thereby broadening students' understanding of how varied callings contribute to the life and mission of the church.[247]

Recognizing that many students require guidance and companionship in discerning their vocation, Coe also advised that faculty should walk alongside students throughout this process of discernment.[248] He recommended that seminaries offer a course on the theology and praxis of calling and vocation in order to support students as they discover and respond to God's call.[249]

In addition to curriculum design and classroom instruction, faculty can support students' holistic formation by cultivating "a biblically nurtured Christian education community."[250] In their study of 206 seminary students, TenElshof and Furrow found that "secure adult attachment was a stronger predictor of faith maturity when compared to measures of parental bonding."[251] Such relationships foster the confidence and relational capacity necessary for effective ministry.[252] Accordingly, they suggested that faculty intentionally provide secure attachment experiences for students, helping them deepen their relationships with both God and others.[253]

Similarly, Pennington's research demonstrated that "spiritual parenting" relationships between faculty and students often establish a

244. Coe, "Seven Deadly Disconnects."
245. Coe, "Seven Deadly Disconnects," 8.
246. Coe, "Seven Deadly Disconnects."
247. Coe, "Seven Deadly Disconnects."
248. Coe, "Seven Deadly Disconnects."
249. Coe, "Seven Deadly Disconnects."
250. TenElshof and Furrow, "Secure Attachment," 106.
251. TenElshof and Furrow, "Secure Attachment," 99.
252. TenElshof and Furrow, "Secure Attachment."
253. TenElshof and Furrow, "Secure Attachment."

secure adult attachment that powerfully shapes the mentee's spiritual development.[254] In this way, faculty play a vital role not only as academic instructors but also as companions in the transformative process of spiritual formation, modeling the love and presence of Christ within the seminary community.

Additionally, Holm emphasized that the spiritual maturity of faculty members profoundly influences the spiritual growth of their students.[255] TenElshof and Furrow likewise proposed that, in order to nurture students' formation, professors must attend to their own spiritual maturity by following God's leading and strengthening healthy adult attachments.[256] Barber and Baker further suggested that seminary faculty should receive continual soul care so that they can shepherd students with authenticity and compassion.[257]

Henri Nouwen insightfully wrote that teachers and ministers "need a place where they can share their deep pain and struggles with people who do not need them, but who can guide them ever deeper into the mystery of God's love."[258] When faculty receive this kind of care, they are better able to attend to the souls of their students and to model a spiritually integrated life grounded in grace and humility.

In summary, faculty in theological education facilitate students' holistic spiritual formation by intentionally designing curricula, engaging meaningfully in classroom practices, offering secure attachment and mentorship, and attending to their own souls through ongoing formation in Christ.

Concerns About Spiritual Formation

While spiritual formation has been widely employed and has proven effective in equipping ministerial leaders within seminaries, a number of concerns have also emerged from diverse theological perspectives. This section examines several of these critiques, which may also help illuminate how many Chinese Christians perceive and respond to spiritual formation.

254. Pennington, "Dynamics."
255. Holm, "Identity Formation Through Classroom."
256. TenElshof and Furrow, "Secure Attachment."
257. Barber and Baker, "Soul Care."
258. Nouwen, *In the Name of Jesus*, 50.

Roberts expressed concern that spiritual formation could become a superficial response to deeper spiritual problems.[259] He questioned the legitimacy of the term *spirituality*, noting that it does not originate in Scripture.[260] Furthermore, he argued that the phrase *spiritual formation* itself is non-biblical and maintained that seminary students should have their identities shaped primarily through participation in the communal life of the local church.[261] Nevertheless, Roberts acknowledged the value of studying "the piety of the desert fathers, the discipline of the different monastic orders, and so on."[262]

Langer likewise affirmed "many points that are praiseworthy" in the spiritual formation movement while expressing unease about its potential excesses.[263] He cautioned that an overemphasis on spirituality could lead to neglect of the physical world, that many spiritual disciplines are often inherited uncritically from monastic traditions, and that Scripture may at times be employed in hermeneutically questionable ways.[264] While Langer acknowledged that spiritual formation has contributed meaningly to the growth of both seminary students and the church, he concluded that it must be practiced with discernment and caution.[265]

Other concerns have also been raised. Some critics argue that spiritual formation places excessive emphasis on subjective experience. Bloesch, for example, warned that "the great mystics of the church" at times compromised the truth of God through overly introspective forms of meditation.[266] Others caution that the practice of spiritual disciplines can devolve into legalism or behaviorism. Richard Foster himself, in *Celebration of Discipline: The Path to Spiritual Growth*, warned that "an outward life-style of simplicity without the inward reality leads to deadly legalism."[267] He further cautioned that disciplines pursued apart from a focus on the kingdom of God risk degenerating into "legalistic trivia."[268]

259. Roberts, "Seminaries."
260. Roberts, "Seminaries," 46.
261. Roberts, "Seminaries," 47–48.
262. Roberts, "Seminaries," 49.
263. Langer, "Points of Unease," 182.
264. Langer, "Points of Unease."
265. Langer, "Points of Unease."
266. Bloesch, *Spirituality Old and New*, 78.
267. Foster, *Celebration of Discipline*, 80.
268. Foster, *Celebration of Discipline*, 87.

Another concern centers on the use of extra-biblical sources of wisdom. In *Systematic Theology: An Introduction to Biblical Doctrine*, Grudem asserts that Scripture alone provides the wisdom necessary for faithful living.[269] He wrote, "If we simply keep the words of Scripture, we will be 'blameless' and we will be doing 'every good work' that God expects us."[270] Finally, some critics have observed that excessive focus on the interior life may lead practitioners of spiritual formation to neglect evangelism and engagement with the world.[271]

Response to Concerns About Spiritual Formation

While concerns about spiritual formation persist among evangelicals,[272] many scholars nonetheless affirm both its necessity and its effectiveness in cultivating Christian maturity. Far from being a recent innovation, spiritual formation has deep roots within the Christian tradition. As Porter explains, spiritual formation may be understood as "simply the Protestant doctrine of sanctification in a new key."[273] Likewise, Chandler observes that "evangelical spirituality rides upon the shoulders of a long and robust Christian tradition, predicated on the various eras of church history including the patristic, medieval, and Reformation eras through to the present time."[274]

Throughout history, leading Protestant figures, such as John Calvin, Martin Luther, John Wesley, and Jonathan Edwards, practiced devotional disciplines inherited in part from the monastic tradition and produced a rich legacy of writings on Christian spirituality.[275] According to Chandler, the "contemporary spiritual formation movement" is built upon this heritage and continues to draw from modern authors such as Richard Foster, Dallas Willard, and Robert M. Mulholland.[276]

Concerns have also been raised about the perceived association of spiritual formation with Catholicism. In response, Porter argued that all

269. Grudem, *Systematic Theology*, 127.
270. Grudem, *Systematic Theology*, 128.
271. Mason, *Active Life and Contemplative*.
272. Keely, "Spiritual Formation"; Roberts, "Seminaries."
273. Porter, "Sanctification," 129.
274. Chandler, "African American Spirituality," 159.
275. Houston, "Living Through"; Porter, "Sanctification."
276. Chandler, "African American Spirituality," 159.

Protestant theology, including doctrines such as the Trinity, the incarnation, and sanctification, is historically "rooted in the pre-Reformation Catholic Church."[277] While the Protestant Reformation arose in opposition to certain doctrinal errors, it did not reject "fifteen centuries of reflection on the nature of spiritual growth."[278] Indeed, many of the spiritual disciplines practiced within the Catholic tradition have continued to shape Christian spirituality throughout the history of the church.[279]

Porter further asserted that, whether emphasized or neglected in different eras, the church always bears responsibility for articulating a clear and practical theology of spiritual growth for believers.[280] What must be carefully guarded against, he cautioned, are the "unbiblical theology and practices" that can distort authentic formation.[281]

Regarding the concern that spiritual formation may be hermeneutically erroneous, Hall asserted,

> The fathers never split theology off from spirituality, as though theology was academic, mental exercise best practiced in one's study, while Christian spirituality was more appropriately focused on the heart and centered in a church sanctuary. Any split between mind and heart, theology and spirituality, study and sanctuary would have met with scant toleration from the fathers.[282]

In other words, spiritual formation is firmly grounded in Scripture and reflects a holistic understanding of sanctification in which believers actively cooperate with the Holy Spirit in the transformation of their lives.[283]

With respect to the concern that spiritual formation places excessive emphasis on experience, Edwards and Houston argued that Christian spirituality is necessarily experiential, since "all Christian practice is experienced."[284] They further explained, "Our inward knowledge of God will dominate our religious experience, or holy practice."[285] Similarly,

277. Porter, "Sanctification," 132.

278. Porter, "Sanctification," 133.

279. Scorgie, "Overview of Christian Spirituality"; Sittser and Peterson, *Water from a Deep Well.*

280. Porter, "Sanctification."

281. Porter, "Sanctification," 133.

282. Hall, *Learning Theology*, 10.

283. Howard, "Advancing the Discussion."

284. Edwards and Houston, *Religious Affections*, 185.

285. Edwards and Houston, *Religious Affections*, 185.

Calhoun observed that throughout church history, spiritual formation has been closely linked to believers' longing for deeper relationship with God.[286] For Christians, the practice of spiritual disciplines has long served as a visible expression of godliness.[287] As Edwards and Houston affirmed, when believers follow God's leading in their experiential spiritual journey, authentic spiritual practice does not culminate in legalism but in grace-shaped transformation.[288]

Concerns have also been raised about the use of worldly wisdom independent of Scripture in spiritual formation. Porter responded that while "Scripture is the believer's highest authority and the sole authority that defines what constitutes Christian belief and practice," extra-biblical sources of wisdom, such as psychology, church history, and the social sciences, can assist believers in understanding and applying Scripture more deeply.[289] Sheldrake likewise emphasized the interdisciplinary nature of Christian spirituality, explaining that "Christian spirituality . . . is an interdisciplinary field shaped by scripture, theology, and Christian history, but which may also draw upon psychology, the social sciences, literature, and the sciences."[290] He further noted that "the study of Christian spirituality is also 'self-implicating,' in the sense that it is not treated in a purely theoretical way but includes a quest for practical wisdom."[291]

Finally, in response to the concern that spiritual formation might become cloistered and neglect evangelism or social engagement, research suggests that genuine formation fosters spiritual maturity that naturally contributes to the expansion of God's kingdom.[292] Chittister warned against romanticizing spirituality as a means of escape,[293] noting its potential for distortion when detached from engagement with the world. Echoing this insight, English and Tisdell observed that when "applied to the workplace, community, or higher education . . . spirituality is neither a thing to be manipulated for the bottom line nor an escape."[294]

286. Calhoun, *Spiritual Disciplines Handbook.*

287. Edwards and Houston, *Religious Affections.*

288. Edwards and Houston, *Religious Affections.*

289. Porter, "Sanctification," 141.

290. Sheldrake, "Christian Spirituality," para. 4.

291. Sheldrake, "Christian Spirituality," para. 4.

292. Howard, "Advancing the Discussion"; Porter, "Sanctification"; Scorgie, "Overview of Christian Spirituality."

293. Chittister, *Rule of Benedict.*

294. English and Tisdell, "Spirituality and Adult Education," 291.

In this sense, spiritual formation does not withdraw believers from the world but equips them to participate more fully in God's redemptive mission. Authentic formation integrates contemplation and action, nurturing a spirituality that transforms people inwardly while directing them outward into faithful service, witness, and social responsibility.

SPIRITUAL FORMATION IN ASIAN CONTEXTS

In the previous section, I examined spiritual formation as practiced within the North American context. Yet understanding how spiritual formation should be contextualized across diverse cultures remains an essential task. Chandler observed that spiritual formation is shaped by "location, historical setting, and culture,"[295] noting that "culture within historical and spiritual context has a powerful shaping quality."[296] Likewise, McMinn explained that "spiritual formation, like parenting, educational systems, values around sports and beauty, notions of civic duty and civility, develops from within a cultural context."[297] As Chandler emphasized, it is therefore essential to recognize and honor the distinctive ways Christian spiritual formation is practiced within particular cultural and historical frameworks.[298]

In this section, I explore how spiritual formation has been practiced in selected Asian contexts, specifically in South Korea, Hong Kong, Taiwan, and mainland China. These regions share a common Confucian cultural background. Examining these contexts offers valuable insight into how formation is both enriched and challenged by the deep moral, relational, and communal traditions shaped by Confucian thought.

Spiritual Formation in the South Korean Context

This section examines how spiritual formation has been practiced in South Korea, a nation whose cultural heritage, like that of China, has been deeply shaped by Confucian values.

295. Chandler, "African American Spirituality," 160.
296. Chandler, "African American Spirituality," 161.
297. McMinn, "Perceiving the Cultural Sea," 148.
298. Chandler, "African American Spirituality."

Contextualized Spiritual Formation for Korean Seminarians

In recent decades, spiritual formation has been intentionally contextualized for Korean Christians. Since the twentieth century, increasing numbers of international students have attended North American seminaries to study theology, including many from South Korea. Through their exposure to Western models of spiritual formation, some of these students have learned formative practices abroad and subsequently adapted them to serve their own cultural, ecclesial, and pastoral contexts upon returning home or ministering within Korean diasporic communities.

Among these efforts, MacEwen developed a contextualized spiritual formation strategy specifically for Korean Christians.[299] She noted the rapid growth of Christianity in South Korea during the twentieth century, as well as its stagnation and decline in more recent decades. MacEwen identified several underlying challenges, including "performance-based spirituality, legalism, and other problems associated with spiritual immaturity," which she traced to "syncretistic elements in Korean Christianity related to Korean traditional religions."[300] She further observed that "the influence of Korean traditional religion on Korean Christianity and spiritual formation creates obstacles that cause some Korean Christians to become stagnant in their spiritual lives or experience burnout."[301]

MacEwen's findings demonstrated the effectiveness of contextualized spiritual disciplines and underscored the urgent need for spiritual formation courses within Korean seminaries.[302] Her research showed that spiritual formation functions as "a bridge that connects sound theology to day-to-day spiritual practices."[303] She affirmed that "the consistent practice of spiritual disciplines can strengthen Christians' spiritual lives and contribute to dispelling syncretistic beliefs and practices."[304] Furthermore, she proposed that "contextualized spiritual formation can be taught and implemented in an adult Sunday school setting," enabling believers to cultivate spiritual growth through disciplined practice.[305] Recognizing South Korea's significant role in global missions, MacEwen also urged

299. MacEwen, "Impact."
300. MacEwen, "Impact," 2.
301. MacEwen, "Impact," 2.
302. MacEwen, "Impact."
303. MacEwen, "Impact," 199.
304. MacEwen, "Impact," 199.
305. MacEwen, "Impact," 199.

Korean mission organizations to incorporate "contextualized spiritual formation classes in their missionary training programs" and to develop formation strategies appropriate to indigenous cultural contexts.[306]

Spiritual Direction for Korean Directees

Spiritual direction constitutes a central element of spiritual formation. As increasing numbers of Christians from diverse cultural backgrounds seek spiritual direction from North American directors, scholarly attention has increasingly turned to the dynamics and challenges of cross-cultural spiritual direction.[307]

Spiritual direction has a long history within the Christian tradition. Silver defined it as "a unique one-to-one relationship in which a trained person assists another person in the search for an ever-closer union of love with God."[308] "By its very nature," he noted, spiritual direction is "a relationship of unusual intimacy and trust."[309] It "involves the relationship of the directee to God and that of the director to God as well as the relationship of the directee to the director."[310] Both directors and directees affirm the "reality of the spiritual" and the primacy of relationship with God.[311] Within this process, the true director is the Holy Spirit, who works through "two poor sinners sitting down together."[312] As director and directee discern the Spirit's activity in their lives, both grow in their relationship with God. Throughout church history, clergy and laity alike have practiced spiritual direction as a vital means of spiritual guidance and transformation.[313]

When spiritual directors and directees come from different cultural backgrounds, the process of spiritual direction becomes more complex.[314] For example, although many Korean directees reported overall satisfaction with cross-cultural spiritual direction experiences with North American directors, they also described difficulties relating to directors

306. MacEwen, "Impact," 200.
307. Lee, *Christian Spiritual Direction.*
308. Silver, *Trustworthy Connections*, 117.
309. Silver, *Trustworthy Connections*, 39.
310. Silver, *Trustworthy Connections*, 39.
311. Silver, *Trustworthy Connections*, 117.
312. Silver, *Trustworthy Connections*, 19.
313. Silver, *Trustworthy Connections.*
314. Lee, *Christian Spiritual Direction.*

who were unfamiliar with Korean culture, which has been deeply shaped by Confucianism.[315] Confucian values strongly influence key dimensions of Korean relational life, particularly "hierarchy, gender, and age," and consequently shape how Koreans understand their relationships with God, with others, and with themselves.[316] Without careful cultural contextualization, spiritual direction across differing cultural frameworks can therefore present significant challenges.

At the same time, attentiveness to directees' cultural backgrounds can greatly enhance the effectiveness of spiritual direction. In K. Lee's study of Korean directees' experiences, participants reported difficulties "in the areas of emotional exchange, covenantal characteristics of relationship, and asking for and receiving advice," challenges they attributed to the influence of Confucianism.[317] Lee's research makes a significant contribution to the field of spiritual formation by expanding understanding of spiritual direction within an Asian, particularly Korean, context. He offers "some perspectives to understanding how Confucianism influences the Korean directee's self-construction and relation making," insights that are especially valuable for North American directors who have been trained in non-Confucian cultural settings and who frequently accompany directees shaped by Confucian traditions.[318]

These findings suggest that cross-cultural spiritual direction requires not only theological sensitivity but also cultural intelligence, an awareness of how deeply ingrained relational norms, hierarchies, and values shape a directee's spiritual expression. When such understanding is present, the practice of spiritual direction can transcend cultural barriers and become a more effective means of grace.

Spiritual Formation in the Hong Kong Protestant Evangelical Context

In recent years, increasing attention has been given to spiritual formation in Chinese-speaking contexts. Since the beginning of the twenty-first century, numerous studies on Christian spiritual formation have been published or translated into Chinese, providing rich resources for

315. Lee, *Christian Spiritual Direction.*

316. Lee, *Christian Spiritual Direction*, 272.

317. Lee, *Christian Spiritual Direction*, 272.

318. Lee, *Christian Spiritual Direction*, 273.

spiritual growth among Chinese Christians. This development has been especially evident in Hong Kong, where churches and seminaries have historically enjoyed broader access to theological education and international Christian literature. As a result, "many protestant theological seminaries in Hong Kong have begun offering courses in Christian spirituality, spiritual classics and spiritual formation to church leaders and lay people."[319]

Ng observed that although spiritual formation in Protestant Chinese churches remains "in the very early development stages," it has already demonstrated effectiveness in nurturing Christian maturity.[320] To evaluate its impact, Ng examined "the reflections of Western female authors on Ignatius of Loyola's *Spiritual Exercises*" and explored "how these insights might be applied to Protestant Chinese churches."[321] Ignatius's *Spiritual Exercises*, a Christ-centered model of formation, has long helped Christians "enter into a holistic, life-transforming journey toward Christlikeness."[322] Ng found that Chinese female leaders in Hong Kong experienced spiritual growth comparable to that of Western female participants who had practiced Ignatian spirituality, despite their differing cultural contexts.[323]

Nevertheless, Ng also recognized that contextualization is essential for the spiritual formation of Chinese Christians.[324] Given Hong Kong's distinct cultural environment, she observed that "Chinese female retreatants can learn from Western female authors' integrations of Ignatius' *Spiritual Exercises* only after suitable adaption of their insights to the Protestant Chinese context."[325] She further emphasized the importance of cultural awareness, noting that "Christian spirituality is a new discipline in Protestant Chinese churches" and that "it may need an interdisciplinary approach to explore the new development of contemporary spirituality in new and different contexts."[326]

In her research, Ng examined "how the old Christian spiritual classics and traditions can be applied in a contemporary context and how far

319. Ng, "Ignatius' Spiritual Exercises," 187.
320. Ng, "Ignatius' Spiritual Exercises," 187.
321. Ng, "Ignatius' Spiritual Exercises," 187.
322. Warner, *Journey with Jesus*, 9.
323. Ng, "Ignatius' Spiritual Exercises."
324. Ng, "Ignatius' Spiritual Exercises."
325. Ng, "Ignatius' Spiritual Exercises," 187.
326. Ng, "Ignatius' Spiritual Exercises," 203.

Western experience can be applied in a Chinese context."[327] She concluded that attentiveness to cultural uniqueness and "appropriate adaptation" is essential for developing authentic spiritual formation among contemporary Protestant evangelical Chinese Christians.[328] In other words, while the underlying principles of spiritual formation may be universal, their practice must be carefully contextualized to address the distinctive spiritual, emotional, and communal needs of Chinese believers.

Spiritual Formation in Taiwanese Theological Seminaries

Research over the past few decades has shown that many Taiwanese seminaries have emphasized students' cognitive development while often neglecting their spiritual formation.[329] In response to this imbalance, Huang implemented a contextualized spiritual formation curriculum within a Taiwanese seminary.[330] She found that many seminary students had converted from Buddhism and therefore lacked familiarity with Christian spiritual disciplines.[331] To address this need, Huang integrated biblical study with spiritual practices throughout the formation process.[332] This contextualized approach enabled students to renew their understanding of God and equipped them to guide others toward deeper intimacy with him.

Spiritual Formation for Mainland Chinese Christians

Since the late twentieth century, the Christian community in mainland China has experienced notable growth,[333] creating an increasing need to understand the spiritual formation of Chinese believers.[334] Research has highlighted both the vitality and the vulnerability of this development.[335] Ro noted that his research among Chinese churches revealed a

327. Ng, "Ignatius' Spiritual Exercises," 203.
328. Ng, "Ignatius' Spiritual Exercises," 203.
329. Huang, "Evaluating the Effectiveness."
330. Huang, "Evaluating the Effectiveness."
331. Huang, "Evaluating the Effectiveness."
332. Huang, "Evaluating the Effectiveness."
333. Liao, *God Is Red.*
334. Pennington, "Dynamics"; Williamson, "Stress or Burnout."
335. Pennington, "Dynamics"; Williamson, "Stress or Burnout."

continuing emphasis on equipping pastoral leaders through training in counseling and spiritual formation.[336] Similarly, Williamson conducted a "quantitative research study analyzing responses or reactions of personal and professional stress-related factors that can lead to ministry stress or burnout in Chinese pastors."[337] He found that Chinese ministers experience "ministry stress and/or burnout at an alarming rate of 94.8%."[338]

In addition, the influence of Chinese culture on spiritual formation warrants careful examination. Pennington recognized that Chinese culture profoundly shapes Chinese Christians' spiritual formation[339] and conducted a case study of "a university-educated, urban Chinese man" in order to explore the distinctively Chinese contours of formation.[340] He proposed a biblical model of formation centered on spiritual parenting, patterned after the relational dynamics between Jesus and the Father, Jesus and his disciples, and Paul and his converts.[341] Pennington found that this model resonates with Chinese cultural patterns and may be effective in facilitating spiritual growth. Nonetheless, because Confucianism, the predominant cultural ideology in China, has historically fostered fear toward authority figures, it remains unclear whether such hierarchical mentor-mentee relationships encourage or inhibit honest relational engagement with the mentor, and consequently with God. This unresolved tension calls for further exploration.

Since the early twenty-first century, several American women have served Chinese Christian women in mainland China by introducing contextualized spiritual formation curricula.[342] They invited Chinese women to participate in retreats and introduced "additional practices and biblical concepts that will nourish their souls and sustain a deepening relationship with God as His grace."[343] After more than a decade of ministry with approximately one hundred Chinese women, these leaders found that although spiritual formation was initially unfamiliar to many participants, the curricula they developed produced meaningful and lasting changes

336. Ro, "Globalization's Impact."
337. Williamson, "Stress or Burnout," 5.
338. Williamson, "Stress or Burnout," 5.
339. Pennington, "Dynamics."
340. Pennington, "Dynamics," iv.
341. Pennington, "Dynamics."
342. Russell et al., "Making Disciples."
343. Russell et al., "Making Disciples," 200.

in the retreatants' lives.[344] While acknowledging that their "plan for spiritual formation is a costly work—costly in terms of time and personal investment," they expressed amazement at witnessing God's work among the participants.[345] As they listened to and encouraged these women, they testified to the "deep work in the hearts of these particular women in China"[346] that emerged through sustained spiritual formation practices.

In addition, some organizations have recognized that cultural factors necessitate the contextualization of guidelines for spiritual directors.[347] One such organization, Spiritual Directors International, describes itself as "an inclusive, global learning community of people from many faiths and many nations who share a common passion and commitment to the art and contemplative practice of spiritual direction."[348] The organization encourages the practice of spiritual direction with deliberate attentiveness to cultural contexts.[349] This emphasis reflects a growing awareness of the need to contextualize spiritual formation. However, the degree of cultural awareness that is both necessary and sufficient remains an open question.

SPIRITUAL FORMATION IN NORTH AMERICAN SEMINARIES FOR CHINESE STUDENTS

The application of spiritual formation among Chinese students studying in North American seminaries warrants careful examination. In many North American evangelical contexts, spiritual formation has been intentionally integrated into theological education as a means of nurturing believers' spiritual growth.[350] Its teachings and practices encompass "the process of sanctification, personal spiritual disciplines or practices, discipleship, intimacy with God, contemplation, *lectio divina* or sacred reading, Christian mysticism, soul care, and spiritual direction."[351]

However, little is known about how Confucian cultural values interact with these principles of spiritual formation. For example,

344. Russell, Lewis, and Ro, "Making Disciples."
345. Russell, Lewis, and Ro, "Making Disciples," 200.
346. Russell, Lewis, and Ro, "Making Disciples," 200.
347. Silver, *Trustworthy Connections.*
348. Spiritual Directors International, "About Us."
349. Silver, *Trustworthy Connections.*
350. Chandler, "African American Spirituality."
351. Chandler, "African American Spirituality," 159–60.

Confucianism's emphasis on filial piety and the cultivation of shame may influence how Chinese Christians express vulnerability or honesty when sharing their life stories with spiritual directors. Likewise, Confucian collectivism, which prioritizes communal harmony and often restrains personal expression, may shape how Chinese believers engage in one-on-one spiritual direction, a practice that typically emphasizes individual spiritual development.

Therefore, this study seeks to explore how participation in spiritual formation within a North American seminary context influences Chinese students' relationships with God, with themselves, and with others.

3

Methods and Procedures

THIS STUDY EXPLORES HOW a spiritual formation program at a North American seminary has impacted the lives of Chinese students influenced by Confucian cultural values. This chapter outlines the methods and procedures used in conducting the research. It addresses the research paradigm and approach, data collection strategies, data storage and preservation, data analysis procedures, researcher positionality, validation strategies, and ethical considerations.

RESEARCH PARADIGM

The research paradigm adopted for this study is qualitative inquiry. Qualitative research follows an inductive and emergent process that seeks to explore and understand "the meaning individuals or groups ascribe to a social or human problem,"[1] as described by Creswell. Rather than testing predetermined hypotheses, qualitative researchers seek to understand how people interpret their experiences and construct meaning within the contexts of their lives.[2]

In this study, I sought to understand how a spiritual formation program at a North American seminary has influenced the lives of Chinese students shaped by Confucian cultural values. Data were collected

1. Creswell, *Research Design*, 4.

2. Merriam and Tisdell, *Qualitative Research*.

through open-ended questions, allowing for close examination of how these students interpreted their experiences within the seminary's spiritual formation program. Although previous research has explored the impact of spiritual formation in various North American seminaries, comparatively little attention has been given to Chinese students' own perceptions of such programs. For this reason, qualitative research provided the most appropriate methodological framework for this inquiry.

Among the diverse approaches to qualitative research, constructivist grounded theory was well suited to this study because it generates substantive theory grounded in empirical data.[3] Consistent with this approach, I remained open throughout the research process to what I saw, heard, and observed, seeking to address the research questions through participants' interpretations of their lived experiences. In this process, I constructed an understanding of reality in dialogue with participants through iterative cycles of data collection and analysis.

As a constructivist grounded theorist, I regard reality as "holistic, multidimensional, and ever-changing."[4] Accordingly, I sought to understand participants' perspectives and to present a comprehensive, interpretive account of their experiences.[5] At the same time, I acknowledge that my theoretical constructions represent interpretations of participants' interpretations.[6]

The strength of a constructivist grounded theory approach lies in its systematic yet flexible guidelines, which allow concepts to emerge inductively from the data. As I analyzed how participants interpreted their experiences, I engaged in processes of coding, constant comparison, and memo writing. With each analytic cycle, the level of theoretical understanding deepened. When new questions or conceptual gaps emerged, I returned to data collection to address them and refine developing categories. In this way, grounded theory enabled me continually to "check and refine the emerging analytic categories"[7] and ultimately to develop a substantive theory explaining how this group of Chinese students made sense of their experiences within a North American spiritual formation program.

3. Corbin and Strauss, *Basics of Qualitative Research.*
4. Merriam and Tisdell, *Qualitative Research*, 242.
5. Merriam and Tisdell, *Qualitative Research.*
6. Charmaz, *Constructing Grounded Theory.*
7. Charmaz, *Constructing Grounded Theory*, 4.

DATA COLLECTION STRATEGIES

Qualitative researchers intentionally select participants and sources of data that will help them understand the research problem.[8] In this study, I collected data through semi-structured face-to-face and distance intensive interviews.

Participant Selection

By 2018, approximately thirty Chinese students had graduated from the spiritual formation program at a seminary in the western United States. All participants had completed the same required courses, participated in group spiritual direction, attended both corporate and individual retreats, and received one-on-one spiritual direction as part of the program.

I contacted potential participants by email and conducted face-to-face interviews with those residing locally. For participants who could only be reached online, I conducted distance interviews using Facebook audio chat and WhatsApp. Because all participants were graduates of the program, they were able to offer firsthand accounts and reflective interpretations of how the seminary's spiritual formation program had influenced their lives.

Grounded theorists conduct as many interviews as necessary to achieve theoretical saturation rather than mere adequacy.[9] Accordingly, I continued interviewing until saturation was reached, that is, when additional data no longer yielded new conceptual insights or revealed new dimensions of the emerging categories.[10] Once saturation was achieved, data collection ceased and theoretical integration proceeded.

In total, I interviewed eighteen participants. Sixteen had completed either an MA or MDiv degree with a spiritual formation emphasis between 2010 and 2018, and two had completed the emphasis courses but had not yet graduated. Most participants had served in Chinese churches or Christian organizations prior to entering the seminary. Some had grown up in Chinese Christian families, with parents who were pastors or active church leaders. As a result, participants were well acquainted with both family and ecclesial dynamics within Chinese Christian contexts.

8. Creswell, *Research Design*.

9. Charmaz, *Constructing Grounded Theory*.

10. Creswell, *Research Design*.

Although participants came from various regions of the world, all had at least one Chinese parent. The eighteen interviews lasted between one and two hours each; ten were conducted in person and eight at a distance. Participants ranged in age from twenty-five to fifty-five, with equal representation of men and women.

Role of Participants

Participants were invited to recollect and reflect on their experiences within a North American seminary's spiritual formation program and to describe how those experiences had influenced their lives. My aim was to interpret what participants had seen, heard, experienced, and understood as faithfully as possible. In this sense, participants functioned as co-constructors of meaning, contributing to the development of grounded theory through the sharing of their life stories and the articulation of their interpretations.

Data Sources

To collect firsthand data, I conducted intensive interviews designed to elicit participants' perspectives, interpretations, and lived experiences. These interviews enabled participants to describe in depth how they experienced spiritual formation within the seminary context through the use of open-ended questions (see Appendix). During the interviews, I also followed up on unanticipated themes, implicit meanings, and underlying assumptions as they emerged in the conversation.[11] After each interview, I promptly transcribed the recordings and began preliminary analysis.

Face-to-Face Interviews

Face-to-face interviews are a widely used method of data collection in qualitative research because they allow researchers to ask clarifying questions and attend closely to participants' own interpretations of their experiences.[12] Such interviews facilitate rapport and foster an atmosphere

11. Charmaz, *Constructing Grounded Theory*.

12. Creswell, *Research Design*.

of mutual trust, while also allowing flexibility within a semi-structured format.[13] At the same time, face-to-face interviews present certain limitations. They typically occur in designated settings rather than natural environments, participants may differ in articulateness or self-awareness, and the researcher's physical presence may influence responses.[14] To mitigate these limitations, I sought to cultivate genuine rapport and to create a setting in which participants felt safe to express themselves freely and authentically.

Distance Interviews

Although many qualitative researchers prefer face-to-face interviews, technological advances have made distance interviewing an effective alternative through the use of smartphones, digital recorders, and online platforms.[15] I conducted distance interviews in order to include participants who were unable to meet in person because of geographic distance. These interviews enriched the study by incorporating diverse voices and perspectives, thereby enhancing the richness and trustworthiness of the data.[16] Each distance interview was scheduled at a mutually convenient time. Throughout these conversations, I practiced empathetic listening and sought to foster a sense of care and understanding that encouraged participants to share their experiences openly and deeply.

Data Recording

All interviews were recorded using a Sony digital recorder and the voice recorder application on my MacBook Pro. Immediately following each interview, I transcribed the recordings verbatim using the ExpressScribe application. This practice allowed me to remain close to the data and to capture participants' words, tones, and nuances accurately while the interviews were still fresh in my memory.

13. Creswell, *Research Design*.
14. Creswell, *Research Design*.
15. Dzubinski, "Distance Interviews."
16. Dzubinski, "Distance Interviews."

Data Storage

I maintained exclusive possession of all interview recordings and transcriptions. To protect confidentiality, all participants were assigned pseudonyms. Because each participant already used an English name, I created corresponding English pseudonyms to ensure consistency throughout the study. All digital files, including audio recordings, transcripts, and analytic memos, were securely stored on a password-protected computer and an external hard drive. These materials will be retained for a minimum of five years, in accordance with institutional research ethics standards and data protection policies.

DATA ANALYSIS

In grounded theory, data analysis is dynamic, recursive, and flexible, involving continual interaction between the researcher and the data.[17] I analyzed the data through systematic coding, assigning concise labels to segments of text in order to capture their essential meaning. Through this iterative process, I engaged deeply with participants' accounts to understand how they interpreted their experiences. Repeated and intensive coding enabled me to immerse myself in the data and to apprehend participants' worldviews with increasing clarity. The analytic process unfolded in four major phases: initial coding, focused coding, theoretical coding, and memo writing.

Initial Coding

Initial coding constituted the first analytic step, moving the analysis "from concrete events and descriptions of them to theoretical insight and theoretical possibilities."[18] At this stage, I remained open to exploring conceptual possibilities emerging from the data. Following Charmaz's guideline that "initial coding should stick closely to the data,"[19] I coded inductively, keeping my codes "short, simple, active, and analytic."[20] This approach enabled me to identify both explicit statements and implicit

17. Merriam and Tisdell, *Qualitative Research.*
18. Charmaz, *Constructing Grounded Theory*, 137.
19. Charmaz, *Constructing Grounded Theory*, 116.
20. Charmaz, *Constructing Grounded Theory*, 120.

concerns within participants' narratives. Through initial coding, I began to discern the underlying structure of participants' experiences and to develop preliminary theoretical directions.

Focused Coding

Focused coding represents the second analytic step, in which the researcher uses "the most significant and/or frequent earlier codes to sift through and analyze large amounts of data."[21] During this process, I identified and refined the initial codes that best represented patterns across the data set. Focused coding enabled me to synthesize and conceptualize earlier findings while highlighting key categories that guided subsequent analysis.[22] When new insights emerged, I returned to the raw data to examine previously unnoticed or developing themes. Because focused codes are generally "more conceptual" than initial codes, they provided clearer "theoretical direction" and laid the groundwork for the final stage of analysis.[23]

Theoretical Coding

Theoretical coding followed the focused coding stage and guided the conceptualization of relationships among the focused codes, leading to the development of a coherent theoretical framework. During this phase, I moved iteratively between focused and theoretical coding, refining categories and clarifying their conceptual relationships. By integrating and relating conceptual categories, I theorized the data and developed a substantive theory that explains how Chinese students interpreted their experiences of spiritual formation within a North American seminary context.

Memo Writing

Memo writing is an essential component of grounded theory, serving as an analytic bridge between coding and theory construction.[24] I wrote memos throughout the research process to capture emerging insights,

21. Charmaz, *Constructing Grounded Theory*, 138.
22. Charmaz, *Constructing Grounded Theory*.
23. Charmaz, *Constructing Grounded Theory*, 138.
24. Charmaz, *Constructing Grounded Theory*.

questions, and reflections. During interviews, I recorded brief notes by hand and elaborated these notes into analytic memos after each session. As new insights emerged, I documented them in both a physical notebook and a digital memo folder within NVivo. Memo writing enabled me to trace the development of analytic categories and remain attentive to my evolving theoretical perspective.

Qualitative Data Analysis Program

I used QSR International's NVivo software for data storage, coding, and memo organization. Nvivo proved helpful for managing large volumes of qualitative data efficiently. However, I used the software solely as a technical aid rather than an analytic substitute, because in constructivist grounded theory, the researcher—not the software—conducts the analysis and constructs meaning.[25]

INTERNAL VALIDITY

For qualitative researchers, internal validity is emphasized and examined throughout the research process.[26] Internal validity addresses the question of "how research findings match reality."[27] In this study, I sought to understand how participants perceived and interpreted their experiences within a spiritual formation program; therefore, internal validity served as a central measure of the study's trustworthiness. I presented my findings through participants' own interpretations and employed several strategies—reflexivity, positionality, rich description, and peer debriefing—to enhance both internal validity and the overall trustworthiness of the study.

Reflexivity

Researchers' backgrounds inevitably shape how they design, conduct, and interpret their studies.[28] Reflexivity is therefore essential for maintaining

25. Charmaz, *Constructing Grounded Theory.*
26. Lewis, "Redefining Qualitative Methods."
27. Corbin and Strauss, *Basics of Qualitative Research*, 242.
28. Creswell, *Research Design.*

rigor and guarding against distortion.[29] According to Creswell, reflexivity requires that researchers "reflect about how their biases, values, and personal background . . . shape their interpretations."[30]

As a middle-aged Chinese woman who had also studied in a North American seminary's spiritual formation program, I recognized that my experiences could influence how I interpretated the data. I was mindful that not all participants shared my background or perspective. Accordingly, I practiced reflexivity by examining how my personal history shaped my interpretations and by continually checking my analysis against participants' own words and intended meanings.

Positionality

Positionality complements reflexivity by requiring researchers to acknowledge their social and relational location as well as their potential presuppositions.[31] Throughout this study, I remained attentive to my dual role as both an insider—sharing cultural and theological experiences with participants—and an investigator responsible for systematic analysis. I intentionally included data that did not support my emerging theory and refrained from privileging interpretations that merely confirmed my expectations.

My own journey through a North American seminary's spiritual formation program significantly shaped my understanding of transformation and culture. Through this program, God brought healing to my heart and revealed inner barriers—such as shame, fear of authority, and performance orientation—that hindered intimacy with him. My study of intercultural education further clarified how these patterns were culturally embedded within Confucian norms emphasizing hierarchy, honor-shame dynamics, comparison, and fear of failure. This awareness enabled me to approach participants' narratives with humility, recognizing both points of resonance and divergence between their experiences and mine. Such attentiveness reduced interpretive bias and enhanced the credibility and rigor of my analysis.

29. Corbin and Strauss, *Basics of Qualitative Research.*

30. Creswell, *Research Design*, 247.

31. Merriam et al., "Power and Positionality."

Rich, Thick Description

In grounded theory, rich, thick description enables readers to enter participants' contexts and grasp the depth of their experiences.[32] By providing detailed narrative accounts and incorporating direct quotations, I sought to help readers perceive the lived realities of Chinese students engaged in spiritual formation. This narrative richness strengthens the validity of the findings by grounding theoretical analysis in concrete, contextualized experience.

Peer Debriefing

Peer debriefing strengthens the credibility of a study by incorporating perspectives beyond the researcher alone.[33] Throughout this research, I consulted Chinese Christians and theological educators who had received seminary training and were serving in Chinese churches. Their insights resonated with and helped verify many of my emerging findings. My dissertation committee also provided ongoing feedback and critical reflection at each stage of the research process. I intentionally included discrepant data and reported the "full range of findings," including those that challenged or nuanced initial themes, in order to preserve analytic rigor, complexity, and trustworthiness.[34]

ETHICAL ISSUES

Because qualitative research involves the collection and analysis of personal experiences, ethical considerations are essential for protecting participants and ensuring the integrity of the research process.[35] The primary ethical concerns in this study included informed consent, confidentiality, and participant protection.

Prior to data collection, I obtained approval from the Protection of Human Rights in Research Committee (PHRRC). At the beginning of each interview, I introduced myself, explained the purpose of the study, and described participants' rights. I guaranteed confidentiality, informed

32. Creswell, *Research Design*; Lewis, "Redefining Qualitative Methods."

33. Creswell, *Research Design*.

34. Creswell, *Research Design*, 99.

35. Creswell, *Research Design*.

participants of potential risks, emphasized that participation was voluntary and that participants could withdraw at any time, and provided contact information for follow-up questions.

Each participant signed an informed consent form containing the "standard set of elements that acknowledges protection of human rights."[36] Some participants provided signed forms in person, while others submitted them electronically by email. Both face-to-face and distance interviews were conducted in private, interruption-free settings. To protect privacy, I used pseudonyms for all participants and omitted identifying details. These measures ensured the ethical soundness of the research and strengthened the credibility of the findings.

CHAPTER 3 SUMMARY

This chapter outlined the methods and procedures employed in this study. I explained the rationale for adopting a constructivist grounded theory paradigm and described the strategies used for data collection and analysis. I also discussed the approaches employed to ensure validity, reflexivity, and verification of findings, as well as the importance of recognizing my positionality as a researcher. Finally, I addressed ethical issues related to participant protection and confidentiality. Together, these methods provided a rigorous and ethically grounded foundation for exploring how Chinese students experience spiritual formation in a North American seminary context.

36. Creswell, *Research Design*, 96.

4

The Impact of Spiritual Formation on Chinese Students

The central finding of this study is that participation in a Western Christian spiritual formation program facilitated Chinese students' transformative learning in three interrelated ways. First, the program prompted participants to reexamine their upbringing—a countercultural and often challenging process for those shaped by Confucian values. Second, it provided a safe and accepting environment in which students could explore and disclose vulnerabilities that their cultural background frequently associates with shame. Third, the program equipped students with conceptual spiritual knowledge, a range of spiritual disciplines, and hands-on apprenticeship experiences.

Through these processes, participants experienced substantial transformation in their meaning perspectives, particularly in their views of themselves, God, and others. Many described a shift away from an autonomous, self-reliant mode of living—an orientation shaped in part by Confucian ideals—toward a life increasingly characterized by awareness of God's presence and dependence on God.

In this chapter, I present the data related to each of these dimensions of transformation.

THREE NARRATIVES ON THE INTENSIVE INWARD RETREAT

First, I present three narratives that exemplify the transformations participants experienced. These narratives are drawn from participants who attended the intensive inward retreat, a significant component of the spiritual formation program. Although not every student participated in the retreat, the experiences described here reflect broader patterns of transformations that participants reported throughout their studies.

Mia's Story

Mia attended the intensive inward retreat and described the experience as both effective and life-changing. Reflecting on the retreat, she explained that she "uncovered a lot of [her] relational issues with [her] parents" and became aware of her judgmental and perfectionistic tendencies. Through the retreat, she also discovered her desire to fix things and recognized how strongly her parents had shaped these patterns.

She further described the structure of the retreat and its impact, noting that although it was a silent and solitary retreat, she met daily with a spiritual director who was also a trained clinical psychologist. She found this rhythm "very valuable and interesting" and observed that many of her interpretations of childhood memories shifted during the retreat, differing from the understandings she had carried for years.

Although Mia recalled familiar events from her childhood, she began to perceive them differently. She noted that her earlier memories had been shaped largely by her parents' narratives. For example, she described being taken every weekend to her paternal grandmother's home and having been told throughout her life that she loved being there and was very close to her grandmother. During the retreat, however, she realized that she had actually felt lonely and abandoned in that environment, surrounded by adults and separated from her parents.

Through sustained reflection and emotional engagement, Mia was able to reconnect with feelings she had long suppressed. She explained that the emotions her parents labeled as "joy" and "wonderful" were not truly hers, and that as she grew up, she lost touch with her own desires in favor of meeting adult expectations. This realization helped her understand how her people-pleasing tendencies had developed.

Mia emphasized that the guidance of the spiritual director played a crucial role in this process. Early in retreat, he invited her to choose a parent and begin speaking freely. Although the exercise initially felt awkward, suppressed memories soon surfaced. As emotions emerged, she cried and expressed feelings of loneliness and abandonment, asking her mother why she had been left behind.

The retreat provided a safe place for these emotions to surface. Mia reflected that being in solitude and feeling safe with the spiritual director allowed her to "let go and say whatever came up," and that previously inaccessible memories began to unlock. As these emotions surfaced, she was able to process them and receive healing and comfort from the Lord. Toward the end of the retreat, the spiritual director offered her a powerful image that helped her integrate her experience:

> He said there has always been a little Mia locked up inside me—the part the adult Mia does not accept. That's why little Mia's emotions sometimes burst out, and I couldn't control or understand them. The director helped me accept little Mia and bring my person into a whole rather than a split self. Emotions like rejection, abandonment, loneliness, and fear belonged to little Mia, and the adult Mia tried to suppress them. Through the retreat I realized these are all part of me. When they arise, I shouldn't suppress them but seek to understand why I feel that way and how to find resolution.

Mia described little Mia as a fearful child who carried feelings of rejection, loneliness, and abandonment. When she pictured herself holding little Mia on her lap, she experienced a profound shift. The spiritual director invited her to imagine taking little Mia anywhere and everywhere, an exercise that helped her integrate emotional awareness with a growing sense of acceptance and love.

> The director said, "Today, picture yourself taking little Mia anywhere, everywhere." As I walked on the beach, listening to the birds, I sensed little Mia with me. I drew pictures—birds, seagulls, and more. I felt a lot of love. Loving little Mia was equivalent to loving myself—learning how to love myself—and in that process, I felt God's love in me and around me.

Because of her Chinese upbringing, Mia explained that her adult self had learned to reject or suppress negative emotions. The retreat allowed her to reexperience her childhood with greater emotional awareness and to feel accepted and loved by God as she embraced her true self. She described the spiritual director as kind, gentle, and experienced, noting that his calm presence helped her feel free to speak openly. Meeting with him daily for extended sessions, she was encouraged to continue conversations with her parents, and as emotions surfaced, he helped her process them within the context of spiritual direction.

For Mia, healing ultimately came from God. She explained that understanding what was happening in her heart was the first step, followed by bringing those emotions honestly before the Lord. Through prayerful conversation with God, she learned when to speak the truth in love—sometimes returning to others to express how their words or actions had affected her.

Mia had studied in the spiritual formation program for several years before attending the retreat. She described her journey as an "ongoing unlocking of the real self," noting that earlier coursework prepared her for what she eventually experienced more fully during the retreat. Only then did she begin to grasp that spiritual formation involved opening the true self before God. When she imagined holding little Mia on her lap, she felt God's love and realized that going deep into the core of the self was, in fact, an encounter with God.

Looking back, Mia came to distinguish moral formation from spiritual formation. Although she had diligently practiced prayer exercises and journaling, she recognized that much of her earlier effort involved forcing herself toward a version of the "true self" while continuing to suppress little Mia. The retreat enabled her to touch emotions she had previously avoided and to understand what the program had been guiding her toward all along.

By the end of the program, Mia experienced newfound freedom. She learned to name her emotions, understand their origins, and process them with the Lord and, when needed, with her spiritual director. Over time, this reduced her reliance on avoidance behaviors and enabled her to speak the truth I love, even when fear remained.

> When I felt hurt, I learned to honor the reality of my feelings. After I processed and understood what happened, I sensed the next step was to let the person know. If I didn't, resentment would grow, and there would be no resolution. I still felt fear, but speaking up is the loving thing to do—even for the other person—because it opens the possibility of reconciliation. The director said that if I don't tell the truth of my feelings, the other

> person won't know and may repeat the same behavior, creating a cycle. Speaking the truth in love is what God wants in relationships. I still have to pray for courage, but God has reinforced this through fruitful results; a couple of times, after I shared, the other person apologized.

Now that Mia can name and understand what is happening in her heart, she brings her emotions to God, entrusting them to the Holy Spirit's ongoing work of transformation and experiencing increasing freedom in Christ.

George's Story

Everyone's experience of the intensive inward retreat was different. For George, although the retreat "was extremely painful," it ultimately helped him find his voice and encouraged him to be himself—most concretely through developing a long-desired hobby. He initially approached the retreat with a mindset of self-cultivation and achievement, expecting to "go through some stuff and then come out a new person for the better and all put together." Instead, he left feeling "in pieces" and returned "very discouraged." Reflecting on the experience, he explained that during the retreat, he felt deep despair about his life, his relationship with his parents, and their inability to help him develop his own voice. He had expected improvement, but "it did not happen the way [he] thought."

George acknowledged that he had assumed there was a standard, "correct" way to do the retreat and found himself constantly evaluating whether he was doing it right. Even in prayer, he questioned his experience: while he was supposed to be resting during the final days of the retreat, he wondered whether what he was experiencing truly counted as rest.

He reflected that he had grown up in a "relatively shame-based family," where he was constantly compared to others, particularly his sisters. Being a "good boy," he explained, meant not being disruptive, achieving academically, and obeying his parents—an identity that left little room for his own voice. As a result, he was continually preoccupied with whether he was doing things correctly. The retreat exposed these deep-seated wounds, along with his long-suppressed voice and emotions. When he returned home, he struggled to talk about the experience, feeling pressure to report something positive rather than admit that he felt despair and loneliness.

Over time, however, George came to realize that "God wasn't done with that experience." In the year following the retreat, he noticed repeated opportunities to exercise his voice—something he felt he had lacked for much of his life. Although the wounds remained palpable both during and after the retreat, he also sensed that he was being held and loved in the midst of the pain. Gradually, he came to see that his story was not only about woundedness but also about being embraced by God in his brokenness. He illustrated this shift with a concrete example:

> There are small things, but they felt significant. For example, I always wanted to go surfing and had tried once or twice. It was terrifying, and I thought I was going to die, but I also thought it would be fun. It wasn't very practical—I lived about forty-five minutes to an hour away from the beach. I wanted to buy a surfboard and get lessons, but I was undecided. I talked about it in therapy and with my wife. They encouraged me: "You can do it." I felt the freedom of that voice, and that's very meaningful—seemingly small, but meaningful. It's still terrifying, but I felt that this is me doing something for myself with God. That came as a result of the intensive inward retreat and afterwards too.

Through the retreat and the process that followed, George became aware of his own voice and gained the courage to express it. Symbolized by his new hobby, this emerging freedom reflected a growing acceptance of himself and a deeper trust in God's love and presence.

Jack's Story

Jack also attended the intensive inward retreat and described his experience as deeply embodied and transformative. Reflecting on the retreat, he recalled,

> On the retreat, I was asked to talk to my parents, and when I talked to Mom, my chest felt like crashing on itself. I felt I couldn't breathe when I spoke to Mom, and I ended up writing later that my mom and I were enmeshed. I was actually being suffocated by my mom. To put it more poetically, when I was born, actually my umbilical cord wrapped around my neck, and it was almost like my mom never took it off. She choked me throughout life and

> constantly taught me to choke life—press, control, control. And on the retreat, for the first time, I felt that pain.

Jack explained that confronting his relationship with his father also produced strong physical sensations. When speaking about his father, he felt pain in his throat and described his father as narcissistic, noting that in his family, "either Dad has a voice or no one has a voice." As a result, Jack experienced himself as voiceless and emotionally constrained. Returning to these memories during the retreat, he became acutely aware of how his body had carried this pain.

Jack further recounted how his mother had instilled fear in him from an early age, repeatedly training him to "be vigilant." She would tell him, "If I die, you die," a message that shaped his understanding of the world as dangerous. During the first weeks of the retreat, he confronted these fears intensely. Staying alone in a large, dark house heightened his anxiety; he recalled locking himself into a room at night with food and water, realizing that the isolation amplified the fears his mother had planted in him.

He also described recurring "fear fantasies," brief imagined scenarios in which danger arose but he always survived. These fantasies, he explained, functioned as a way to manage fear and maintain a sense of safety. His spiritual director, who also served as his therapist, encouraged him to confront these fears directly. Each day, Jack intentionally entered situations that triggered fear, gradually learning to remain present rather than avoidant. Over time, he found himself sleeping near open doors and even beginning to enjoy the darkness.

One night during the retreat, Jack experienced a profound turning point:

> I imagined a death figure slithering up the stairs and choking me. I was about to defend myself, but I decided to let him choke me. Eventually, he stopped and sat beside me as we watched the sun set. I realized these fear fantasies weren't intruders but lost pieces of myself—my loneliness. Jesus told me, "You are not alone. I'm here." The fantasies were parts of me crying out, saying, "I'm scared." Maybe the world isn't one of fear like Mom taught me, but one of love.

After the retreat, Jack found that the fear fantasies largely subsided. For the first time, he felt deeply and reconnected with parts of himself that he believed Jesus was healing. The retreat also gave him what he described as "options." As he released the expectations imposed by his parents, he felt freed from the roles he had long carried—particularly his role as the "golden child" and family fixer. He described setting boundaries with his mother for the first time and experiencing a new sense of freedom in choosing when to say "yes" or "no."

Jack summarized the impact of the retreat succinctly, noting that he was released both from the death figure and from the expectations his parents had imposed on him.

These three narratives illustrate how the intensive inward retreat, a major component of the program, facilitated profound transformation in participants' lives.

REASONS FOR ENTERING THE PROGRAM

According to the data, participants entered the spiritual formation program primarily to become better equipped to help others in ministry, while also recognizing their own spiritual needs and limitations.

To Help Others

Most participants had been serving in ministry before entering the program and sought a deeper understanding of how people grow spiritually. Bonnie, for instance, had been in full-time ministry for approximately ten years. While serving college students, she wondered why "some students would take off and grow and run with whatever they learn, and some would just be stuck." Her desire to understand how the Holy Spirit transforms people to become more Christlike led her to enroll in the program.

Similarly, Lucas, who served youth in a Chinese church, was deeply aware of the pain many young people carried because of difficult family circumstances. He explained, "I knew they had much pain because their family life was tough. A lot of them were unsatisfied." As a pastor's son, Lucas understood these struggles firsthand but felt ill-equipped to address them. He joined the program after being drawn to its emphasis on spiritual formation.

Amelia, another participant who had also been serving in the church, expressed a similar concern. She reflected, "I did not know how to help people. Sometimes I felt like I could only give them Bible verses, but they needed more than that." Although she had studied both theology and psychology, she found that "psychology itself was not enough," and that the program's integration of theology and psychology enabled her to care more holistically for herself and others.

Other participants articulated comparable motivations. Ethan, who had been involved in youth ministry, explained that counseling teenagers from broken families revealed his need for deeper understanding of spiritual growth, even though he was trained in theology and counseling. Leo was drawn to the program's retreat center and envisioned establishing a similar space for Chinese pastors. He observed that many Chinese Christian leaders suffer silently under cultural expectations of moral perfection, leading to isolation and burnout. Likewise, Sophia noted that "many Chinese church leaders worked hard to serve the Lord," yet experienced significant burnout, motivating her to seek counseling skills and spiritual formation training to alleviate their burdens.

Several participants emphasized the limits of their existing knowledge and resources. Mia spoke of church leaders' exhaustion from striving to please God. Olivia hoped to better understand human development for ministry purposes. Isabel, a practicing therapist, wanted to address clients' spiritual concerns while deepening her engagement with Scripture. Emma, who served in a Chinese church, summarized this shared experience succinctly: "It felt like I had reached the end of my advice and knowledge. I couldn't help people anymore. I had reached the end of me."

Taken together, these accounts suggest that participants entered the program with a dual motivation: to be more effectively equipped to serve others in ministry and to experience personal spiritual renewal themselves.

For Their Own Struggles

Many participants also expressed awareness of their personal struggles in spiritual life and a deep longing to grow in their relationship with God. They sensed that there must be something "more" about the Christian life—a deeper experience of knowing God and walking with him.

Ethan, although trained in pastoral care and counseling, acknowledged ongoing struggles in ministry. Reflecting on his context, he observed, "In the Asian context, ministry is perhaps the biggest challenge in a pastor's life. Sometimes we are trapped by busyness and demands and fall into burnout after many years of service." He entered the spiritual formation program seeking "to be equipped," not only for ministry but also for his own spiritual well-being.

Jack similarly recognized his need to tend to his inner life. He desired time and space to understand "what happened in my past, who I am, what are my tendencies," describing this self-examination as "big" for him. Harry likewise entered the program with expectations of significant personal change. He hoped for what he described as "radical change"—that the program would "change [his] life 180 degrees," making him "a completely different person" who could see life differently. Both anticipated deep personal transformation.

Several participants entered the program during periods of spiritual struggle or disorientation. Olivia enrolled at a time when she experienced God's absence and found herself confused and "struggling with many signature sins." Amelia recalled a similar longing for healing and change: "I wanted to be healed and also wanted to change my life. I didn't want just more degrees and knowledge without living out the life I wanted to live. I had hurts and needed healing. I also had many questions about life in general."

Participants were keenly aware of their inner struggles and sought a way forward. In addition to her desire to help others, Bonnie acknowledged that a second motivation for entering the program was her own spiritual journey. After ten years of service in a Christian organization, she found herself drained and nearing burnout amid disillusionment and unresolved questions about ministry. She began asking foundational questions: "What does it mean to be a Christian? What does it mean to have a relationship with God?" Reflecting on this season, she explained, "I was tired. All I wanted was to go away for a season, to have space and time to rest—with the hope that I would be refreshed or renewed or reenter into God again. I just needed to go away and find some answers about growing."

Similarly, Noah—who had earned an MDiv from a Chinese seminary and served as a pastor for fifteen years—recognized that he was approaching burnout due to excessive workload. He reflected, "I felt very dry and desolate in ministry. I worked day and night without noticing the days. Every day was the same—work, work, and more work. I seemed to be serving God, but I was wondering, 'Where is God?' He seemed so far away." Fearing burnout or depression, Noah resigned from his church and entered the program "to get away from ministry."

Amy also found herself near burnout, burdened by expectations from both herself and others. With what she described as a "performance-driven mindset," she felt "overburdened" when meeting evangelism goals became the central focus of her ministry. This sense of disorientation and pressure drew her to the program to seek a deeper understanding of spirituality.

Emma, who grew up in the church and had previously experienced spiritual consolation, similarly longed to deepen her relationship with God. After reading the Bible and various spiritual books during college, she later experienced what she described as "a huge loss of Christian community" and struggled to sustain spiritual disciplines. "Reading the Bible became dry, reading spiritual books became dry, and praying became dry," she explained. Emotionally, she no longer felt drawn to prayer or Scripture, which "didn't seem relevant to my life" and felt "more like literature than personal relationship." She interpreted this season as "a kind of dark night of the senses experience—it felt like the Lord had withdrawn His presence."

As Emma watched others grow while she felt stuck, she experienced increasing loneliness and despair. "It seemed like I wasn't getting anywhere but kept trying," she recalled. "When I felt alone in this, I didn't want to keep trying anymore, but still did because I didn't know what else to do." She added that continual improvement had long been part of her identity: "Spiritual growth is important and constant improvement is part of me. I just had to improve continually." During this "dark night" period, she found her church "not helpful" and felt she had no one with whom she could connect spiritually or personally. Feeling trapped yet deeply thirsty for renewal, Emma entered the program seeking restoration.

Likewise, George became aware of what he described as a moralistic striving for God's love. He recognized a pattern of "constantly hitting the wall but trying to get up and activate [his] will to make things better." Influenced by Chinese cultural expectations of "saving face," George found it difficult to be honest with God or others. "Deep down, I've always felt something repressed and hidden but wanting to come out," he reflected. He wondered what it would be like to be fully honest before God and himself. Initially, he entered the program hoping "to come out holier."

Clara likewise joined the program with instrumental expectations. She anticipated learning "how to counsel people and help them fix problems by giving them Bible verses." Instead, she encountered unexpected self-examination: "I didn't expect to be forced to look at myself and delve into being broken down. I didn't know that this program was going to be about me."

Across these accounts, participants recognized not only their exhaustion and inner fragmentation but also their longing for deeper spiritual growth and a freer life grounded in God's love rather than performance or striving.

To Deepen Their Relationship with God

Alongside their desire to help others and to find relief from struggles in ministry and personal life, participants also expressed a longing to deepen their relationship with God through studying in the spiritual formation program.

Ethan, who had previously studied in a Chinese seminary, hoped for "a different experience" from his earlier theological education, where he felt "trapped learning spiritual things based on theory without experience." He wanted to have "personal experience of God's work" in his heart and sought spiritual guidance for his journey. Similarly, Noah desired to "learn more about prayer," and Jack hoped to "grow a deeper relationship with Jesus." Having served in ministry, Jack had heard "bad stories about seminary where people just go get head knowledge and then stop knowing the Lord anymore." He did not want to "walk away with some theological content about Jesus" without maintaining a living relationship with him.

Other participants voiced similar longings. George, for example, wanted to see himself "transformed" during his seminary years and worried that "seminary would become a cemetery" for his soul. Recognizing the importance of spiritual formation for both personal and ministerial growth, he transferred into the program.

Mason likewise transferred after two years in seminary, drawn by the program's emphasis on knowing both God and self. He explained, "I wanted to go on a journey to discover what is going on in my life because I didn't want to end up being a pastor or minister who might be good at ministry skills but lose myself somewhere. I didn't want something wrong or some big moral failure to happen without knowing why."

Harry, too, was attracted by the program's focus on helping people grow closer to God. Amelia, originally enrolled in another focus area, also transferred because she wanted to learn more about relationship with God and how to live out the life of Jesus. After more than ten years as a Christian and six years of ministry service, she entered seminary with many unresolved questions. Reflecting on her experience, she said,

> The more I studied in seminary, the more questions I had. I realized that even though I could memorize the Bible, that didn't mean I loved God. These are two different things. Having much theological knowledge doesn't mean that your relationship with God is good. So after two years, I transferred to the spiritual formation program because I had friends studying it. I saw their lives—they were more loving and living out the love of Christ, unlike some people who focused on debating theology but didn't show Christ. For me, the more important thing about Christianity is the relationship with God, not merely knowledge.

Mia similarly entered the program seeking a well-grounded relationship with the Lord and a deeper understanding of the work of the Holy Spirit in Christian transformation. Fred also desired to understand his own spiritual life more deeply. After transferring into the program, he found that professors and peers were willing to ask questions he had "learned to stop asking" in the Chinese church. He explained that at church, he had "learned to stop asking questions about spiritual life, growth, and prayer," noting that the community focused only on answered prayer and thanksgiving, while questions about unanswered prayer were rarely addressed.

Although Fred had long silenced these questions, they remained "deep" in his heart. Like him, many participants entered the program with a desire to explore and experience Christian spirituality more fully—to know God more deeply and to cultivate a closer, more authentic relationship with him.

REEXAMINING CONFUCIAN UPBRINGING

In this section, I present participants' perceptions of their experiences reexamining their Confucian upbringing within the context of a Western Christian spiritual formation program.

Encountering Cultural Differences

After entering the program, several participants reported encountering significant cultural differences. Shaped by their Chinese cultural background, they described struggling with various cultural assumptions and practices embedded in the Western context of the spiritual formation program.

Western Context

Some participants reflected on the program's predominantly Western setting. Olivia described the environment as "pretty Eurocentric" and "a very European American experience," noting that "all of the major professors there are not Asian American. All of them are Caucasian." Similarly, Leo observed, "Many theories or theological perspectives are not based on Asian culture, so sometimes they didn't make much sense to me." At the same time, he added, "I was aware enough of those differences and appreciated them, recognizing that reality doesn't have to be the way I think." Sophia acknowledged that faculty and staff "wanted to be culturally sensitive," yet she noted, "I don't feel they were very supportive to people other than the main culture and didn't have many resources for them."

Coming from a collectivistic cultural background, Noah felt that the program lacked sufficient opportunities for communal learning. He explained that there was not enough "cohort group" time and that "no one cared about you while you worked alone, studied alone, and practiced alone." He associated this experience with what he perceived as American individualistic culture, suggesting that "students could have encouraged each other to learn more and explore deeper if we were in a group, not just alone."

Amy also found the program's "mostly Caucasian American setting" challenging. She explained, "The cultural part is missing, and there's no cultural integration. For example, there isn't enough teaching on what it's like to do spiritual direction with an Asian or an African." As a result, she felt that students from non-Western backgrounds were expected to internalize and translate the material on their own. Reflecting on her experience after graduation, she added, "When I started meeting my Chinese directees, I realized I didn't know how to put spiritual formation language into Chinese or how to express emotions in Chinese. I had to explore that myself."

Fred likewise described having to adjust from a collectivistic to an individualistic cultural framework. He observed, "The biggest cultural difference was that the program is still very individualistic. There isn't really a sense of formation in community." Drawing on his understanding of Christian tradition, he noted that "most believers are formed in the local church, not necessarily in a seminary." By contrast, he felt that the program at times positioned itself as compensating for what local churches lacked, which he found troubling: "There's something unfaithful about that. In Asian contexts, formation is not just individual; it takes place within the community."

Ethan spoke more directly about interpersonal and racial dynamics. As an Asian student, he struggled "more specifically with white people, with American people, who cannot easily connect with us." He described difficulties with language and communication and noted that some classmates "didn't want to engage with us, even in spiritual formation classes." While those with missionary experience connected more readily, others did not. In group settings, Ethan felt excluded and believed he had to demonstrate academic competence to gain respect: "After I presented my paper, people respected me more and engaged with me. It's common in Western culture—people want to see first what we can give to them."

In sum, many participants experienced tension with the program's dominant Western orientation, which contrasted sharply with their Chinese collectivistic backgrounds. Communication barriers often reflected limited intercultural understanding on both sides—among Asian students as well as Western faculty and peers.

Emotional Issues

Several participants described difficulty accessing and expressing emotions, often linking this struggle to their Chinese cultural upbringing. Mia admitted that it took her longer to be "in touch with [her] core emotions and core self," and she wondered whether this was related to how she had been raised. She explained, "In Chinese culture, emotions were primarily seen as something negative and were to be suppressed. So the deeper I suppressed my emotions, the longer it took to uncover them."

Mia recalled an exercise in which one of her spiritual directors "tried to stimulate my faculty of feelings with photographs and asked me to pick one that spoke to my emotions." She reflected, however, that

"I didn't get much out of it because I was trying to perform." Although the photographs did not resonate with her emotionally, she attempted to choose one that appeared appropriate: "I tried to find one that kind of related to my emotional state." She added that "the spiritual director didn't understand Chinese culture," which intensified her struggle in the process.

Bonnie similarly described difficulty engaging in emotionally intensive practices. She recalled struggling with therapy because she was unaccustomed to emotional openness: "It wasn't easy to go through such intense weekly therapy for a long period—seventy months. It was emotionally draining." Although she acknowledged its importance—"I worked through a lot of hurts and received much healing"—she emphasized the toll it took: "Every time after therapy, I couldn't do anything for another day. I was emotionally exhausted." Reflecting on her cultural background, she added, "Being Asian, I wasn't very in touch with my emotions, so it wasn't easy to work through that."

Strong Sense of Shame

Several participants also reported challenges related to a strong sense of shame, particularly in response to evaluative feedback within the program. Some struggled acutely with professors' comments during spiritual direction training.

Mia shared, "I struggled with the comments professors gave me in supervision. I had to look for the perfect segment for them to listen to, but still, they gave negative feedback, and I really felt rejection. It was me being rejected." Reflecting on her practicum experience, she explained, "In my first practicum class, I didn't fully grasp what spiritual direction was. My perfectionism got in the way—the more I wanted to do it perfectly, the more I struggled, because spiritual direction is about listening to the Holy Spirit. When I started thinking about myself, I wasn't really listening." She further observed that "Asian students have a big hurdle because professors don't understand us. Harsh comments often drive Chinese students to strive more, but that striving goes against what spiritual direction is about."

Noah also described struggling with shame during his practicum experience. He explained, "I was so self-conscious, self-protective, and ashamed because of my upbringing. The shame pushed me to do more to cover it up." He associated this shame with his family background and a drive for achievement: "I was ashamed of my family, my background, everything. I just wanted some big achievement to cover that shame." Practicum, in particular, felt exposing to him: "Practicum was horrible—having to let others supervise me felt like being naked. When teachers asked, 'What were you doing?' or 'What were you thinking?' my mind went blank. It was very hard."

Fred similarly observed that "Americans don't really know the extent of Asian guilt and shame, how deep it runs." Mason echoed this perspective, describing shame as "a big piece" of his life and suggesting that "if programs could help students navigate their cultural issues with someone familiar with that context, it might help draw those things out earlier."

Not all participants, however, interpreted these experiences in the same way. Isabel offered a contrasting perspective, noting, "Of course, one or two Asian students thought the professors were not culturally sensitive, but for me and my friends, if there were misunderstandings, we just clarified them." In her experience, the professors were "humble and open," and she emphasized that "all of us received a lot of blessings from the program." For Isabel, open communication between Asian students and faculty helped resolve cultural misunderstandings.

Taken together, these accounts highlight the varied ways participants experienced cultural difference, emotional unfamiliarity, and shame while studying in the spiritual formation program. For many, the program's Western context—combined with deeply ingrained patterns shaped by their Chinese upbringing—posed significant challenges. At the same time, some participants found that relational openness and mutual clarification mitigated these difficulties. The following section examines how the program enabled participants to reexamine their Confucian upbringing more deeply.

Reexamining Upbringing

While studying in the spiritual formation program, participants were led to reexamine their upbringing and reflect on the values with which they had been raised. Although participants came from different regions of the world as members of the Chinese diaspora, all acknowledged being raised "in Chinese ways," strongly shaped by the values of their parents and families. As they reflected on their formation, many recognized the pervasive influence of Confucianism on their family systems and parenting practices.

Harry observed that his mother was "culturally Chinese," explaining that these values had been "passed down" from her parents. Mia likewise affirmed that she was raised in a "primarily Chinese culture," noting that "my parents' parenting is primarily Chinese." Similarly, Fred stated that he had been "brought up in a predominantly Chinese culture."

Bonnie reflected on how Chinese identity remained central even within diaspora contexts. She explained,

> I have been very aware that I am Chinese ever since I was born. Even though we are Chinese diaspora, which means we left mainland China, there is still a very close-knit Chinese community that keeps the ties very strong. I was brought up in a family that still practices many Chinese customs, traditions, and beliefs. So, I never doubted that I was Chinese.

She continued, "We still keep traditions like Chinese New Year and other festivals that mainland Chinese people celebrate, including visiting ancestors' graves. At one point, we even had an altar for ancestral worship at home."

Regardless of geographic location, participants' families actively preserved Chinese traditions and social values. In the following discussion, I examine how participants perceived the influence of Confucianism on their upbringing in both family and church contexts. For analytic clarity, these perceptions are organized into three interrelated dimensions: hierarchy, shame, and performance. Although closely intertwined in everyday life, these categories illuminate the ways Confucian values permeated nearly every aspect of participants' formative experiences.

Hierarchical Social Structure

Participants described how Confucian hierarchical social structures shaped their experiences in both family and church contexts. Many reflected on the ways hierarchical assumptions were embedded in everyday relationships, influencing authority, obedience, and expectations across generations.

Generation Hierarchy

Within Confucian-influenced Chinese culture, participants emphasized the importance of generational hierarchy, including reverence for ancestors and deference to elders. This orientation was most visibly expressed through filial piety and corresponding patterns of parenting that emphasized obedience and conformity.

Filial Piety

Filial piety occupies a central place in Chinese cultural formation. It not only emphasizes honoring and respecting elders but also involves strong expectations of obedience to parents and older relatives. Mia recalled that in her upbringing, "Family and respect for the elderly is very important."

Bonnie reflected on the persistence of these values even within families that viewed themselves as reflective or adaptive. She explained, "Even though my parents call themselves rethinkers, they still practice Chinese customs influenced by Confucian teachings." She noted that family and community were consistently prioritized over individual desires, adding, "Whatever you do, you must think about how it will affect others in the family. Does it bring shame or honor? This is the whole aspect of filial piety: honoring your parents and showing respect to people older than you." She continued,

> In my family, it was always emphasized that we must respect the elders. You don't talk back or question their decisions. Growing up, my parents decided my life path and how I should live, and I went along because we always listen to our elders. Hierarchy is stressed, and respect is given to those who are senior in generation.

Clara described her parents' approach as "very traditional and typical Chinese," explaining that "whatever they say goes" and that children "should always respect the elders." She characterized her upbringing as highly directive: "My parents taught me to do as you're told and do what we say. It felt very much like a military style of parenting. It didn't matter what we children wanted; it was what the parents said that went."

Fred likewise recalled that his parents rarely invited his input: "When I was growing up, my parents very seldom—perhaps never—asked me, 'What do you want?'" As a result, he felt his capacity for self-awareness and decision-making was limited: "Very early on, I didn't develop the tendency to recognize what I actually wanted or how I felt about certain things, and that aspect of me became stunted."

Lucas similarly described how Chinese parenting norms emphasized unquestioning obedience. He explained, "I grew up with the mindset, 'I'm going to obey; my obligation is to fulfill whatever anyone says to me,' but I never learned to use my brain or think for myself."

Across these accounts, participants described parenting patterns that strongly emphasized compliance and respect for authority. For many, this Confucian hierarchical structure shaped not only family dynamics but also their perceptions of authority within church and broader social contexts.

Duties and Expectations

Within Confucian thought, people are expected to fulfill duties associated with their social roles. Several participants described how these expectations shaped their upbringing. Fred explained that Chinese culture, strongly influenced by Confucian ideals, "emphasizes duties and obligations to family and society" and "underscores the importance of being virtuous people who fulfill their duties regardless of how they feel about it." He elaborated, "Suppression of self-desire is encouraged and even exalted. Good and moral people are those who fulfill their duties even when they do not feel like it." Reflecting on his formation, Fred noted that these expectations "formed me deeply—I just inherited this idea of duty."

One widely shared expectation was the obligation to care for aging parents, a central expression of filial piety. Burdened by both his parents' expectations and his own internalized sense of responsibility, Fred recalled growing up with the fear that he would fail to provide his parents with a secure future. He explained that this concern became "the driving factor" behind his academic pursuits.

Bonnie similarly described a strong sense of obligation toward her parents: "As a child to my parents, there are obligations, duties, and expectations. As they grow older, I need to take care of them and make sure they are well fed and cared for." She understood these responsibilities as intrinsic to relational life within the family: "That is simply responsibility—how we live in relationship with one another." For many participants, such intergenerational expectations created a persistent sense of moral pressure shaped by both family and community norms.

Influential Mothers

Many participants indicated that their mothers played a primary role in their upbringing, often because fathers were frequently absent due to work. Harry explained, "I grew up closer to my mom because my dad worked and wasn't home much." Jack similarly noted that his mother was the central caregiver: "As kids, it was all my mom. She raised us. She was the soul of the household."

Several participants described maternal involvement that extended into high levels of control. Jack characterized his mother as a "helicopter mom" who managed nearly every aspect of his life. He recalled being unable to make basic decisions for himself and described a deep sense of enmeshment: "A lot of my identity as a child was wrapped up with my mom." He perceived that his mother sought to fulfill her unrealized aspirations through her children, particularly through him as her "golden hope."

Jack later interpreted his mother's controlling behavior as rooted in fear and anxiety rather than malice. He explained that her vigilance was driven by a desire to preserve life and prevent loss. Even in adulthood, he noted, she continued to exert influence over his choices, reflecting unresolved fear and ambivalence toward her own cultural identity.

Other participants shared similar experiences. Olivia described her mother as authoritarian and emotionally dominant, noting that her mother's emotional state governed the household. Only later did Olivia recognize the relational impact of this dynamic, reflecting that her upbringing had centered on meeting her mother's emotional needs rather than supporting her own development. Lucas likewise recalled becoming an outlet for his mother's accumulated stress and anger, describing an environment of constant emotional tension.

Across these narratives, participants described maternal relationships marked by high expectation, emotional intensity, and strong authority. These patterns were often understood as expressions of Confucian ideals emphasizing filial duty, parental authority, and moral responsibility. For many, such dynamics significantly shaped their sense of self, agency, and relational patterns well into adulthood.

Distant Fathers

Whereas some participants described enmeshed relationships with their mothers, others reflected on emotionally distant relationships with their fathers. In many Chinese families, fathers were experienced as less present in children's daily lives, particularly in emotional and relational terms.

Ethan remarked, "I did not have father figures in my own life." Mason similarly recalled that although his father granted him considerable freedom, he "didn't communicate with me very much." Reflecting on his father's background, Mason explained,

> My dad told me that my grandfather used to work twelve to fourteen hours a day. As a doctor, he would just keep seeing patients all day, then go upstairs to study or work some more. Every day was the same. When I look at my dad's life, it's the same pattern. He works hard, comes home, goes upstairs, and keeps drawing because he designs landscapes for new homes. He saw that example in his father and draws strength from it. He has an excellent work ethic—very responsible, a provider for his family.

Mason recognized that this dedication came with emotional limitations. He reflected, "On the other side of the coin, he doesn't give himself space to feel or to process what he's going through because he doesn't know how." While his father functioned well socially, Mason noted that deeper emotional engagement remained difficult: "When it comes to deeper things—his feelings or emotions—it's hard for him to navigate." As a result, Mason explained that he now attempts to share his own vulnerabilities with his father "without expecting anything in return."

Olivia likewise described her father as "very passive and distant, definitely more of the provider type." Although her father was physically present, she felt he did not invest relationally: "He would go to work and be around, but not invest in our lives or ask how our day was." Reflecting further, she said, "He was out of the picture." She associated this distance with her father's work patterns, describing him as a workaholic who spent little time at home despite occasional family activities.

Summarizing her experience, Olivia observed, "He was like many Chinese dads—usually not very available." She reflected that "many Chinese fathers think that because they provide for the family, that means they love the family." While she expressed appreciation for her father's provision, she also articulated a longing for relational connection: "I don't want just what he can give me. I want him as a person." She concluded that although her father had more to offer emotionally, "it's just hard for him to connect in those ways."

Poor Parental Relationships

Beyond strained parent-child dynamics, many participants also reflected on their parents' conflicted or emotionally distant marriages. Noah shared that his father had been abusive toward his mother and described his family as "not a good family." Although Jack's parents remained together, he characterized their household as "a kind of broken family."

Harry likewise recalled, "Growing up, I was never close to them. I don't think they were close to each other. So the whole family wasn't super close." At the same time, he added, "I know they care for me, and I care for them," indicating the presence of affection alongside emotional distance.

Olivia described similar patterns in her family. She reflected that family members often "took each other's presence for granted" and recalled realizing as a teenager that her parents' relationship was deeply strained. She described her parents as emotionally disconnected and recalled persistent conflict between them. Reflecting on these dynamics, she observed,

> My dad didn't respect my mom or her gifts and talents, and my mom was basically a doormat for him. I grew up with an imbalance of power because there wasn't mutual respect or partnership. My mom expressed Christian women's submission by being a doormat—emotionally manipulative, saying, "I'll just go along with whatever your dad says," while actually abusing herself spiritually and emotionally. If my dad had truly been a man—able to make leadership decisions and respect my mom's gifts—they could have partnered together. They would be in a much more robust place than they are now.

Across these accounts, participants described family environments marked by emotional distance, power imbalance, and unresolved relational wounds. These dynamics were often understood as shaped by Confucian hierarchy and traditional gender expectations, and they left enduring effects on participants' formation and relational patterns.

Traditions Inherited

Several participants reflected on the uncritical transmission of Chinese traditions within their families. Some described their parents as following inherited practices "blindly," without reflection or questioning. Jack noted that although his mother expressed ambivalence toward her Chinese heritage, she nevertheless held certain "folk beliefs" that she had absorbed unconsciously. He observed similar patterns among many Asian directees from different cultural backgrounds and described this inheritance as a form of unexamined tradition.

Lucas likewise described Chinese culture as "very family-oriented and continually built up generation after generation," noting that people are often trained to inherit what is passed down rather than to question it. Participants suggested that these patterns extended beyond families into church contexts as well.

Sophia reflected that within her church, there was limited space for self-awareness or questioning: "You don't have much room to know yourself, to explore why you say no, why you don't want to do something, or why you don't want to follow." Lucas similarly lamented what he perceived as unreflective tradition within Chinese churches:

> Chinese churches follow their cultures closely—they uphold and hold onto their traditions. Whatever was laid out to them, they follow. Do they know why? No. Do they know their faith? Not really. Do they have faith? Maybe. Why do they do it? Because their parents did.
>
> At the same time, I recognize that this is what they inherited. The parents do this only because they learned it themselves, and it just becomes an endless cycle. Is it disappointing? Yes. Is it frustrating? Yes. But spiritual formation has taught me that it's a deep chain. They see their parents' hypocrisy and yet repeat it.
>
> Of course, this is a generalization—not every Chinese person or church is like that. Still, in many cases, families understand Christianity primarily as behavior modification rather than relational transformation.
>
> The main characteristic of the Chinese church is tradition. That isn't entirely bad—there are good ways to keep tradition—but for many, it has become attending functions without knowing why, without understanding the reason for it, and without taking God seriously.

In this sense, participants described Chinese traditions as transmitted not only within families and communities but also within church life, often shaping faith practices in ways that emphasized conformity over reflection.

Gender Hierarchy

Some participants identified gender bias within hierarchical social structures shaped by male dominance. Clara described sensing her parents' preference for boys, even though it was never stated openly: "It wasn't a spoken thing, but you could tell it was there." Although her father raised his four daughters "like boys"—encouraging sports and physical activity—he nevertheless enforced gender-based restrictions: "Girls don't do this; girls don't do that." Clara recalled wanting to learn Chinese Kung Fu but being forbidden to do so because "girls don't do that." Over time, she became aware that certain behaviors were discouraged simply because she was female.

Bonnie similarly observed that in her family—"like any other Chinese family"—boys were valued more than girls. She explained, "From when I was very young until now, boys are obviously preferred. My brother gets better treatment and more opportunities than me and my sisters." She added that in many families, parents questioned the value of investing in girls' education if daughters were expected to marry and leave the family.

Several participants also noted that these gendered assumptions extended into church contexts. Clara felt that "boys were more valued than girls" in her church, and some female participants described feeling ignored or dismissed because of their gender. Amelia described serving in a church environment marked by subtle but persistent gender bias: "They would never say it aloud. It's subtle—you can feel it. If you speak up as a woman when a male pastor is talking, people look at you strangely." Despite equivalent training and education, she felt that women's voices were often disregarded. Emma echoed this experience, observing, "No one says this, but there's an underlying belief that a male leader is definitely better than a female one. I've struggled with that a lot, being a woman in ministry."

Across these accounts, female participants described how gendered expectations within both family and church contexts shaped their experiences, often creating obstacles in their personal development and ministerial calling.

Position Hierarchy

Some participants reported that church structures mirrored broader patterns of social hierarchy within Chinese culture. Fred described his church as having a "very authoritarian and strict hierarchical structure," shaped largely by the senior pastor's personality and vision. He explained, "The church basically becomes an extension of the senior pastor's personality and his goals." He likened this model to an Old Testament leadership framework, adding that cultural norms reinforced unquestioning obedience: "You don't question authority; you listen and submit."

Because Clara's parents were church leaders, she experienced similar dynamics at home and in church. Reflecting on her upbringing, she said, "I don't think I've ever been given space to explore or question my spirituality or faith." She associated this lack of space with both familial and ecclesial authority structures that discouraged questioning and self-reflection.

Taken together, these narratives suggest that hierarchical patterns rooted in Chinese cultural norms shaped participants' experiences of authority, obedience, and self-expression within family and church contexts.

Shame

Many participants affirmed that they grew up in a "shame-based" Chinese cultural context in which guilt and shame were deeply embedded. As Fred remarked, "Honor and shame was the second reason for parents' emphasis on their children's achievement at school." The following subsections examine how participants reflected on their upbringing within this shame-based cultural framework.

Superficial Communication

Within such a cultural context, matters involving failure, weakness, or vulnerability are often avoided; as a result, communication tends to remain "superficial" and focused on outward appearance. Several participants noted that deep communication with their parents was largely absent. Interactions were typically one-directional, characterized by parental instruction or judgment rather than dialogue. As Clara admitted, "I have never had a one-on-one conversation with my parents."

Mason recalled, "Growing up, I learned many things through observation. My parents didn't sit down and explain things to us. Although both of them were nurturing, there was a void in verbal communication." He elaborated,

> Like many Chinese parents, mine cared deeply about material provision but invested little in our emotional or spiritual growth. They made sure we were fed and well rounded—music, swimming, Taekwondo, painting, and SAT classes. We were busy and physically cared for, but emotional connection was lacking. They had not learned this from their own parents, so we did not receive it either.

George described a similar dynamic: "My parents had their own business and were always busy. When they were around, they were not really present. Communication felt one directional—'This is what to do.' When I said, 'I want to do this,' they would reply, 'No, that's a bad idea.' I felt unknown by my parents."

Olivia summarized her household as "not very emotionally or relationally close," while Harry observed that family communication remained largely superficial: "When we were younger, it was about funny things that happened at school or church—nothing deep, nothing spiritual. As we got older, it felt forced and minimal. We did activities like biking or watching TV so we didn't have to interact. We were trained to stay in superficial areas."

Amelia explained that her parents' primary expression of love took the form of practical service rather than emotional connection:

> My parents made sure I had food and clothes, but they didn't have the capacity to talk about feelings. There was a lot of "should"—you should be a good student, a good daughter, work hard. They were too tired and probably never received emotional care from their own parents. Talking about feelings was a luxury.

She added that, while some Chinese parents might be different, her own parents' ethic of hard work reflected a generation shaped by physical survival and the demands of rebuilding after hardship.

Additionally, some participants noted that illness was regarded as a form of weakness and therefore concealed. Mason recalled, "My mom had cancer when I was growing up. My parents didn't want my brother and me to know. They shielded us from her pain. She went through a bone marrow transplant and chemotherapy, but we were told everything was fine. When she died while I was in junior high, I was lost. No one took me to counseling. There was nowhere to talk. That left a huge hole in my development." Raised in a shame-based environment, many participants similarly lacked support to face vulnerability or to process painful emotions.

Emotions Ignored

Participants consistently emphasized that emotions were rarely acknowledged within their families. Mia recalled, "Feelings were not talked about. Emotions were to be suppressed. During dinner, if I got emotional, my dad would tap my head with chopsticks. He wanted us quiet. No conversation during meals. In Chinese culture, emotions aren't to be expressed or even explored."

Noah echoed this pattern, observing, "Chinese people are more on a thinking mindset than a feeling one. It's hard to use words to express emotions. People feel safer talking about thoughts because feelings are vulnerable. Being sad or worried seems improper; people just want to show, 'I'm strong. I'm okay.'" As Isabel concluded bluntly, "Chinese people don't talk about feelings. Period."

Lucas's Story

Lucas's story illustrates the emotional consequences of growing up in a shame-driven home. His older brother, frequently punished for disobedience, redirected his anger toward Lucas, who appeared compliant and "good." Beneath this surface obedience, however, emotional harm went unrecognized and unaddressed. Lucas recounted, "I don't have many childhood memories. Elementary and middle school were the toughest. My brother sometimes beat me. I was never taken to a psychologist, but I think I was depressed. Every day was about avoiding getting yelled at."

He internalized the family's turmoil as personal failure: "Anytime someone was angry, I thought, 'I caused it.' It wasn't just my mistake; it was a failure for my family." Over time, anger and isolation intensified: "At church or school, I'd burst out in anger—the only place I could. I lost friends. I couldn't tell anyone what was happening at home; it would only start the cycle again."

By seventh grade, suicidal thoughts emerged. "My brother collected swords and knives. I knew where they were. Every day felt like the possibility of ending it. Fear was constant." At his lowest point, Lucas described a moment of divine encounter that altered his trajectory: "I heard a voice: 'Give me a chance to change this.' Slowly, the yelling stopped. At a summer retreat I, heard again, 'I showed up.' That's when I said, 'Yes, You did.' It became the point where faith became real—not behavior management but relationship."

Even as an adult, Lucas continues to wrestle with the lingering effects of his upbringing: "I'm afraid of marriage, afraid of having children. I've seen my anger hurt people. I don't want to become like my father. Maybe celibacy isn't a bad idea—for now, I'm not ready."

Lucas's experience exemplifies how emotional suppression and shame can foster fear, depression, and self-blame, even across generations. Yet his story also points toward the beginnings of healing—through faith, honest self-reflection, and the gradual integration of grace into emotional life.

No Encouragement and Comparison

Many participants reported that affirmation was rare within their families. Words of encouragement were scarce, while judgment, criticism, and corrective discipline were common. Rather than fostering confidence or secure identity, this parenting pattern often left participants feeling shamed and chronically "not enough."

Absence of Praise

Mia described her parents' approach as fundamentally shaming: "I seldom received praise. Instead, they were always criticizing me and judging me. Now that I think about it, the words and the manner were quite shaming. Spanking was very common at home." Reflecting further, she linked this pattern to a cultural suspicion of praise: "They considered praising a young child a no-no, lest it make the child prideful. Criticism and judgment were thought to form virtue. So parenting focused on punishing vice rather than building up the child."

Clara echoed the same dynamic: "In our family, we never encouraged each other. My parents didn't say, 'Good job!' They'd say, 'Be better.' If someone complimented me, they'd dismiss it—'Oh, she's whatever.' It felt like I wasn't allowed to exist outside the family unit. No one felt permitted to be encouraging." Across these accounts, the absence of affirmation combined with frequent censure produced a pervasive atmosphere of shame.

Relentless Comparison

Participants also described constant comparison—among siblings, cousins, and peers—as a defining feature of their upbringing. Clara recalled, "I was a curious kid who liked taking things apart. I didn't know how to put them back, so my parents would say, 'You're bad. You break everything. You're hyper.' My whole life I heard, 'Why can't you be like your sister? Why can't you be like that person?'" She recounted a particularly painful moment at church: "A friend spoke as a missionary. Afterward, my mom thanked her and said, 'I hope you can teach Clara to be better.' It made no sense and felt very shaming—as if I needed to be made into someone else."

Jack connected comparison to his mother's unfulfilled aspirations: "Mom compared us to her sisters' kids: 'Your cousin's a pharmacist—that's your track. Your other cousin's becoming a lawyer—that's what you should be.' Since she hadn't finished school, her parenting became, 'Because I couldn't make it, you must.'" He also noted how identity and shame intersected with assimilation pressures: "She associated her Taiwanese heritage with shame, while America represented opportunity. Her biggest fear was that we would be 'going back.'"

George summarized the broader cultural climate: "I grew up with honor/shame, saving face, passive aggression, duty—looking like you have it all together. If I brought home a B or A-, my parents said, 'As long as you did your best,' which really meant, 'If it were your best, it would be an A.'" Lucas similarly reflected on "blindness to the shame-and-honor culture," while Bonnie described shame as an intentional pedagogical strategy: "Chinese culture uses shame to teach—to scare you into discipline. The shame hits not just you but your family."

For Noah, economic hardship intensified these dynamics: "I was ashamed of everything—our old building, my family. I never invited classmates home. We say, 'Family disgrace shouldn't be aired,' so I drove myself to achieve more each day to cover my shame."

Across these accounts, comparison functioned as a moral accelerator—fueling perfectionism, face-saving, and relentless self-pressure—while simultaneously eroding secure identity and emotional safety.

Sex as Taboo Subject

Several participants reported that sexuality was rarely discussed within their families. In many Chinese households, topics related to sex, bodily development, and desire were regarded as shameful or inappropriate, leaving children uninformed and emotionally unsupported.

Silence and Shame

Mason explained that his parents "never talked about sexuality." As a teenager, he struggled privately: "I never told anybody because there was a lot of shame associated with that. My parents didn't sit down and explain our bodies or sexuality. I was curious, feeling the changes happening in my body, but I had no guidance."

He described the absence of both instruction and emotional care: "My parents didn't provide emotional comfort. No one said, 'This is your body; this is how you steward it.' They didn't know about the internet either, so I was left exploring online, dabbling in unhealthy practices." Without formative guidance, Mason sought comfort through online sexual exploration, which quickly produced guilt: "It felt good, but afterward I felt bad—guilty. I thought something was wrong with me because I couldn't control it. It felt too powerful."

Relief came only when he encountered a Christian peer group that addressed sexuality openly: "In high school, I met some Caucasian Christian guys reading a book about sexuality together. I was shocked—they were actually talking about this! It was the first place I learned that I could be honest and vulnerable about these struggles."

Similarly, Lucas recognized that both his family and church had failed to provide constructive teaching: "I wasn't educated about sex or attraction. My only education was what the world told me, not the church. All I heard was, 'If you feel something, don't do it.' When the topic came up, I had no idea what to do." The absence of explicit instruction left participants confused and burdened with shame during their sexual development.

Female Experiences

Female participants likewise described silence and discomfort surrounding sexuality. Olivia recalled that during adolescence, her father's withdrawal intensified her confusion: "When I was a teenager, my dad recoiled from my body. It created distance. I wished he could have said, 'Olivia, you're a woman now, and I respect you as a woman. We can still hug, but some parts of your body are sacred.'"

Although her mother attempted to discuss sex, the conversation felt unsafe: "Talking to anyone about sex is vulnerable and requires trust. Unfortunately, my mom wasn't trustworthy—she would share my secrets with others. So I couldn't talk to her about anything confidential." Olivia reflected that this breach of trust made intimate or sacred conversations impossible: "Sex is sacred because of its importance. My mom never understood what trust meant—she wasn't willing to respect boundaries. She'd claim to respect me, but her actions proved otherwise."

Cultural Barriers to Emotional and Sexual Wholeness

Across these accounts, participants' stories revealed that in many shame-based Chinese families, superficial communication and relational distance left little space for healthy discussion of sexuality. Silence surrounding sex—rooted in fear of shame, discomfort with emotion, and lack of relational trust—hindered holistic development. For both male and female participants, sexual formation was shaped more by secrecy and guilt than by love, wisdom, or embodied grace.

Shame of Vulnerability in the Church

Participants observed that in many Chinese churches, people—especially leaders—rarely share their weaknesses. Within Chinese seminaries, where future pastors are trained, vulnerability is often neither modeled nor taught.

Ethan reflected on his seminary experience: "The professors in my country never share their weaknesses—never ever. They talk only about success, ministry, and reputation. They tell us, 'Remember, students, your congregation is watching.' Professors teach us to perform ministry based on people's evaluation. We cannot be ourselves."

This pattern extends into congregational life. As Noah remarked, "In Chinese culture, a pastor must appear strong. Leaders act as if they have answers to all problems. Chinese people hide their shame by showing wealth or power to prove they're OK. But there's shame inside."

Clara confirmed that this dynamic shaped everyday church interactions: "I noticed a lot of false humility—parents bragging about their children: 'Oh, your kid's at Stanford.' Then the other replies, 'Your kid's doing so well, too!' It's all ego-stroking, not genuine care."

Lucas likewise described the superficial nature of church communication: "Conversations go like, 'How was your week? Nice.' It's small talk. The deepest it gets is acknowledging that life isn't fun right now—but never exploring why. People don't face reality in love."

Emma, a pastor's daughter, felt the burden of image and expectation especially acutely: "Growing up, there was a lot of shame and guilt dumped on me. If you didn't fulfill expectations, it felt shameful. Bad grades meant making my parents look bad—as if our family wasn't put together. That gave me guilt." She explained how this culture shaped church relationships: "It was easy to see what everyone was doing but not to know who they really were or how they felt. There were many misunderstandings. Even now, I'm leaving my church because I don't feel known or loved."

Across these accounts, participants concluded that in environments where weakness is concealed in order to appear strong, individuals feel unseen and unaccepted, and genuine community becomes difficult to sustain.

Fixing Problems Instead of Attending to Emotions

Several participants noted that Chinese churches often emphasize solving problems rather than attending to emotional needs. Noah admitted, "As a pastor, when I heard a problem, I wanted to fix it quickly—give people a way out. In Chinese culture, we don't allow time to process. We want a quick fix."

Lucas observed the same pattern and described it as pervasive in both leadership and congregational life: "When you have a problem, someone tells you what to do. There's no talk about how you feel. Pastors tell you how to fix your problems instead of dealing with your emotions." He illustrated this with an example: "A missionary came back from the field feeling lonely and discouraged. The senior pastor called him only once—and the next time, months later, was to say, 'We're cutting your funding.' No one asked how he felt." Lucas explained that emotions were not misunderstood so much as deliberately managed: "Chinese churches don't misunderstand emotions—they just manage them. Feeling less means you're better. It becomes a contest: who can feel the least. Those who hide best seem stronger and more blessed." He also critiqued a subtle prosperity mindset: "Many Chinese churches unconsciously buy into the prosperity gospel. If life is going well, God is blessing you. When things go wrong, people will pray for you but won't walk with you." In this context, emotional distance masquerades as politeness: "People say, 'How are you?' and 'Let me pray for you,' thinking they've done their job. But they never talk about what's going on inside. The church teaches wisdom, but wisdom becomes about outward behavior—being polite, doing the right things."

Emma added, "Chinese people don't like to look at themselves. They look forward, set the next goal, and work hard. We're driven, but we avoid self-examination."

Clara echoed this pattern in her own church experience: "Even in church, it wasn't safe to be vulnerable. You don't share your struggles—people might gossip or use it against you. I've never experienced real fellowship where people love one another. It was always, 'You're doing this wrong; change.' It was a shame-based, behavior-driven culture at church and at home." She eventually distanced herself from church life: "I was born in church but didn't become a real Christian until my mid-twenties. In college, I stopped going altogether."

In this shame-based culture, participants learned to hide their weaknesses and brokenness in order to seek approval and self-worth. As Lucas concluded, faith became a matter of "behavior management"—appearing good outwardly while concealing inner pain.

Performance

Participants described being trained to focus on outward performance. In both family and church contexts, appearance, achievement, and social conformity were prioritized over authenticity or inner life.

Outward Appearance

Many participants explained that in the honor-shame culture of Chinese society, looking good externally carries great importance. Lucas summarized,

> Chinese culture is about making sure we appear OK on the outside—that's our standard. People care a lot about jobs, income, and how their families look, especially compared with others. Outward appearance matters more than inward reality. Parents don't understand what's happening in their children's hearts.

Mia observed that parents often teach behavior through rules rather than relational understanding: "They tell you how to behave—what you should and shouldn't do. It's basically dos and don'ts. My mother was always protecting the family image, wanting us to behave properly with relatives or friends. Shameful things in the family were never to be mentioned outside."

Similarly, Emma noted that the emphasis on "giving face" and maintaining appearances pervades Chinese life: "Chinese people, generally speaking, care a lot about how they look and how to give face."

For these participants, preserving external harmony and reputation took precedence over honest emotional or relational engagement.

Behavior Modification at Church

The same pattern extended into church life. Lucas remarked, "Church has become a place for behavior modification. Raising kids is about making sure they look good. They don't know how to handle emotions because that's the inner heart, and parents don't know how to deal with that either. Families just keep looking good on the outside."

Clara recalled that this moralism defined her early church experience: "Growing up, I was always told, 'You're bad, so change your behavior.'

The church was judgmental, legalistic, and hypocritical. I thought, if this is what church is like, I don't want to go. So I stopped attending."

Emma likewise felt burdened by expectation as a pastor's daughter: "As a pastor's kid, I felt I had to act a certain way, lead others, take care of the group. Everyone expected something from me because of who my dad was."

George summarized his church as being "all about trying to be good," while Fred commented that Chinese Christians "put a premium on having it all together—being in control, well put together, and presentable."

Lucas described how this moralism distorted his early faith: "As a child, I loved God deeply, but church became another place to perform. Every altar call, I would say yes again, asking, 'Am I really a Christian?' Each time I'd promise to get my act together, but it never worked. I kept thinking something was wrong with me." He concluded that Christianity had become a behavioral system rather than a relationship: "Church made faith seem like a list of activities. It was never about belief—it was about doing the right things."

Thus, an emphasis on appearance and conformity often replaced genuine transformation, creating confusion about grace and identity.

Performance Orientation

Alongside the emphasis on outward appearance, achievement and performance were central to participants' upbringing. Fred described a culture shaped by Confucian work ethic and economic anxiety, noting that "growing up under Confucian values, it was all about studying hard and getting good grades," because academic success was understood as the only path to college, employment, and stability. Reflecting on the emotional impact, he explained, "I never felt seen. . . . Everything was about behavior, not the inner life," describing how love was delayed and conditional rather than experienced in the present.

Amy similarly recalled that her parents equated love with academic success, observing that "they took pride when our scores were high and celebrated our achievements." Lucas added that this emphasis often reflected parental anxiety and care rather than hostility, explaining that Chinese parents "want the best for their children, but it becomes all about performance."

This performance orientation extended into theological education. Ethan observed that some Chinese seminaries were "performance-driven," where regulations were strictly enforced and students were evaluated primarily on outward compliance. He concluded that "spiritual performance doesn't solve heart problems," noting that unresolved issues of identity and character often emerged later in ministry. Fred summarized the broader impact by stating that Confucian performance orientation had led many Chinese Christians toward legalism, with a focus on rules and outward behavior while neglecting the heart.

Burnt-Out Church Leaders

Within a collective culture that prizes performance, obedience, and self-sacrifice, church leaders are often expected to work tirelessly without rest. Participants consistently described how this performance-driven ethos produced exhaustion, loneliness, and neglect of both family life and interior spiritual health.

Unending Demands in Ministry

Ethan observed that in many Asian church contexts, ministry becomes "the biggest challenge in a pastor's life," as leaders are trapped by constant busyness and demands that eventually lead to burnout. Noah, a former pastor, echoed this experience, explaining that pastors are expected to "give, give, without receiving," which left him feeling lonely and unseen despite his hard work.

Leo described how such expectations devastate families, noting that leaders are often expected to be available to the church "twenty-four hours a day." When church is placed above family, he explained, children grow up without a father and spouses without a partner, yet family members are discouraged from speaking up lest they be accused of being unfaithful to God. As a result, family issues among Christian leaders become especially severe.

Rest Denied, Even at Retreats

Even spiritual retreats often failed to provide genuine renewal. Ethan noted that retreats were designed primarily for "equipping others," emphasizing teaching and worship rather than rest for pastors and leaders themselves. Harry described Chinese church retreats as tightly scheduled, filled with sermons and activities that left little room for silence, reflection, or restoration.

Faithfulness as Exhaustion

Sophia, a long-time church minister, described how she once equated faithfulness with relentless effort, explaining that she believed being a faithful servant of God meant "working really, really hard." This mindset eventually led to burnout and spiritual disorientation. In her context, she observed, people "do right things to prove they are faithful," and obedience is valued over self-awareness. Saying yes signals faithfulness, while saying no is often interpreted as rebellion or selfishness. She traced this mentality to her Chinese evangelical church, which emphasized obedience and right behavior but offered little guidance on how to address weakness, inner conflict, or personal limits.

Fortitude and Suppressed Vulnerability

Amelia noted that Chinese culture emphasizes fortitude, which can promote discipline and responsibility but also leads people to be judged primarily by behavior. She explained that to be a "good Christian," one must do certain things while avoiding topics that signal weakness. As a result, vulnerability becomes taboo. When fortitude is exalted and weakness is silenced, even within the church, believers learn to suppress pain rather than bring it into the light of grace.

5

Transformation Through the Program

According to the data, participants reported that their study in the spiritual formation program brought significant changes to their lives. At the beginning of chapter 4, three narratives illustrated examples of transformation experienced by some participants. This chapter focuses on how all participants described their experiences of transformation through the program.

PERCEPTIONS OF TRANSFORMATIVE EXPERIENCES

Participants repeatedly described the spiritual formation program as life changing. Jack called it "incredible and life-changing—quite the most life-changing thing I have ever been part of," explaining that it accelerated his spiritual growth and spared him from "a neurotic path." He described the program as "a significant grace," adding that God used it to deliver him from years of pain and to "speed up what might have taken years to mature."

George likewise described the experience as "deeply formative and life changing," noting that it helped him see himself more clearly and relate to God more deeply, especially by allowing him to be "held in some very painful places."

Isabel described the program as intense and transformative, saying it moved her from knowing God only intellectually to experiencing God "in my heart." She spoke of enjoying "a very intimate relationship with God" and reflected that the ten years she spent in the program taught her how to seek God, listen to him, and submit herself to him within a loving community.

Fred emphasized relational transformation, observing that spiritual growth involved learning to accept who God is for us and realizing how deeply we are loved, which in turn reshapes character and behavior. Harry noted that the program helped him become more aware of God's presence, slow down, and appreciate both God and himself more fully.

Lucas highlighted the program's Christ-centered focus, explaining that its greatest contribution was helping him realize that spiritual formation "isn't an end in itself—it points to Christ," and that the ultimate goal is relationship with him.

Cross-Cultural Transformation

All participants reported that the program changed how they viewed themselves, God, and others—particularly as Chinese students engaging a Western approach to spiritual formation. Noah described the experience as "eye-opening," noting that it expanded his understanding of how God works through deep self-knowledge alongside knowledge of God. He was especially struck by the openness with which students shared vulnerabilities during retreats, observing that such disclosure, particularly around sensitive topics, was rare in Chinese culture but deeply meaningful to him.

Ethan likened the experience to spiritual surgery, explaining that the program brought hidden aspects of his heart into the light. He described this exposure as painful but necessary, as it revealed inner darkness that God was addressing.

Lucas described the program as a season of weakness, noting that while his life had taught him emotional control, the program revealed how little control he actually had. He explained that he learned he could not change others and that "apart from Jesus," he could do nothing good. At the same time, the program taught him that he did not need to do everything on his own.

Experiencing God's Love in Weakness

Through the program, participants learned to experience God's acceptance amid weakness and brokenness. Emma shared that the program gave her language for feeling "stuck" and helped her see such experiences as part of spiritual maturation rather than something shameful.

Mason similarly learned to hold brokenness and belovedness together, explaining that the program helped him see that God loves him "even in pain and weakness." While many Chinese people, he noted, are trained to ignore pain, he came to recognize that pain is part of who we are and that "it's healing to know God still loves us there." This awareness enabled him to walk with God "more as a whole person," integrating strengths and weaknesses, virtues and vices, pains and joys within the embrace of God's love.

A Lifelong Journey of Union with Christ

Participants also recognized that transformation is an ongoing process rather than a one-time event. They spoke of learning about union with Christ, walking daily by the Spirit, and trusting that God meets them wherever they are in their journey. George explained that he learned they are "one in Christ" and forgiven in him, and that God continues to shape their story. While churches often emphasize theology, he noted that the program highlighted "the slow, everyday journey with God."

Harry appreciated learning how to be with God and to be still before him, realizing that "it's OK not to be OK." Mason similarly observed that "people don't change overnight," yet even years later, when he experiences shame or weakness, he knows that God is with him and loves him.

Awareness of the Holy Spirit

Participants reported that the program heightened their awareness of the Holy Spirit's work through spiritual disciplines. Ethan shared that he now understands his identity "not in human ways but in God's way," learning to approach spiritual disciplines not legalistically or through fortitude but as ways of being with God. He explained that personal effort cannot bring true change, emphasizing that "only the Spirit" can transform lives.

Sophia likewise reflected that learning about the ministry of the Holy Spirit opened a new way of following Jesus. Rather than relying on fortitude, she learned to abide in Christ through spiritual practices, which she continues years after graduation. This shift also reshaped her ministry, moving her from solving problems to teaching others to pray and listen for God's guidance.

Rest and Renewal

Several participants testified that the program provided space for rest and renewal. Bonnie, weary from ministry, described finding "a place to rest and be refreshed." Harry similarly shared that the program allowed his "soul to rest" through retreats and helped him learn to be kind to himself, embracing rest and enjoyment as part of faithful living.

Summary

Overall, participants described the program as painful, yet healing; unexpected, yet eye-opening; demanding, yet freeing; and intense, yet deeply transforming. The pain emerged largely from the cultural and personal shifts required, particularly the movement from performance-based identity toward grace-based self-understanding.

For these Chinese students, engaging a Western spiritual formation model involved cultural tension, reflection on formative family patterns, and reexamination of deeply held assumptions. Through this process, however, participants encountered God's love in new ways and began to live more integrated, Spirit-led, and relationally grounded lives.

IMPACT OF THE PROGRAM

This section presents how participants perceived the impact of the spiritual formation program on their lives, particularly in their relationships with themselves, God, and others.

Changed Views of Self

Participants described significant changes in how they understood themselves, frequently noting that their self-perception was "different" after completing the program. To appreciate the depth of this transformation, it is necessary first to examine how participants viewed themselves prior to their study.

Old Views of Self

Self as Lost or Repressed

Raised within traditional Chinese parenting patterns, many participants described a sense of self that had been lost, muted, or repressed. Mia explained that because family and community were prioritized, "there is a de-emphasis of the self," and growing up meant learning to follow parental desires rather than attending to one's own feelings.

Clara similarly reflected that this upbringing left her without direction, noting that she lacked purpose or goals because she simply did what she was told. She explained that she never learned how to think for herself or discern what was attainable, since she was not given space to express herself or ask questions.

Jack described his identity as deeply enmeshed with his mother's, recalling that she would say, "If you die, I die." He explained that their identities were emotionally fused, so that his actions reflected directly on her sense of honor and shame. As a result, his personal desires and autonomy were buried beneath expectations shaped by emotional control. Olivia likewise recognized that she and her brother had been raised primarily to meet their mother's emotional needs. She described becoming people-pleasing, enmeshed, and codependent, explaining that her mother had been the center of her world while her own desires were repressed and her voice silenced.

Through the spiritual formation program, Olivia became more aware of how this pattern had shaped her identity. When a professor discussed how parents sometimes form children to meet their own needs, Olivia realized that her mother had been shaping her in this way. Following an intensive retreat and therapy, she came to recognize that she had not been raised as God intended and described her healing as an ongoing process.

Because participants were often parented in ways that demanded obedience while neglecting emotional attunement, many concluded that their sense of self had been suppressed or erased.

Negative Self-Perception and Low Self-Esteem

Several participants admitted that their upbringing left them with deep self-rejection and low self-esteem prior to the program. Fred described himself as lacking confidence, noting that he had "pretty low self-esteem" and often questioned whether he was acceptable to others. Isabel similarly confessed, "I didn't like myself before," explaining that she constantly doubted her value and believed she was unlovable. Emma echoed this struggle, sharing that she viewed both her introversion and her identity as a woman as weaknesses, particularly in contexts where authority was associated with men.

For others, low self-worth was shaped by family dynamics, gender bias, and distorted views of embodiment. Olivia traced her struggle to her father's rejection and her mother's belief that embodied life held little value. Bonnie likewise recounted growing up with gender bias, explaining that as the youngest daughter, she felt insignificant and voiceless. Amelia reflected that her parents' high expectations fostered perfectionism and self-criticism, noting that when she failed to meet those expectations, she judged herself harshly and "didn't like [her]self" before entering the program.

Several participants connected their low self-esteem to shame-based formation rooted in performance and achievement. Noah observed that his upbringing trained him "to do something and be somebody," while beneath the surface, he carried fear and shame. Emma similarly recalled that "a lot of shame and guilt" had been placed upon her within the church. George confessed that he often felt whatever he did was never enough, describing a persistent sense of shame that, though diminished, still lingered.

Before encountering the spiritual formation program, participants' sense of self had been shaped by cultural, familial, and ecclesial expectations that emphasized performance, obedience, and perfection, leaving them with little awareness of their intrinsic worth.

Performance Orientation

Many participants recalled being trained to work hard in order to gain approval and avoid shame, describing a deep fear of "not measuring up." Noah explained that achievement became a way of covering shame, noting that he wanted "to do something and be somebody," but that "deep inside, it was shame that pushed me to do more in order to cover it up." He described being ashamed of his family, upbringing, and self and using achievement as "a mask to wear."

Fred similarly reflected that his upbringing offered no constructive way to deal with inner brokenness. He explained that in his culture, "we don't know what to do with our bad, except to be good," and that shame and guilt attached to unwanted thoughts and desires were managed through outward compliance. While good behavior was meant to resolve inner conflict, he found that it instead increased dissonance, leaving him feeling that he was pretending to be someone he was not. Being good, he concluded, only intensified the shame and trapped him in a vicious cycle.

Fred further connected this pattern to cultural expectations that discouraged questioning authority. Because blaming parents was unacceptable, failure and disappointment were internalized, leading him to assume that he alone was at fault and had not worked hard enough.

Other participants echoed this experience of performance-driven identity. Jack recalled "a lot of pressure and shame for not being good enough" across academics, music, and sports. Amy described constantly trying to improve herself and measure up, yet never being able to accept who she was. Clara similarly shared that she had been taught to "be better, be smarter, be more," explaining that failure meant shame and confirmed that she was not good enough.

False Self-Identity

The emphasis on performance, pleasing others, and meeting expectations led many participants to develop what they described as a "false self" identity. George explained that "being a good boy" had become his primary identity marker. Ethan similarly admitted that he had rooted his identity in ministry performance and others' approval, noting that "seeking people's acceptance has been my major issue," and that he could not truly see his identity in Christ.

Reflecting on his experience in traditional Chinese churches, Ethan added that busyness and visible roles were treated as signs of spiritual success. Praise from pastors or congregations made him feel accepted, leading him to become "a people-pleaser rather than a God-pleaser." Ministry performance thus functioned as a substitute for secure identity.

Amelia traced her false identity to growing up with a mother who was difficult to please. She recalled internalizing many religious "shoulds," including being a good Christian and serving others faithfully. Over time, this produced what she recognized as a "savior complex," driven by a need to be needed. Although being a "good Christian" became her identity, she acknowledged that it ultimately prevented her from discovering her true self in Christ.

Self-Reliant

Several participants also recognized that their upbringing shaped them into highly self-reliant individuals who felt compelled to depend solely on themselves. Noah recounted growing up in survival mode, explaining that hardship taught him that "everything depended on [him]self" and that no one would care for him except himself. He described pushing himself relentlessly for achievement, living like a "warrior," until he eventually broke down.

Leo similarly recalled that he was harsh on himself, forcing himself to work hard for God until he eventually burned out. Bonnie likewise observed that growing up in a culture that "prizes achievements and productivity" bound her to constant expectations. She explained that Chinese parenting emphasized strength over vulnerability, teaching children to "pick yourself up" rather than express pain, which led her to rely on her own abilities, gifts, and strength to navigate life.

Taken together, participants recognized that Confucian-influenced parenting and ecclesial formation shaped them into persons marked by repressed or lost selves, low self-esteem, performance orientation, false identities, and pronounced self-reliance.

Transformed Views of Self

After studying in the spiritual formation program, participants described significant changes in how they viewed and related to themselves.

Emotionally Aware

Participants reported a new capacity for emotional awareness and integration. Lucas noted that the program matured him "not only to think with my mind but also feel with my heart." Rather than downplaying emotions, he learned to "sit with them," describing this integration as embodying "the part of theology that the church has been missing."

George similarly observed that he had learned to "feel much deeper," explaining that the program helped him navigate his internal world more effectively. As a result, he came to trust himself more and became more aware of internalized lies, which he now actively resists.

Mia described increased awareness of her "inner movements" and recognized patterns of false self-talk she had previously used to suppress emotion. Instead of numbing discomfort through substitutes such as food or television, she learned to discern and express emotions such as anxiety and anger. Noah likewise affirmed that he became more conscious of "the movements of my heart," including desires, longings, struggles, and burdens, through practices such as prayer and meditation.

For Bonnie, emotional awareness involved recovering her voice. She explained that growing up, she believed she had nothing to offer, but the program helped her recognize that she has a voice and an opinion, which she described as freeing. Amy identified self-awareness as her most significant learning, noting that greater awareness of her inner motivations enabled her to be more gracious toward herself.

Through this growing emotional awareness, participants reconnected with their real selves rather than remaining confined to culturally formed false identities.

Liking Themselves

Through inner healing of past wounds, participants reported a newfound ability to like and love themselves, in sharp contrast to earlier patterns of self-rejection. Emma shared that she no longer interprets life through a "shame and guilt lens" and is now "much more OK with brokenness," adding simply, "I like myself now"—a shift she described as previously unimaginable.

Bonnie likewise described the program as correcting the narratives that had shaped her identity. She explained that it restored her sense of personhood and freed her from equating worth with productivity, realizing that "it's not what I do that matters but who I am," which she experienced as deeply releasing. Olivia echoed this transformation, noting that the first change she noticed was also basic, yet profound: "I like myself now." She described the joy of embracing embodiment, creativity, and value, recognizing herself as part of God's plan.

Several participants connected self-acceptance with freedom from fear and regret. Olivia reflected on healing rooted in 1 John 4:18, explaining that God had been detaching her from fear-based patterns, particularly in relationships, and helping her reclaim her voice. Lucas similarly described becoming more at peace with who he had been and what he had done. He explained that he learned to stop replaying "if only" narratives, recognizing that he had acted out of who he was at the time and could not have done otherwise. This realization enabled him to accept himself and, as he stated, "love myself more" than before.

Sophia likewise testified that her image of God changed through the program, allowing her to love herself more deeply even as she became more aware of her brokenness. She emphasized that this self-love was not self-generated but sustained by the power of God. Clara also described the impact as "huge," explaining that the program reinforced the belief that she is enough and that God loves her for who she is rather than what she accomplishes. She described the experience as life-giving, providing space to internalize God's love and, in turn, learn to love herself.

Across these accounts, participants consistently expressed that the program enabled them to accept and love themselves even as they became more aware of their weaknesses and failures.

Freedom to Be Themselves

Another significant change participants described was a newfound freedom to be themselves. Bonnie explained that the program helped her discover "inner freedom," releasing her from expectations tied to roles and others' demands. Being away from home gave her "the space to just be myself and not live up to anyone's expectations."

Others echoed this sense of liberation from performance and evaluation. After years of ministry pressure, Ethan experienced renewed freedom, while Amelia identified "the freedom to be myself" as a central takeaway from the program. In Chinese collective church settings, she noted, individual needs and feelings were often subordinated to institutional expectations. As a female minister, she also struggled with unspoken hierarchical and cultural constraints that shaped what she was permitted to do or express.

Several participants described freedom as the ability to enjoy who they were without shame. Emma shared that she had begun to explore hobbies she once suppressed, realizing that "it is OK to have fun," even if others considered her interests childish. Clara similarly reflected that she was learning to extend grace to herself, no longer fearing judgment for enjoying "quirky" things. She described growing confidence in saying, "This is me, and I'm OK with this—and I have fun doing it."

For others, freedom involved releasing shame and embracing self-acceptance. Noah observed that when he opens up, he experiences freedom rather than shame, recognizing that he now has a choice to expose it and be released. Leo likewise discovered that God's priority was relationship rather than productivity. Learning to receive forgiveness not only from God but also from himself enabled him to "be [him]self, not a saint trying to be what [he] can never achieve."

Participants also described freedom as permission to rest and care for themselves. Harry shared that the program taught him that it was acceptable "to play when you are on retreat," a foreign concept in the ministry culture he had known. Learning to rest and enjoy life allowed him to become "kinder to myself." Lucas summarized his transformation as learning "to be OK with who [he is]," explaining that seeing God more clearly enabled him to accept himself rather than striving to be someone he was not.

Clara recalled that her professors repeatedly encouraged her to extend grace to herself—an unfamiliar concept because she had always been pushed to be "better, smarter, more." Failure had been shameful because it meant she was "not good enough or could not measure up."

Overall, participants learned to stop concealing weakness through performance and instead embrace freedom to be themselves—accepted and loved by God in both strength and brokenness.

Knowing That God Loves Them as They Are

Participants reported that through the program, they encountered God's love amid weakness and struggle and came to trust that they are loved as they are. Leo reflected on a shift in both motivation and freedom, explaining that he now works hard not out of fear or obligation but out of enjoyment of being with God. Formerly unable to like himself when he failed to perform well, he summarized the change as working hard not "because of shame or guilt but because of God's love and grace."

Lucas described grasping God's love in the midst of personal "messiness," explaining that Scripture now made sense to him because God knows his history and still calls him to live with him. This realization helped him experience God's invitation not as condemnation but as presence and faithfulness.

Several participants testified that knowing they were loved as they are freed them from people-pleasing and relentless productivity. Ethan described being released from the pressure of others' evaluation, explaining that criticism or lack of recognition no longer mattered as long as he was pleasing God. Noah likewise learned to unlearn a harsh rhythm of productivity, discovering that resting—even "wasting time"—was a way of trusting that God still loves him when he does nothing.

Amy described the process as coming home to her true self, explaining that early deconstruction removed false identities and masks so that she could finally "be who [she] really [is]."

Finding Identity in God

As the program exposed weakness and sin, participants testified that it led them not to despair but to receive God's unconditional love and live from a truer identity. Ethan described the process as divine surgery, explaining that the program revealed the darkness of his heart while helping him see his true identity as a child of God—fully forgiven and accepted.

Because she experienced God in places of weakness, Bonnie chose to face painful emotions with him rather than avoid them. She explained that she now invites God into dark places, trusting him to bring healing, and has developed a greater capacity to embrace pain as part of growth rather than something to fear.

Sophia similarly noted that the program enabled her to see deeper into herself, including darker places. Mia echoed this awareness, explaining that understanding her sin and desperation for God's grace transformed how she treated others. Recognizing shared helplessness before grace made it easier for her to forgive and show compassion rather than judgment.

Fred summarized the unveiling he experienced by acknowledging that although he often appeared put together, the program helped him accept that he did not "have it all together." Through therapy and spiritual direction, Amy likewise described growing in acceptance of herself, learning to receive her emotions and inner life as God's precious child, secure in belonging to him.

Together, these testimonies show how participants moved from performance and people-pleasing toward receiving love, rest, and identity in Christ—and from that foundation, began to relate to themselves and others with greater honesty, compassion, and freedom.

Accepting Self

Many participants reported that they could accept themselves as God's work in process. Jack summarized this shift succinctly: "I became much more gracious with myself." Before the study, he explained, he had internalized his parents' constant pressure to "be better, do better, and try harder," shaped by moral expectations of maturity and perfection. Reflecting on the program's impact, he described how it gave him freedom to be in process rather than striving for completion:

> The spiritual formation program allowed me to have freedom to be in process, to be broken, and to be growing. It has allowed me to be maturing, because I am always becoming. I cannot "be" something; I am always growing into something else. The program has allowed me to be much more patient with myself. Jesus has been patient with me and allowed me to grow. Before, sin was shame and led me away from Jesus, because I thought I needed to be perfect and make myself not need Jesus. But now, even sin is, in a sense, another means to seek the Lord. When I see my sinfulness, it reminds me that I need Jesus. So the program allowed me to be much freer and lighter with myself.

Lucas's experience echoed this movement away from self-fixing toward repentance and grace. Although he still sometimes felt anger and annoyance, he learned to resist the old "loop of improving myself" and sensed God reminding him that he could not fix himself. He concluded that the program taught him to care for and forgive himself, explaining that "the best thing I can do is not to be perfect; the best thing I can do is repent and go back to God when I am confronted with my badness." He acknowledged that practicing this posture remained uneven.

Fred likewise emphasized developing patience and grace toward himself, especially as he came to understand how deeply his character had been shaped by forces beyond his control. Through the program, he learned to engage in compassionate self-reflection and to recognize the formative influence of family, culture, and social context, which helped him release excessive self-blame and become gentler with himself:

> The primary thing that I learned is how to have grace for myself and to forgive myself. I learned to be much gentler with myself, much more understanding with myself. I learned to have conversations with myself—"Why do I feel this? Why do I think this way? Why did this feeling come up rather than other feelings? What are the roots to this feeling?" One of the things the program gave me was helping me see how much of my character was formed by external factors not in my control—my family, my parents, their childhood, their characters, the society, our culture, Asian values. None of these were in my control. They formed me in deep ways, so it was never simply up to me. Seeing how strong those connections were helped me have much more patience and grace with myself.

Amelia similarly described learning to accept herself with greater grace, especially by recognizing her limits and releasing a former "savior complex." She reflected that she now accepts herself as a human being with sins, struggles, and needs, no longer believing that she was responsible for saving others. Through repentance, she experienced freedom from this burden and no longer felt compelled to justify her worth through ministry achievement:

> I accept myself more as a human being who has sins and struggles. I now accept myself as a person with different needs. I'm not someone God appointed to save people. I need people to help me too. My former mentality—that I needed to do much to be someone to save people—was not healthy at all. I couldn't get out of the circle of wanting to help God, to do God's ministry, and to save others. The program helped me repent before God, which was really helpful. I was released from the savior complex and no longer felt that I had to have a special call.

As a result, Amelia explained that she continues to serve and share the gospel not because she "should" or "needs to" but because she loves people and trusts that God loves people.

Bonnie likewise described learning to give herself grace and to set healthy boundaries rather than pleasing others. After graduating from the program, she found herself less harsh and critical, releasing untransformed parts of herself to God rather than scolding herself for not changing fast enough:

> After graduating from the program, I've become more gracious to myself. I don't have to be harsh on myself when I make mistakes. I understand that growth and transformation take time. I remember what was stressed in the program—that spiritual growth is the slowest motion on earth—so give yourself grace and time. It's been really good for me. I'm not harsh and critical of myself anymore. When I discover a part of me that's still untransformed or a lingering habit that isn't good, instead of scolding myself—"How come I'm not done yet?" or "I can do better next time; I'll fix it"—I release it to God and say, "God, it's good to know this part is here. Can you help me?"

Clara offered a more tentative account, acknowledging slow and ongoing growth. She admitted that she still struggles to like herself and to define what is lovable, especially on difficult days. While she is not "100 percent there," she described her journey as a slow, steady process of learning to extend grace toward herself:

> I'm still struggling with this. I've never liked myself—growing up, I was told I'm not enough, not this, not that. Naturally I felt, "Why does the Lord love me?" It doesn't make sense because I don't feel lovable. On hard days—if I had a bad day at work, or something went wrong—I still struggle to be OK and to have grace for myself. I'm very hard on myself, including my appearance. I still struggle with how I define what is lovable. I'm not 100 percent there. I don't know if I will be, but it's a slow, steady growth of learning to love myself and have grace for myself.

Olivia, deeply shaped by her mother's dismissive view of embodiment and her father's rejection of her as a woman, similarly acknowledged ongoing difficulty. While she had experienced significant healing, she admitted that she still struggled at times with accepting her appearance.

Overall, while participants continued to recognize areas of weakness and incompleteness, they increasingly moved away from self-improvement projects and toward receiving themselves as people in process—being patiently and graciously transformed by God.

Dependence on God

Participants described a growing awareness of their dependence on God. Lucas explained that the program helped him resist cultural habits of quick fixes and self-sufficiency, noting that it taught him to recognize his limits and "fight against the Chinese tradition of fixing problems or giving quick solutions." He summarized this shift by confessing, "Apart from you, Jesus, I can do nothing good."

Bonnie similarly recounted being stripped of self-reliance. She described losing confidence in her own strength, abilities, gifts, and talents and coming to realize that "life doesn't work without God." Through the program, she reached a point of acknowledging her need for God, recognizing that "apart from him, [she] can do nothing."

In sum, participants described a transformation in their view of self—from lost or repressed identity, performance-based value, and self-reliance toward emotional awareness, freedom to be themselves, and deepened dependence on God. Through the program, they experienced God's love and learned that they are accepted as they are, finding identity in God and increasingly relying on him.

Changed Relationships with God

This section first presents how participants described their relationships with God before studying in the spiritual formation program and then examines how those perceptions changed afterward.

Old Views of God

God Was Scary

Several participants recalled perceiving God as frightening prior to the program. Jack admitted bluntly, "God was fearful. God was scary." He explained that God felt like "a combo of my mom and my dad," both of whom were highly shaming and demanded perfection. Because mistakes were interpreted as personal failure, God appeared to him as "always disappointed and upset," a projection shaped by his parents' expectations.

Ethan similarly described viewing God as punitive, explaining that God would punish wrongdoing "like what parents would do to their kids." Influenced by his relationship with his earthly father, he believed that God would discipline him harshly if he failed to obey. This left him wrestling with whether God could truly accept his failure, weakness, and struggle.

Amelia traced her fear of God to confusion between her mother's voice and God's voice. She recalled that when things went wrong, her mother would say, "I told you so," and punish her, leading Amelia to assume that misfortune signaled divine displeasure. As a result, her prayers took on what she called a "repent mold," focused on identifying wrongdoing to avoid punishment. She later recognized this image of God as manipulative and controlling, shaped both by her family dynamics and by legalistic church teaching that emphasized behavior over grace.

Isabel likewise acknowledged projecting a culturally authoritative image onto God. She believed God demanded obedience regardless of personal capacity or context, recalling church leaders who urged members to "press on and just follow God's word" without attending to individual circumstances. Over time, this reinforced her perception of God as forceful rather than relational.

God Was a Commander and Slave Driver

For Sophia, the most significant change resulting from the program concerned her image of God. Before entering the program, she explained that although she believed God was loving in theory, she experienced him primarily as a commander. Faithfulness meant obedience and performance: if she succeeded, she pleased God; if she failed, she failed God. Her relationship with God resembled that of commander and soldier, centered on duty, responsibility, and her capacity to carry out God's work.

Sophia traced this image to her former Chinese evangelical fundamentalist church, which emphasized doing the right things to prove faithfulness while offering little guidance for engaging weakness. Saying no was interpreted as rebellion, laziness, or self-centeredness, leaving little room for honest discernment or limitation.

Jack described a similar perception of God, explaining that God felt like a place where he received assignments, accomplished tasks, and met expectations. When he failed, God seemed angry and demanding—"a slave driver." He connected this image to his mother's perfectionism and relentless work ethic, noting that leisure produced guilt rather than rest.

Because affirmation was absent in his upbringing, God likewise felt unaffirming, critical, and driven by results rather than relationship.

My Duty to Do God's Will

Mia described her relationship with God as grounded in obedience by effort. She believed God was pleased with her only when she obeyed, explaining that if she did what God asked, she was "on good terms" with him. Despite decades of faithful service, she felt the burden of maintaining the relationship through confession, discipline, and perseverance, often pushing through exhaustion until she felt "spiritual" again.

Fred similarly described Christianity as primarily activity-oriented. Because he had not experienced his parents' love emotionally, he assumed God's love was distant and abstract. Faith became a matter of doing the right things—evangelism, prayer, Bible reading—without deep engagement. Ethan echoed this pattern, describing his earlier spiritual life as marked by constant activity and difficulty responding to God in silence, noting that stillness and solitude were especially challenging within Chinese pastoral culture.

Fear of Being Punished

Participants also described fear of punishment or rejection that limited honesty with God. Sophia admitted that although she believed God already knew her, she avoided bringing her weaknesses into prayer. Amy similarly recalled suppressing sadness or discouragement by forcing herself to focus on gratitude rather than speaking honestly with God. When she felt sad or disappointed, she explained she would "force [her] self not to talk about it with God" and instead try to "muster up that thankfulness" by telling herself, "It's OK—let's count God's blessings now and don't be discouraged."

Amelia described a more subtle form of distance. Although she believed God was loving, she felt compelled to pray in particular ways—such as kneeling during crises—to ensure effectiveness. Because emotional openness had been rare in her family, she found herself only partially open with God, hiding certain parts of herself out of habit and fear.

God as Distant

Several participants perceived God as distant, often reflecting experiences with emotionally distant parents. Harry, who had not been close to his father, explained that because his relationship with his father lacked emotional intimacy, he struggled to understand what it meant for God to be an intimate Father. Although he could imagine God as a friend, closeness felt foreign.

George shared a similar experience. Raised by hands-off parents who issued instructions but were not actively involved in his growth, he learned early that being a "good boy" meant obedience, good grades, and non-disruption. This pattern carried into his faith, shaping a relationship with God defined by effort and performance rather than presence.

Other participants described God as distant in more impersonal ways. Fred recalled that his church reinforced a performance-based relationship with God, teaching him to stop sinful behavior and "read the Bible more" in order to improve the relationship. Olivia similarly described God as abstract and factual—"just the Bible and whatever the Bible tells you," rather than a personal being. Leo echoed this distance, explaining that God handled divine matters while he managed earthly responsibilities, leaving little sense of relational connection.

Mason offered a more introspective account. Although he believed God heard his prayers, he lacked awareness of God's presence in daily life. Because he could not name his emotions or understand his inner world, he struggled to recognize how God met him in weakness. During seasons when God felt absent, Mason assumed the problem was insufficient discipline and advised himself—and others—to pray more or do more to regain a sense of God's presence.

Because many participants experienced emotional distance in their families, they often struggled to recognize God's nearness, particularly during times of difficulty and inner confusion.

Old Views of Prayer

Many participants reported that their understanding of prayer prior to the program was shaped by obligation, correctness, and performance. Sophia explained that she had been taught to pray "right and biblically," leading her to focus on accuracy rather than honesty. As a result, she rarely revealed herself fully to God or understood what it meant to be led practically by the Holy Spirit in prayer. Ethan similarly described prayer as formal and dutiful, something he performed in response to needs or responsibilities rather than as relational engagement.

Mia experienced prayer as a heavy responsibility that was "all on me." She confessed frequently yet felt exhausted, believing it was her duty to maintain the relationship with God through rigorous devotion and service. Amelia likewise recalled praying out of fear, feeling compelled to kneel—especially in serious situations—to ensure effectiveness. Prayer, for both, was shaped by anxiety rather than trust.

Fred described how guilt and shame made prayer difficult. He had not been taught how to experience God in seasons of darkness and assumed that God's absence signaled personal failure. He traced this understanding to a Confucian moral framework that emphasized virtue, behavior, and self-cultivation while neglecting the inner life, desires, and intentions of the heart.

Clara traced her prayer life to parental expectations of goodness and compliance. Because her parents discouraged emotional "mess," prayer felt like another reminder that she was not good enough. Scripture reading and prayer became obligations marked by silence rather than conversation, leaving her without a sense of connection or response from God.

In these ways, Confucian-influenced parenting and church formation shaped participants' views of prayer as duty-driven, fear-based, and emotionally constrained rather than relational and honest.

Transformed Views of God

All participants reported that their study in the spiritual formation program transformed their relationships with God. Several interrelated themes emerged from the data: participants developed healthier images of God by separating parental and cultural voices from God's voice; they experienced God's acceptance and gentleness; they became able to be honest about weakness and struggle; and they recognized God's nearness and personal involvement in daily life.

Healthier Image of God

After studying in the program, participants described a significant shift toward healthier images of God, often by recognizing how parental and cultural influences had shaped their earlier perceptions. Amelia realized that her former "fear-repent-mold" of prayer stemmed from fear of a "manipulative and controlling" God modeled after her mother. After intensive inward therapy, she learned to see God as loving and accepting and no longer assumed that suffering or difficulty meant she had done something wrong or deserved punishment.

Jack described a similar process of disentangling his parents' voices from God's voice. He reflected that God had once felt associated with slavery because of how deeply his parents' expectations shaped his inner world. During intensive inward therapy, he created two icons—one representing Jesus and the other his mother—to externalize and confront these internalized images:

> I had an icon of Jesus, and then I made an icon of my mom. I'd put them on two sides. The icon of my mom was a black figure with a ball and chain. She was chained to Confucius, to her Chinese heritage, because for her, all she knew was the slave driving of needing to make her kids perfect. Then I was chained to that. I also made an icon of Jesus as the great high priest on the throne. I would talk to both of them. Jesus' is freeing, and I'd imagine myself back under my mom's rule. Her life was a life of slavery. The program helped me separate these two images so I could cling to the true image of God. My mom's love language was shame and guilt, which she used a lot. There's a particular style in Asian shame and guilt that I experienced deeply from my mom.

As Jack became aware of how shame and guilt—common to all cultures but intensified in his Asian upbringing—had shaped his image of God, he experienced a profound reorientation. Whereas God had once seemed frightening and demanding, he began to encounter God as safe and loving:

> Through the journey of studying in the program, God became a safe place and a place of love for me. I began to see that I had projected my parents onto God. Slowly God began taking those pieces off, freeing me from my parents and allowing him to be himself rather than them. God is different today than he was then. It's been very freeing.

Jack summarized this transformation succinctly, emphasizing that what surprised him most was God's gentleness. Contrary to his earlier assumptions, he discovered that God does not relate through pressure or coercion but through patient, inviting love.

Other participants echoed this internalization of God's love. Olivia shared that although she had intellectually believed that God loved her, she had never known what that love felt like until after the program. She now described God as loving, gracious, faithful, and generous. Lucas summarized his experience simply: "I get that God loves me." Sophia likewise testified that after three years of formation, her image of God became firmly rooted in God as loving Father.

Reflecting on this shift, Olivia noted that where she once lived in fear of not doing enough for God or the kingdom, she now understood God as love itself. Her understanding of God moved, in her words, from "black and white to colorful," no longer grounded in achievement or obedience but in unconditional love.

God Is Accepting

Another significant change participants described was experiencing God's acceptance and love amid weakness and failure. This was foreign to many, as they had been raised to behave well, avoid mistakes, and please authority figures. Amelia shared that where God had once felt fearful, she came to understand—especially after intensive inward therapy—that "God knows everything, and he accepts every part of me."

Ethan similarly testified that he learned God loves him like this: "As I am and as I was," freeing him from striving to please God through fortitude or ministry performance. Through the program, he came to understand God as a gracious Father and learned to distinguish discipline from punishment. He described God as patient and restorative, giving "a second chance" after failure, and explained that this helped him grasp what it means to be a new creation in Christ.

Lucas echoed this discovery, explaining that he learned God knows him intimately, including his weaknesses, failures, and limitations. Coming from a family marked by anger and abuse, he found it especially difficult to believe that God could continue to love him after repeated failure. Through the program, he realized that God is neither ashamed nor disappointed, because God fully knows what to expect from human beings. He described this season as one of weakness and learning to be at peace with that reality, grounded in the assurance that God's love is not dependent on performance.

Through the program, participants moved from fearing God's rejection toward trusting his unconditional acceptance of their whole selves.

Being Honest with God

Knowing that God loved them in their weakness enabled participants to become honest with him. Sophia described one of her most significant changes as being able to "reveal myself honestly to God." Amy similarly explained that the program helped her become transparent with God, trusting that God would not leave or abandon her when she was deeply honest. She shared that she now feels safe bringing what is happening "at the depth of my heart" into prayer.

Noah also testified that honesty brought freedom. He explained that when he opens up and names his shame before God, he experiences release rather than being driven by it. The program empowered participants to expose vulnerability to God as they experienced his full acceptance and forgiveness.

God Is Close

While some participants had previously experienced God as distant—often reflecting relationships with emotionally distant parents—after studying in the spiritual formation program, they described God as present and personally involved. Ethan noted that the program helped him develop a personal relationship with God. Clara likewise shared that God became more accessible, explaining that she no longer needed to be "good" to come to God but could approach him honestly as she was. Harry reflected that the program helped him recognize God's presence throughout his life story, not only in major events but also in ordinary moments.

Others emphasized discovering God as a personal, relational being rather than an abstract concept. Olivia shared that although she once had only head knowledge of God, she came to realize that "God is a person" who has emotions and feels deeply. Leo echoed this shift, explaining that while he had known God intellectually, the program led him to experience God personally, describing it as moving from knowing about God to truly encountering him.

Participants also described how correcting distorted images of God led to deeper intimacy. Sophia explained that replacing her former image of God as commander or slave driver with God as loving Father transformed her relationship with him. Isabel similarly testified that God became "much closer" and more intimate than she had previously experienced. Fred added that the program helped him understand what God was doing in his life and how to respond relationally rather than performatively.

Having grown up with emotionally distant parents, Harry admitted that he was still "wrestling with the idea that God is an intimate Father," yet he felt he was "getting a little bit closer to understanding what it means for a spiritual Father to be intimately close." For Noah, this growing sense of closeness culminated in a profound experience during a long retreat after graduation. Continuing the spiritual rhythms formed in the program, he encountered God affirming him as a beloved son. He described this father-son relationship as a deep and lasting foundation for his life with God, independent of achievement or failure.

Olivia, who once read the Bible diligently but understood God primarily as "a bunch of facts," recounted a turning point during the program when she was invited to move from propositional knowledge to relational knowing:

> It has been fascinating because in my second year, God very gently—not abruptly—said to me, "You already know your Bible. Stop reading your Bible and get to know Me." I felt puzzled because I was in seminary and God asked me to stop reading the Bible. However, I sensed that God was inviting me to know him as a person—to know the love that he has for me, which I had never been able to experience through years of inductive Bible study. Although the Bible is essential for knowing God and forming right theology, God is so much deeper than that. He is present in our anger, sorrow, happiness, and joy. I realized I did not need to be afraid of these emotions, because we have a great high priest who sympathizes with our weaknesses and has gone through what we have gone through.

Through this program, participants became increasingly aware of God's intimacy and closeness, not merely as theological truth but as lived, relational reality.

Aware of God's Presence

After studying in the spiritual formation program, participants reported heightened awareness of God's presence and the work of the Holy Spirit in their lives. Many described learning to recognize God's presence not only in moments of consolation but also in silence, struggle, and darkness.

Mason described the program's impact on his relationship with God as "huge," explaining that he came to trust God's presence even when he felt abandoned. During what he identified as a "dark night of the senses," he learned that God remained with him and loving him. Entering his weaknesses rather than avoiding them enabled him to experience God's love there, which he described as the most significant change in his spiritual life.

Fred similarly came to recognize that God is present in darkness and silence. The program reshaped his understanding of Christian life, helping him see that silence does not signify God's absence. Instead, he learned that spiritual growth involves a deepening awareness of sin and dependence on grace rather than striving for moral perfection. Reflecting on this reversal, he explained,

> As the years go by, especially in the program when I was taken into the depth of my sinfulness, it deepened my experience of knowing that there was a person deep down in me whom I did not even know if I could accept or not. Yet God told me that this is the person for whom Jesus died. I have been slowly learning to internalize that and accept that this is what the Christian life is about. This has been the way to realizing how much I have been forgiven and how much I am loved.

Lucas likewise described becoming more aware of his dependence on God, explaining that the program opened him to his need for God in a way he had not previously recognized. He came to understand abiding in Christ and living in the Holy Spirit as the core of Christian life, acknowledging that "without him, I am nothing."

Several participants described recognizing God as distinct from authoritative figures in their families. Bonnie expressed gratitude for the restoration of her image of God, realizing that God was not like her earthly father but a loving heavenly Father. This rediscovery led her to experience being loved and valued by God in new ways.

Others emphasized increased awareness of the Holy Spirit's personal and active role. Ethan noted that the program helped him see his heart in relation to God and the Spirit in a more personal way. Isabel likewise said that the program clarified misunderstandings and deepened her relationship with God. Emma reflected that without the Holy Spirit, the program would have remained merely intellectual, explaining that genuine transformation, especially integration of wounds and inner healing, was only possible through the Spirit's work:

> I don't think anything would have happened without the Holy Spirit these past five years. It could have just been a very intellectual walk in the park or a very intellectual attempt to get somewhere with my life, but without the Holy Spirit, that would not have happened—nothing would have happened. Without the Holy Spirit, transformation on the spiritual level, like being OK with myself, my inner child, and my wounds, and seeing them as an integrated part of me—I don't think any of that would have happened.

Noah described learning that sanctification could not be achieved through effort alone. The program helped him understand that the "sanctification gap" could only be crossed through the Holy Spirit's guidance rather than self-driven discipline. This realization reshaped his approach to spiritual growth and deeply impacted his relationship with God. Olivia used a metaphor to describe her expanded awareness of the Spirit's work, likening it to having "a wider bandwidth" between herself and God through the practice of spiritual disciplines.

Through their study in the spiritual formation program, participants' relationships with God became more immediate and experiential. False images of God as distant or demanding were corrected, and participants learned to recognize God's loving presence even in darkness and struggle. As they became more attentive to the Holy Spirit's work, they experienced God as actively involved in their lives and increasingly learned to live in honest, dependent, and relational trust.

Transformed Views of Prayer

After completing the spiritual formation program, participants described profound changes in their understanding and practice of prayer. Rather than viewing prayer as performance, obligation, or theological correctness, they came to experience it as honest presence with God, led by the Holy Spirit.

Sophia explained that her understanding of prayer shifted from doing it "right" to bringing her true self before God. Prayer became simpler and more genuine, no longer dominated by concern for theological precision. She described learning to enter silence, surrender herself, and sense how the Holy Spirit was leading her to pray, noting that this change in prayer deeply reshaped her relationship with God.

Mia likewise learned to present her unfiltered self to God rather than a self that was already "cleaned up." She explained that prayer was no longer about maintaining the relationship through effort but about receiving grace. When she felt distant from God, she learned simply to tell him how she felt and to ask for grace, rather than pushing herself through guilt or discipline.

Several participants described learning to pray honestly without first fixing themselves. Bonnie reflected that she once began prayer by asking for forgiveness in order to make herself "presentable" to God. Through the program, she realized that God already knew her fully and loved her as she was. Prayer became a space where she could invite God into her struggles and emotions and allow him to reveal what he wanted her to see, without striving to earn approval.

Fred described how deeper self-knowledge transformed his prayer life. He learned to distinguish between the heart's self-condemnation and God's voice, recognizing that feelings of guilt and shame often arose from internal judgment rather than divine rejection. This insight freed him to remain present with God rather than projecting condemnation onto him.

Others emphasized how prayer became more relational and integrated into daily life. Clara said prayer and Scripture were "way different now," no longer boring or pressured but marked by slowing down, stillness, and awareness of God's presence. George similarly described prayer as woven throughout his day, especially through the prayer of recollection, which continually reminded him of his identity in Christ as beloved, forgiven, and secure. This shift, he said, brought a radical difference to how he lived.

Amelia found new freedom in prayer as fear dissolved. After the program, she no longer assumed that difficulties meant she had done something wrong or that God was displeased. She described God as loving and present at all times, enabling her to pray freely in any place without fear of punishment or offense.

Overall, the data indicate that the spiritual formation program profoundly reshaped participants' prayer lives. Having experienced God's love and acceptance, they learned to approach prayer as honest, relational presence rather than duty or performance. Prayer became a space where they could bring their whole selves, including weaknesses, emotions, and struggles, before a loving, close, and attentive God.

Changed Relationships with Others

Some participants entered the program hoping primarily to learn how to help others but soon realized that meaningful care for others required learning to care for themselves first. Clara reflected, "I cannot counsel or direct someone else when I cannot even have grace or love for myself." She added that recognizing "I matter in this process" was both significant and entirely new. Clara was surprised to discover that the program was "not just about helping someone else" but about developing a mutual relationship with the Lord that transformed her and, in turn, reshaped how she related to others.

This section examines participants' perceptions of how the program influenced their relationships with others. It first describes their relational patterns before the program and then explores the changes that followed.

Old Views

Participants' earlier approaches to relationships were largely shaped by their upbringing and cultural expectations.

Unhealthy Relationships

Several participants described themselves as people-pleasers prior to the program. Amelia admitted that she had carried a "savior complex," while Clara recalled being highly codependent: "In order to keep a person my friend, I would do anything to keep the relationship, because I was not confident enough in who I was as a person." Amy similarly explained that her relationships were driven by performance: "In the past, my relationship with others was more about what I could do for them, or how I could please them or impress them."

Judgmental

Others recognized that they had related to people through judgment rather than grace. Fred confessed, "Previously I was very judgmental," explaining that in Asian cultures where public behavior is emphasized, perceived misconduct is quickly evaluated and condemned, often internally. Bonnie echoed this posture, admitting that she often labeled others as hopeless or irredeemable. Olivia likewise acknowledged that she had been judgmental toward unbelievers and "very fact-oriented and regimented" when discipling other Christians.

Lack of Connection

Several participants also noted a lack of genuine relational connection. Emma reflected that she once tried to connect by emphasizing shared experiences, believing that similarity created closeness. While this approach sometimes helped, she later realized it did not foster the depth required for true soul care. Noah admitted that, before the program, investing in relationships felt like "a waste of time." Sophia similarly explained that although she was regarded as kind and helpful, her care for others was largely technical: she knew how to solve problems and apply techniques, but she did not know how to connect deeply at the heart level.

Through self-examination in the program, participants came to recognize that their earlier ways of relating, marked by people-pleasing, judgment, and superficial connection, limited their capacity for authentic, healing relationships.

Transformed Views

After their study in the program, participants reported that their perspectives on others were significantly transformed.

Aware of the Work of the Holy Spirit

Through the program, participants became more attentive to the work of the Holy Spirit in other people's lives, especially in contexts of ministry, counseling, and spiritual direction. Ethan described a major shift in how he approached helping others. Whereas he had previously relied on his own skills, strategies, and empathy, he came to recognize the "much more influencing role of the Holy Spirit" in revealing people's struggles and guiding response. He explained that he learned not to react merely with human sympathy, but to respond as God responds—relying on the Spirit rather than his own strength.

Ethan described this change as the difference between working "for" God and working "with" God, drawing on the biblical contrast between Martha and Mary:

> Doing everything "for" God and doing everything "with" God are totally different. It is like the theology between Martha and Mary. Martha was doing everything for God, but Mary was doing everything with God. At first, I would try doing business as Martha, and then I complained about my hectic ministry. But sometimes God seemed to ask me, "What are you doing? And for whom are you doing all these things?" I realized that ministry itself had become an idol for me.

Reflecting further, Ethan described learning to minister attentively in dependence on the Spirit:

> Now I need to learn to be Mary. I do everything with God. It is very important to involve God and rely on the Holy Spirit, because I cannot do everything—even ministry—by myself. Dealing with people and the messiness of human hearts is too difficult. I tell my students to open both ears: one ear to listen to people and their problems, and the other ear to listen to the Holy Spirit.

Other participants echoed this growing reliance on the Spirit. Sophia described witnessing the "powerful transformational work of the Holy Spirit" in both her own life and the lives of others. She learned to abide in Christ and follow the Spirit's leading in ministry rather than depending solely on hard work and fortitude. Noah similarly admitted that learning to listen attentively in spiritual direction was difficult, but through the program he learned to sit, wait, and allow the Holy Spirit to guide the process. Leo also shared that spiritual direction training reshaped his counseling paradigm, teaching him to rely more fully on the Holy Spirit rather than technique alone.

Through their study, participants became increasingly aware of the Holy Spirit's active role, not only in their own formation, but also in guiding how they care for and walk alongside others.

Deeper Connection

Participants also reported forming deeper and more intentional relationships with others. Olivia explained that her friendships changed as she learned to listen more attentively. She described developing an intentional posture of slowing down and being present with others "on behalf of the Holy Spirit," which enabled her to notice and honor what God was doing in another person's life. Through this posture, she learned to invest in relationships with greater depth and intimacy.

Noah likewise described a shift in how he valued relationships. Whereas he once considered relationship-building a waste of time, he now recognized its importance. He admitted that he was still learning how to relate to others, not through productivity or problem-solving but through presence, shared enjoyment, and simply being with people.

Through the program, participants learned to build deeper, more intentional relationships rooted in attentiveness, presence, and reliance on the Holy Spirit rather than performance or efficiency.

More Empathetic

Participants consistently reported that the program fostered greater empathy and compassion in their relationships with others. Rather than responding from judgment, problem-solving, or performance, they learned to relate to others with patience, presence, and grace, mirroring how they had come to experience God.

Ethan described becoming empathetic "as God, not in human ways." He learned to see people from God's perspective rather than evaluating them by his own standards. Because of his own healing, he became more aware that others carry "their own hurt and pain" and sought to understand them as God sees them. He emphasized that true empathy required reliance on the Holy Spirit rather than personal strength, especially when relating to those who had hurt or discouraged him. Teaching at a Chinese seminary, he distinguished counseling from spiritual direction, explaining that the latter helps people attend to God rather than merely fixing problems.

Lucas similarly described learning to listen deeply rather than offering quick solutions. The program trained him to hear both himself and others and to recognize emotional movements beneath behavior. He noted that many Chinese people have never learned to face emotions, such as grief or anger, and instead blame circumstances. Through the program, Lucas learned to attend to the heart and to connect emotional awareness with God's presence, which enabled genuine empathy.

Several participants described how empathy grew as they learned vulnerability and grace. Mason said he learned to "enter emotions" previously unfamiliar to him and to express them in relationships with his wife, colleagues, and friends. Recognizing that people are "in a journey," he became more patient and learned that sharing vulnerability appropriately helped others feel free from the pressure to be perfect. Jack echoed this shift, explaining that because he experienced God as gentle, he desired to be gentler with others, even when they held immature or flawed theological views. Leo likewise noted that learning to forgive himself enabled him to forgive others more readily and to release the impulse to judge.

Bonnie reflected that experiencing God's presence in her own pain created space to accompany others in theirs. Although being with others in discomfort could stir unease, she found herself more willing to journey with them, trusting God's presence in difficult places. Sophia similarly testified that through her suffering and the Spirit's work, she became more compassionate, not only technically but emotionally and spiritually.

Harry emphasized learning to respect others by listening without immediately giving advice. Through sharing life stories in the program, he realized that others are not "side characters" but individuals with complex stories in which God is also at work. He became more willing to listen without telling others what to do, recognizing that "everyone has a life that is just as complex as my own." Emma described a similar shift, observing that she had developed "a greater tendency to give other people space to tell me whatever they want," becoming less focused on inserting her own experiences. She realized that she could now recognize others' stories, even when they resembled her own, as genuinely theirs, which allowed her to see them more clearly and to be more receptive to knowing them.

Fred described a parallel shift from judgment to curiosity. As he became aware of how deeply he himself had been formed by family and culture, he grew more curious about how others had been shaped, especially when their behavior confused him. This awareness transformed how he related both to himself and to others.

Empathy also reshaped participants' engagement beyond the church. Olivia, who once felt guarded and judgmental toward non-Christians, said the program strengthened her sense of identity in Christ and helped her relate to others with compassion rather than defensiveness. She came to recognize unbelievers as image-bearers loved by God and expressed a renewed desire to care for them. Lucas similarly said the program reshaped his understanding of evangelism, leading him to pray less for people to be "fixed" and more for them to encounter God.

Noah, who had experienced loneliness as a pastor, developed a particular compassion for other church leaders. Rather than pursuing large-scale impact, he focused on accompanying a few pastors, helping them become vulnerable and attentive to the Holy Spirit. He emphasized patience, silence, and discernment, noting that many Chinese believers carry deep shame that requires gentle, Spirit-led accompaniment.

In sum, the program cultivated participants' empathy by transforming how they understood themselves, others, and God. As they learned to receive grace, attend to the Holy Spirit, and honor the complexity of human stories, they became more compassionate, patient, and present in their relationships with others.

Leave Unhealthy Relationships

Some participants reported that the program helped them recognize and step away from unhealthy relationships. Clara affirmed that the program "helped me to be able to step away from unhealthy relationships." Formerly codependent, she explained that the program enabled her to question her relational motives, asking herself, "Why am I doing this? Why do I feel the need to always pay for food when we go out?" She reflected,

> It helped me to examine my relationships and probe what my relationships with others are revealing about myself and how I feel about them. So the spiritual formation program has helped me step away from unhealthy relationships and identify my motives for relationships, which has been pretty huge. Through the process of learning to have grace for myself and learning to love myself, it really has helped me to be more sensitive to other people. The program has taught me the importance of presence and how to be present with a person. It has changed and deepened many of my relationships, which have become less like "fun times" but more like deep conversations in truth and openness.

Amelia likewise stated that as her former "savior complex" was dismantled, she no longer felt compelled to please others and experienced a new sense of freedom. Isabel described gaining greater discernment in relationships, choosing to step back from unhealthy ties and to invest more intentionally in relationships God placed on her heart. She noted that these relationships became marked by openness and a willingness to engage deeper issues rather than avoiding true needs.

Amy described a shift from "doing" to "being" in relationships. Rather than trying to please, impress, or escape discomfort, she said, "I can be myself in relationships with others because of the acceptance of myself. I do not care so much about whether other people accept me or not because I am who I am."

As participants grew in self-awareness and learned to extend grace toward themselves, they became increasingly able to step back from unhealthy relational patterns and to form relationships characterized by honesty, presence, and freedom.

Relationships with Family

Participants also reported significant changes in their family relationships. Fred, who had previously experienced love as delayed and conditional, said the program helped him learn "to receive love in the present, here and now." Mason described learning to be emotionally vulnerable with his wife, explaining that the program taught him how to recognize and express his feelings rather than suppress them. This vulnerability extended into his marriage and work relationships, where he could now show up more honestly and authentically.

Mason also noted a shift in his relationship with his emotionally distant father. Although sharing vulnerably with his father still felt new and uncertain, he sensed a growing capacity to open himself relationally rather than remain guarded.

Jack described profound transformation in his relationship with his parents, particularly his mother. Her controlling behavior, anger, and shaming messages had deeply shaped his sense of self and his image of God. Through spiritual formation practices, therapy, and intensive inward work, Jack described a process of detaching from his mother's expectations and relinquishing his longing for her approval:

> For me, I began to detach from the pain and hurt in childhood. My mom stressed work a lot. As a child, I tried to make mom happy, and those things were tied up with love. Through the whole process of spiritual formation, including therapy, retreats, and intensive inward therapy, I was empowered to break the ties with my mom. I had to let myself die to my mom's "love." I pondered over the question of "What if mom never will love me?" I had to say yes, I had to take it, and say, "If mom never loves me, Jesus, your love will still be good enough."

He further described grieving the possibility that his mother might never acknowledge the pain she caused, choosing instead to entrust that unmet need to God. Through this process, Jack said he was able to see his mother as another adult rather than the source of affirmation and identity:

> Now when I am around her, although she is still my mom, I see her as another adult. I am not looking to her for affirmation. Rather, I am looking to her as another human being. As I detached from those expectations, it freed me to love my parents more freely.

As a result, Jack testified that the program enabled him "to actually love my parents." By differentiating God's voice from his mother's, he gained greater relational freedom—not only with his parents but also in ministry and spiritual direction, particularly with others who shared similar cultural experiences.

Other participants echoed similar changes. Mason noted that experiencing God's grace made him more patient and understanding toward family members. Olivia said she was now able to relate to her parents more maturely, including setting clear boundaries while maintaining relationship: "This is my limit. This is as far as I am willing to go."

Overall, the program reshaped participants' relationships with their families. Where filial piety and obligation had once fostered enmeshment or suppression of self, participants learned to relate to their parents as fellow adults, loving them freely, setting healthy boundaries, and entrusting unmet needs to God rather than to family expectations.

Transformed Family Dynamics

After studying in the program, participants reported notable changes in family dynamics. Olivia found that her relationship with her brother became "more robust" because their conversations were no longer "all about mom," nor did they feel the need to "pull out the magic rabbit to make her feel good." Instead of striving to please their mother, Olivia said she and her brother were "able to suddenly stop being mom-centric" and develop a "strong relationship," which had previously been impossible because their mother "never allowed space for them" to connect. She concluded, "My relationship with my brother has definitely shifted in a good direction."

Leo likewise described changes that extended across his entire family system. He explained, "I started relating with my family in the way of letting go of my agenda for myself, for other people, and even my expectation on God." As he released control and relinquished long-held expectations, he noticed that "my family started feeling the freedom and joy for me in their lives," and others recognized "the release that God has worked through me through this program."

These changes were especially evident in Leo's marriage. His wife observed that he was "quite a different person" after studying in the program. Whereas he had previously become "very rigid and hard to approach" when stressed, he was now "much less stressful." Leo noted that after an intensive therapy experience, his wife repeatedly commented that he had become "much less agitated." Through spiritual direction, counseling, and opportunities to process long-standing wounds, Leo experienced healing that enabled him to become a "healthier" person relationally.

The program also influenced Leo's approach to parenting. He reflected, "I used to try to force myself to be a strong father, believing that this was all my role was supposed to be." Through the program, he learned to become more vulnerable, to speak honestly for himself, and to extend grace to himself. "I no longer need to be in control," he said, noting that his children appreciated the changes they observed in him.

Having grown up in a troubled family, Lucas similarly came to recognize the formative power of family relationships. He reflected on "how central a family is" in shaping a person's growth and described how the program helped him become less judgmental and more compassionate toward others' backgrounds and struggles. He illustrated this insight through reflection on family influence:

> When a kid is upset and quick to anger, you can look at his parents. When a kid is very much spouting out all these nonsense of "he is rich, why isn't he treated this way," you just look at their parents. The program helped me to sympathize much more. It also leads me to pray for people more because there are so many problems that we cannot fix, and there are so many problems that, when you come to the end of the day, they go back to the family—mom and dad, brothers and sisters.

Through these experiences, the spiritual formation program reshaped participants' relationships with their families, fostering greater freedom, compassion, and maturity in how they related to parents, siblings, spouses, and children.

6

Mechanisms and Applications of the Program

THE CENTRAL UNDERSTANDING EMERGING from the data is that a Western Christian spiritual formation program facilitated Chinese students' transformative learning through several interrelated mechanisms. First, it led participants to reexamine their upbringing—a countercultural and often challenging process given their Confucian background. Second, it provided a safe and accepting environment in which they could explore and disclose vulnerabilities considered shameful within their cultural context. Third, it equipped them with theological understanding, spiritual disciplines, and hands-on apprenticeship training. As a result, participants' meaning perspectives were transformed in relation to self, God, and others, and their Confucian-shaped autonomy gave way to a growing awareness of God's presence and dependence on him.

In chapter 4, I examined how the program prompted participants to reexamine their upbringing, a process that was countercultural and demanding because of their Confucian heritage. In chapter 5, I discussed how their meaning perspectives were transformed with respect to self, God, and others, along with their growing awareness of God's presence and dependence on him. In this chapter, I present findings that show how the program provided a safe and accepting environment for exploring and disclosing vulnerabilities considered shameful in participants'

Chinese background, and how they sought to apply what they learned within their own cultural and ministry contexts.

Most participants expressed appreciation for all components of the program, including teachings on spirituality, retreats, cohort groups, spiritual direction, therapy, the practicum series for training spiritual directors, Ignatian exercises, and the intensive inward retreat.

Speaking of these components, Amy stated, "I appreciate all of them. They make the program work because all of them are important." She added, "At the same time, it's a very well-designed program. It's a very well thought-through program for people to really get to know God and experience God himself."

Fred similarly said that he "appreciated all of them." He explained,

> For me, the goal of the program is really about drawing a believer into his or her relationship with God and coming to comprehend the gospel. It's quite fundamental and basic. It's about learning what it means to believe the gospel and to continue to believe the gospel—what it means for believers that Jesus Christ died for my sin, and I have a restored relationship with God.

He further reflected that the program facilitated "the deepening of the believer's relationship with God" by helping participants navigate that relationship and give themselves more fully to it.

Reflecting on the program's design, Fred observed that "they first draw you in, then they let you experience, and finally, after you experience the darkness, the pains and hurts, and the memories, they help you understand this process." He concluded,

> I think it's necessary because people need to experience certain things themselves before you help them to process. This spiritual formation program is that kind of experience—the experience of yourself. You really need to be allowed to experience yourself first, because it's something that fallen humanity is just fundamentally against. Sinful human beings do not want to experience themselves, all the way back to the garden. The instinct to cover and hide is the deepest instinct. For that reason, people have to be nudged into it, because if you tell them up-front what they are going to do, they will think, "They are making me do this so that I can experience that." That should not be the point. The point is not to accomplish something but to be with—to live in the category of presence. How do I be with God, regardless of what comes from it? It is really a training in being with and

> that purpose is best served by the way the program is currently designed.

Other participants echoed similar appreciation. Noah said he liked "all of it" and that "everything was huge." George indicated that he "appreciated all of it" and "loved every class." Leo said that he valued "the spiritual journey with God through those practices, directions, retreats, and some of the classes." Sophia affirmed that she "really appreciated the professors' teachings and the design of the program." Mia described "all those components" as "instrumental" to her learning and growth.

Isabel likewise expressed appreciation for the integrated design of the program, noting that "each component plays its own unique role." She explained,

> The lecture is definitely crucial for giving us the right understanding of the Bible and theology. The interaction part—such as the groups, classroom exercises, and prayer projects we do at home—reinforces what we learn. Personal retreats, group retreats, and cohort groups deepen what we learn instead of keeping everything in our head. We are led to actually experience what we learn, and it becomes part of our life, not just head knowledge. I appreciate all of them. If I had to choose one, I would choose personal retreat, because it has now become my habit. Even after graduation, I continue to go on retreat. I think it will be a lifelong desire to spend quiet time with God, away from the world.

COMPONENTS OF THE PROGRAM

This section presents participants' perceptions of how different components of the program facilitated their transformation.

Teachings of Spiritual Theology

Participants reported that the program's teachings in spiritual theology not only corrected misunderstandings of Christian spirituality but also accelerated their spiritual growth.

Emphasis on the Double Knowledge

The program emphasized what Calvin termed the *double knowledge*—knowledge of God and knowledge of self—and guided participants toward deeper understanding in both areas. In particular, it began by helping them see themselves more clearly. Lucas observed, "The program always emphasizes the double knowledge of knowing God and self. It helps us understand that the more you know yourself, the more you know God. This interaction was something I learned here."

Through this emphasis, participants were invited to discover their true selves. Emma explained, "So much of what we were taught in the program was about looking at ourselves and our experiences. We looked back at what we did, reviewed our family sculpture, our family of origin in particular, and how these shaped who we have become—our insecurities, tendencies, wounds, desires, and life goals." She acknowledged that the process was difficult, recalling,

> My first year was absolutely the worst. I remember crying almost every day. It was the transition of adding all of this to my plate—things to do, things to read, things to study—along with the responsibilities of being a student again. At the same time, the material brought up many heart issues that I realized I had never really processed or examined.

Growing up in a Chinese church context, Emma came to recognize that "a lot of shame and guilt had been dumped on top of me." Although she continued to experience shame and guilt, naming them enabled her to become "much more open to not seeing everything through shame and guilt lenses" and "much more OK with brokenness." The program helped her accept both herself and others as people who are "still in process."

Isabel echoed this experience, noting that the first year was especially demanding, "The first year actually was the most difficult year. I didn't anticipate that the professors would open up our history and ask us to review our past. All the prayer projects were very personal. The first year was very, very difficult—very dark and challenging. I wasn't prepared for that."

Although reexamining their upbringing and internal worlds was painful and unsettling, participants consistently described this process as essential to growth in both self-knowledge and knowledge of God.

Teachings About Spirituality

Participants expressed deep appreciation for the professors' teaching on spirituality, describing it as formative, clarifying, and often unlike anything they had encountered previously. Ethan noted that the instruction was "totally different from the spirituality that I had learned before in my country." He explained, "During my study, the professor always emphasized two things: we are totally forgiven and totally accepted by Jesus Christ." This emphasis helped Ethan realize that "there is so much more that we can learn about spirituality and about my own journey with God."

Emma likewise said she "really enjoyed the professor's classes," describing them as "very thought-provoking." Isabel emphasized the foundational role of lectures, stating, "The lecture is definitely crucial to give us the right understanding of the Bible and the theology." Sophia shared that the professor "has taught a lot about the human spirit and the ministry of the Holy Spirit," noting that although she had encountered these ideas before, "I have never had anyone present them in this way." She explained,

> I knew concepts like the weakness of the will and the temptation of the flesh before I came to study in the spiritual formation program, but I didn't have people teach them in that way and make them conceptual. During the classes of spiritual theology, the professor repeatedly told us that we have to know the Holy Spirit—which was the missing part that I had never heard in my entire Christian life, because at my church, we seldom, very seldom talked about the Holy Spirit or the ministry of the Holy Spirit.

As a result, Sophia recalled that she "was shocked in the first year," realizing for the first time that she needed to know the Holy Spirit personally. She wondered, "How can I know the Holy Spirit? How can I know the ministry of the Holy Spirit?" and felt confused and unsure. However, during her second year—through spiritual direction, praying the prayer of intention, and practicing *lectio divina*—she found that these disciplines helped her "open up to the ministry of the Holy Spirit." She testified, "Now I truly experience the ministry of the Holy Spirit in my soul." Previously, she had relied almost entirely on what the professor described as human fortitude. "While fortitude is good," she reflected, "it is not enough. You have to know the ministry of the Holy Spirit, not only your fortitude."

Other participants echoed similar discoveries. Harry stated, "The majority of the content that I learned here was really special—things that I had never heard taught in my Christian undergraduate education or emphasized in church." Clara found the teaching transformative because it gave language to her lived experience: "The teaching is phenomenal because it put my experiences and what I lived through into words, which I could never express." When the professor described experiences such as the "dark night of the soul" and seasons of spiritual consolation and desolation, Clara recalled thinking, "Yes! This is exactly what it is." What she had previously interpreted as personal pathology—being "depressed" or "crazy"—was reframed and normalized, bringing her a sense of clarity and relief.

Mia similarly remembered being struck from the very first class: "Wow! It feels like the professor was describing me all the time." She found the theoretical distinctions—especially between spiritual formation and moral formation—"influential and thought-provoking." Noah was also deeply impacted, particularly by the professor's account of his own transformation during a twenty-one-day retreat, which opened "a new horizon." Through the teaching, Noah learned about humanity's tendency to "cover up or hide because of sin, shame, and guilt," and how growth toward the true self requires honest self-examination.

Noah also highlighted the program's teaching on the "sanctification gap," which named a struggle he had long experienced. He explained that although one might push oneself through effort, "there is always a gap that you cannot cross except with the help or guidance of the Holy Spirit." He concluded, "It is all about spiritual work, not your own hard-working, and I learned it from the program, and it impacted me a lot."

Overall, the program's teaching on spirituality helped participants reinterpret their spiritual experiences, provided language for previously unarticulated inner realities, and corrected misunderstandings rooted in moralism, performance, and self-reliance.

Integration of Psychology

Participants expressed strong appreciation for the program's integration of spiritual theology and psychology, viewing this integration as essential to their growth and formation.

Ethan explained that psychology "opened my eyes to see myself." Prior to the program, he said, he did not "see the self" as part of his identity. "Psychology opened my mind to see the self—to see the problem of the self, and how to deal with my own self," he reflected. Through this process, Ethan came to value the integration of theology and psychology, concluding that theology should not be compartmentalized but integrated with disciplines such as psychology, spirituality, and missions in order to equip seminary students for ministry. George likewise observed that "all professors view spiritual formation through a psychological lens," using it to uncover emotions, deeper inner movements, and formative experiences that shape one's image of God and understanding of self.

Lucas described how the program intentionally led students to revisit their personal histories in God's presence. "They're forcing me to look back, to see what I've been through, and to talk with God about that," he said. Although he initially experienced this as uncomfortable, Lucas later recognized its formative value: "That matures me emotionally because now I see what I've gone through. God walks me through it—all the weaknesses, all the failures—and I can be OK with that." Coming from an unhealthy family background, Lucas found revisiting the past painful, yet the integration of theology and psychology taught him to face difficult emotions with God rather than alone. Through guided reflection, professors helped students invite God into their life stories and become aware of his presence and the work of the Holy Spirit in healing and transformation.

Bonnie similarly found the psychology courses "very helpful" in understanding herself and others. She explained,

> I understand what's going on in my mind and my heart, and most of the time that understanding helps me know that I am normal—that there is nothing abnormal about this. It helped me see that these reactions were normal responses to what was done to me or to the circumstances I grew up in. It also gave meaning to my experiences. Even when there were negative emotions, I could see the meaning behind them. Giving meaning to experiences helps a lot in healing and in moving on. Instead of seeing something as simply bad, I can understand why I reacted the way I did and how I can now live differently.

Bonnie added that this understanding helped her become "less critical and judgmental toward others without first understanding their stories." As participants grew in self-awareness through psychological insight, they also developed greater empathy for others.

Overall, participants affirmed that the program's integration of psychology with spiritual theology played a significant role in facilitating emotional awareness, healing, and spiritual growth.

Spiritual Warfare

Although the study of spiritual warfare was not a required component of the program, one participant emphasized its importance for spiritual formation. Ethan reported being "blessed richly" by a class on spiritual warfare and appreciated the seminary's effort to integrate this topic into theological education. He explained that spiritual warfare is "a big issue and challenge for pastors and ministers in my country," where "many people fall into occultism related to dark powers and become demonized." Ethan concluded that it is vital for ministers to be "equipped with spiritual-warfare knowledge through the teaching of professors who have experience working with people in bondage to occultism and spiritual darkness."

The Faculty

Most participants affirmed the significant influence of the faculty on their learning and formation. When Ethan was still discerning the nature of the program, he met with one professor and shared his "struggles, burdens, and challenges in ministry." He recalled that the professor listened patiently and offered thoughtful responses to both his questions about the program and his personal struggles. In contrast to his experience in Chinese seminaries, Ethan noted that these professors openly shared their own weaknesses and struggles. Rather than diminishing his respect, this transparency deepened it: "I respect them more because I see them as persons—as human beings, as who they are." He described the faculty as "totally different from professors with Chinese backgrounds in my country," emphasizing their honesty and openness in sharing their spiritual journeys.

Clara similarly expressed gratitude for the faculty's care and attentiveness. She said the professors were "all so understanding and patient," willing to answer questions, sit with her, and process experiences together. She reflected, "I've never been in a program like this where the faculty care so much about their students. I've never felt so invested in as a person." She concluded, "When I was in the program, I felt that I was a person—I'm Clara, not a student number. I felt loved and cherished. I felt seen."

Beyond classroom teaching, faculty members accompanied students in their life journeys. Fred recalled spending significant time with one professor who became "a big part of my spiritual formation journey." Jack highlighted the professors' wisdom and their ability to give language to students' experiences:

> They would give vocabulary to the experiences I was having—and even to experiences I would have later. Sometimes a faculty member would say something I didn't yet believe, and then I would discover it later. They gave enough of a road map ahead, even while emphasizing that not knowing where you are going can be a good thing. That helped me feel confident moving forward with God.

Amelia was likewise struck by the faculty's integration of competence, humility, and spiritual attunement:

> All the professors are very knowledgeable and professional, but at the same time very humble and aligned with the work of the Spirit. They are not afraid of dark issues or human sin. They know how to use God's healing power to help students. Seeing them felt like seeing Jesus. They are warm, unique, and deeply formative for us.

Through their authenticity, wisdom, and loving presence, the faculty embodied the very spirituality the program sought to cultivate in its students.

Community

In addition to formal teaching, nearly all participants emphasized the central role of community in their formation. This community included faculty, staff, spiritual directors, classmates, and cohort groups, and it provided a safe, trusting environment marked by acceptance rather than judgment.

Amelia recalled that formation never occurred in isolation: "We had spiritual directors, counseling, cohort groups, and retreats. It was a very well-thought-through program for people to really get to know God and experience God himself." Mason described classes and retreats where students sat in circles, sharing vulnerably, and appreciated how the program intentionally modeled vulnerability and discovery within community.

Bonnie described community as "very instrumental" to her growth, noting that it was rare to experience a group where she felt so deeply understood and accepted. Olivia similarly reflected that she looked back on her years in the program "with fondness because of the intentional community it built," one in which vulnerability and spiritual connection were fostered through the work of the Holy Spirit.

George emphasized the program's intentional design in placing students in groups and cohorts, explaining that "we were not meant to go through life—or this program—alone." He reflected that it was within these relationships that he found greater freedom and access to his true self, as others provided a safe context in which to invite honesty and growth. He described a three-week group spiritual-direction experience as especially life-giving, noting the depth of care that distinguished it from ordinary friendships.

Other participants echoed this sentiment. Leo described the program as offering a "unique family-type community." Sophia valued the mutual support and shared experience. Amy noted the intimacy of small groups, where participants processed life together and "spoke truth in love." Emma appreciated how cohort groups modeled relational depth. Fred valued being in a community where "none of us have it together," yet everyone had freedom to be present without shame.

Through this shared life, the program cultivated a community in which participants could disclose weakness, experience acceptance, and encounter God's love in tangible and relational ways.

Apprentice Training Model and Hands-On Application of Concepts

Participants emphasized that the program's apprentice-training model and hands-on application of theory were central to their transformation, enabling them to live out what they learned rather than merely understand it conceptually. Clara remarked, "I love how hands-on they are with their students." She added, "It doesn't feel like a program; it feels like a church community and home—and that has hugely helped, because we are dealing with a lot of heavy things."

These hands-on components included spiritual disciplines such as prayer projects, spiritual direction, Ignatian exercises, therapy, and the intensive inward retreat.

Prayer Projects

Weekly prayer projects were a core practice through which students processed course material experientially. Ethan recalled that professors often concluded class by assigning prayer questions that directly corresponded to the teaching: "The questions helped open my mind and heart." In addition to meditating on Scripture, students practiced the prayer of recollection and kept prayer journals, which, Ethan noted, gave him "different ways of practicing spiritual disciplines."

Amelia similarly remembered that professors frequently instructed students to "wait on God." This practice was unfamiliar to her, as prayer in her previous church experience had been largely one-directional. Through the prayer projects, she discovered that prayer involved listening as well as speaking: "When I started doing prayer projects, I realized that God also talks to me." As a result, she began to incorporate intentional silence and waiting into her regular prayer life, allowing God to reveal himself and speak to her heart.

Although George initially found the prayer projects challenging, he came to value the structure they provided: "They were so good for me to have that forced time to sit for an hour and pray about these things that are important." Over time, the practice became rhythmic rather than burdensome: "Every Friday I would wake up and do it. It wasn't a duty at all. I really received a lot from them."

Jack identified centering prayer as especially transformative. Introduced in a spiritual-theology class, this discipline invited him to be with God without the pressure to perform. Coming from a family culture that emphasized constant productivity, Jack found centering prayer deeply healing: "It was the first time I could come to prayer not having to do anything—just be with God." In contrast to his mother's repeated message to "improve, improve, improve," simply sitting with God was "something I had never experienced before," and he described it as "so transformational."

Sophia highlighted the program's insistence on embodied practice rather than mere conceptual learning:

> For example, they did not merely ask us to read about *lectio divina*. Instead, they asked us to practice it personally and then provided tutorial classes where we could experience it together, which helped us learn the discipline in a concrete and embodied way. Similarly, they did not ask us simply to read about centering prayer or take an exam explaining its steps. Rather, they required us to practice it for four months, five times a week. That made sense to me. If these are truly spiritual disciplines, they need to be practiced as disciplines within the curriculum.

Mia likewise noted that while she grasped the theoretical content cognitively, it was the prayer projects and silent retreats that enabled deeper honesty before God: "Those practices helped me gradually move into my true self." Fred echoed this observation, stating that applying the concepts through prayer projects revealed "what it looked like to experience yourself and God in prayer."

Through sustained engagement in practices such as prayer projects and centering prayer, participants did not merely learn about spiritual disciplines but were apprenticed into them, resulting in profound transformation in their relationship with God.

Receiving Spiritual Direction

The program required all students to receive individual spiritual direction and to participate in at least one semester of group spiritual direction. Most participants described spiritual direction as a vital component of their formation. Bonnie noted that "another component that was very helpful was the individual and group spiritual direction," explaining that both formats were effective in helping her process course material more deeply.

Ethan likewise described his weekly meetings with a spiritual director as "very helpful." Because group settings were limited by time, he especially valued one-on-one spiritual direction, where he could share "my own journey of life, my struggles, and my progress." Initially, Ethan assumed that the spiritual director's role was to solve his problems and provide answers. Over time, however, he came to understand that the purpose of spiritual direction was not problem-solving but discernment:

"Instead, he was to help me see my own heart with the Holy Spirit and relate to God in a personal way." Recognizing its value, Ethan has continued receiving spiritual direction after graduation, explaining, "I still need a spiritual director."

Sophia was similarly grateful that spiritual direction was a required part of the program, even though she initially had little understanding of the practice. After experiencing it firsthand, she became eager to pursue training as a spiritual director herself. Noah added that spiritual direction "pushed me to listen attentively," cultivating a posture of patience and presence rather than control.

Across participants' accounts, spiritual direction emerged as one of the most formative elements of the program, deepening awareness of God's presence and fostering attentiveness to the inner life.

Spiritual Director Training

In addition to receiving spiritual direction, some students followed the soul-care track and received formal training to become spiritual directors. Jack described spiritual direction as "a big piece of the program," noting that both receiving direction and learning to offer it were "huge" for his formation.

Harry found that training in spiritual direction taught him "to be with somebody when they're hurting," which helped him grow in empathy and patience when accompanying others. Noah acknowledged that this training was particularly challenging because it required unlearning habits shaped by pastoral problem-solving. He reflected, "I used to listen to a problem and immediately want to fix it. But spiritual direction is not like that. You have to sit, wait, and not tell the directee what to do—just let the Holy Spirit guide."

Through this apprenticeship in spiritual direction, participants learned to resist quick solutions and to trust the Spirit's work in others. Training to become spiritual directors thus fostered greater patience, empathy, and reliance on the Holy Spirit in their relationships and ministry.

Other Spiritual Exercises

In addition to prayer projects and spiritual direction, students were required to practice disciplines such as silent prayer and the Ignatian exercises. Although Noah had engaged in some disciplines prior to the program, he said that through this training, he "learned a lot by being exposed to various spiritual exercises." Ethan likewise found it valuable to learn "more personal and more intimate spiritual disciplines such as silence and solitude."

Sophia described these practices as transformative for both her personal spirituality and ministry. She explained, "The program changed me a lot. First of all, knowing the ministry of the Spirit and different types of spiritual disciplines opened up a way that I can follow Jesus." Previously reliant on her own fortitude and often exhausted in ministry, she learned instead to "abide in Jesus through the spiritual disciplines," which enabled her to experience the ministry of the Holy Spirit more deeply. She emphasized that this shift was "a very important way the program affected me."

Even three years after graduation, Sophia reported that she continues to practice these disciplines in her daily spiritual life. Moreover, they reshaped her approach to ministry. Rather than equating faithfulness with relentless effort, she now encourages others to open themselves to the Holy Spirit through prayer and practice. Reflecting on this change, she said that the program transformed "my old way of talking about problems and offering solutions." Instead of trying to fix people's issues, she now teaches them how to pray, trust God's work, and learn to face problems in God's presence.

Among the disciplines participants found especially helpful for cultivating an ongoing relationship with God were the Ignatian exercises. Sophia observed that some Chinese churches have begun to explore the Ignatian exercises because of their emphasis on discernment, which she described as "a missing part in many Chinese evangelical churches." Jack similarly affirmed that the Ignatian exercises were "very formative" for his spiritual life.

Through sustained engagement in practices such as silence, solitude, and the Ignatian exercises, participants discovered new ways of encountering God's presence and discerning his guidance in everyday life.

Retreats

Participants noted that the program's retreats differed significantly from those they had experienced in Chinese churches.

Solitude Retreats

A required discipline in the program was retreat, including both personal retreats and faculty-student retreats. Unlike many Chinese church retreats that are densely scheduled and activity-oriented, these retreats emphasized silence, meditation, and solitude as means of cultivating intimacy with God.

Jack described the retreats as "incredible and so formative for me," ranging from forty-eight-hour retreats to three-week and Ignatian retreats. He explained that they helped him "reshape—or rather, helped God reshape—who I am and who he is." Harry likewise appreciated the retreats and the retreat class, noting that they helped him reflect on his personal story and recognize God's work in what had previously felt like an ordinary life.

During a forty-eight-hour personal retreat, Harry chose to abandon structure altogether. He recalled bringing books and a tentative plan but ultimately allowing himself to nap, fast from media, read, hike, journal, and cook without a fixed schedule. Although unstructured, the retreat remained purposeful: "The purpose was still to be with God and be close to him, to pray."

Ethan described the retreats as "enhancing and far-reaching," adding that they became "a model for me when I lead retreats and teach others about them." He has continued participating in such retreats after graduation. Noah likewise maintained this practice, finding retreats "profound, practical, usable, and effective in discerning God's will," particularly because they provided space to encounter his inner life more deeply.

Nearly ten years after graduating, Isabel said that retreat had become "a rhythm of life." She even introduced her son to silent retreat, explaining spiritual practices in language he could understand. She reflected, "The spiritual formation program has done something beyond the classroom," expressing gratitude for both God's guidance and the professors' dedication.

Although George initially felt reluctant and sometimes "forced" to attend retreats, observing the cumulative growth that occurred from one retreat to the next helped him recognize their value and integrate those experiences over time. Amelia said she enjoyed both the regular retreats and the intensive inward retreat. Bonnie similarly identified retreat as a crucial component, especially the three-week intensive inward-journey retreat, which she described as a "very significant transformative point" in her spiritual life.

Overall, solitude retreats provided participants with a new way of experiencing God's presence and intimacy, one marked not by activity or performance but by silence, attentiveness, and being with God.

Intensive Inward Retreat

Several participants attended the intensive inward retreat, which draws retreatants into deeper encounter with God by integrating psychological insight with contemplative spiritual traditions. Participants described the retreat as "unique," "life-changing," "valuable," and "amazing."

Mason said, "The intensive inward retreat was really good. It helped me realize many things in my upbringing." He noted that he would like to attend again now that he is married, because "more is coming out of me." Sophia asserted that the retreat was "necessary" for her healing and spiritual growth and suggested that it should be "compulsory for all who receive soul-care training." She explained, "As a spiritual director, a soul-care provider, if your inner self is not healthy enough, how can you take care of other souls?"

Amy also described the retreat as pivotal: "The intensive inward retreat is very special for me. There was a breakthrough in my life during the retreat. It was very intense, but I think the spiritual director was really good. He was really experienced." She regarded the retreat as "a gift from the Lord."

For Amelia, the retreat marked a decisive shift in her God-image. She explained that she had long confused her mother's voice with God's voice, even after seventeen years of Christian faith. Through the retreat, she became able to distinguish between the two and recognized that her fear of a "manipulative and controlling" God was rooted in her parents' influence. She reflected, "After the retreat, I see that God is loving and accepting." Rather than assuming punishment when difficulties arose, she learned to speak honestly with God, trusting his grace. Amelia concluded, "I had much freedom after the retreat, which was the most important thing to help me mature as a person."

Participants who attended the intensive inward retreat consistently described it as a turning point—a deeply transformative encounter with God that reshaped their understanding of themselves and of divine grace.

Therapy

Some participants reflected that therapy was a valuable component of the program. Olivia distinguished therapy from spiritual direction, noting that "therapy is more relationship- and self-oriented, whereas spiritual direction is more God-oriented—though that does not mean therapy is not God-oriented." Through therapy, she explained, she could also see "the way in which God is influencing me and has changed my relationship with my parents and other people." For her, engaging in both practices together was especially beneficial: "Doing those two things in tandem is really valuable."

Therapy was required for students in both program tracks, with additional hours for those training as spiritual directors. Lucas, who completed only twelve sessions, reflected that "therapy was OK," though he felt it was limited in impact: "Apparently it takes twenty-five or so." Amelia confirmed this, explaining that students in the spiritual-director track were required to complete twenty-four or twenty-five hours of counseling. She completed all the required sessions and continued therapy for another four or five years after graduation, describing the experience as "really healing."

Bonnie likewise testified that therapy was "important and necessary." She explained that it helped her gain insight into her life history and relationships: "I could make sense of many things—why I was the way I was, where I am now, what shaped me, and what my relationships growing up were like." Therapy provided space for her to process formative experiences from childhood, including family roles, gender expectations, feelings of insignificance, and her relationships with her parents, which she described as "an important place for me to talk about."

Overall, participants found that integrating psychology into theological education through therapy deepened their self-understanding and promoted healing, complementing the program's spiritual and formational aims.

Spiritual Directors

Nearly all participants reported positive experiences with their spiritual directors and expressed appreciation for receiving spiritual direction. Few encountered significant difficulties related to cultural differences, despite most directors being Caucasian. Ethan acknowledged that cultural differences existed but emphasized that his director was very "understanding." Mason likewise reflected that he "did not feel many cultural issues." Harry described his experience as "very positive," explaining that his directors consistently slowed down, listened attentively, and responded with patience rather than judgment or surprise. Through their reflective questions and presence, he said, "they really helped me process my life with God."

Several participants emphasized the formative nature of the spiritual-director relationship. Olivia described spiritual direction, alongside therapy, as especially valuable because her director helped her recognize and name what God was already doing in her life. Although she previously had only an unconscious awareness of God's work, she explained that "once you sit down with somebody and they reflect that back to you, it's a very different reality." Lucas similarly described having multiple directors who were attentive and prayerful, noting that they consistently redirected his attention toward God's activity in his life. "Spiritual direction was great," he concluded.

Others highlighted how directors navigated cultural differences with sensitivity. Mia shared that although her director did not fully understand Chinese culture, the way she practiced spiritual direction resonated deeply. Beginning sessions with Scripture and *lectio divina* felt familiar and created a sense of safety. Amy likewise reported no difficulty related to cultural differences and described one director as "very special," noting that working through the Ignatian exercises with him helped her feel affirmed as an individual. Emma said simply that her director understood her "very well."

Isabel offered a long-term perspective, explaining that her Caucasian spiritual director never imposed his own values or worldview but listened attentively to the Holy Spirit. Although she sometimes felt challenged, she was confident that the challenge came "very clearly from the Spirit," not from the director. Having met with the same director for nearly ten years, she described their relationship as one of mutual witnessing to God's work and growth in Christ. She also distinguished spiritual direction from therapy, noting that spiritual direction primarily addressed her relationship with God, while therapy focused more on her relationships with others and herself. Both, she said, were essential at different stages of her journey.

Fred's experience illustrates the depth of impact spiritual direction had on participants. Reflecting on four years with the same director, he described it as his first experience of having his "soul attended to":

> I was with the same spiritual director all my four years there. We just connected really well right from the start. She really was my first experience of being attended, having my soul attended to, and having someone actually listen to me, listen to my heart, and not just the words that I'm saying. . . . She was able to really hear what was underneath, what my heart was really saying. I wasn't aware of myself most of the time, and she was able to show me that she really heard and responded to my heart despite all the words coming out of my mouth.

Fred also described a contrasting experience with a cohort leader who served as a spiritual director and practiced what he called "tough love." Though difficult at the time, this experience proved deeply formative by exposing how his intellectual analysis functioned as a defense against feeling. In retrospect, he recognized this as one of the moments of greatest growth.

Harry summarized the impact of spiritual direction succinctly, noting that his directors' patient and compassionate responses during moments of failure revealed God's character to him. "Their reactions show me what God is really like," he said. "Spiritual direction showed me that God is someone who is intimately involved with my life. He is not far away."

Through these relationships, participants encountered God's love and acceptance in tangible ways, as spiritual directors consistently modeled attentiveness, patience, and care for their hearts and souls.

Life Situations

A few participants recognized that significant life circumstances also contributed to their process of spiritual formation during their studies. For some, studying abroad created a physical and emotional distance from family expectations that became formative in itself. As an international student, Fred reflected, "Being away from home and parents gave me enough space to experience those things without having to think about what they would think about it too much. That was the major component of discovering myself and finding that."

Bonnie likewise emphasized that both the program and the experience of living away from her familiar environment were formative. She said, "Both the program and being away from my home of familiarity was powerful already. I had that space to just be myself and not live up to any expectations of other people on me." To describe her experience, Bonnie used the metaphor of desert and oasis. As an international student far from home and familiar supports, she explained,

> Spiritually, I felt it was a desert because in Christian tradition, some people went to the desert to find God or to encounter God, also to fight demons. That was what the desert fathers and mothers did. I remember going to study in the program in the first year—there was so much intentional deconstruction happening—that I felt stripped of everything I had placed my trust and hope in. All my abilities, my strength, my gifts—almost everything—were removed. I was able to see, at the core, who I am. That was difficult because it required me to face myself deeply. What was good, though, was finding God loving me there at the core of who I am, and not for what I did.

Bonnie continued by describing a second movement in her experience: "Besides being stripped, there was also an oasis—a refreshing experience." Reflecting on the whole process, she concluded, "My experience of study has been both good and bad, but both were necessary to form me in this process of growth."

For these participants, life situations such as geographical distance, cultural dislocation, and freedom from familiar expectations functioned alongside program structures as contexts in which the Holy Spirit worked. These circumstances created space for self-examination, deconstruction, and renewed encounter with God, becoming an integral part of their spiritual formation process.

The Work of the Holy Spirit

Participants consistently reported that the program taught and emphasized the work of the Holy Spirit in their lives. Olivia recalled that although she had encountered the Spirit earlier in life—"When I was sixteen, I went to a conference and experienced the voice of the Holy Spirit speaking to me for the first time"—the Spirit's activity had never been clearly articulated or integrated into her spiritual life. As a result, she said, "I just did things on my own," eventually finding herself asking, "God, where are you? What's happening right now?" In contrast, she explained that the spiritual formation program emphasized a dimension of spiritual life that is often unseen yet actively at work. Through spiritual disciplines, she learned to open herself to "the ministry of the Holy Spirit in my soul."

Noah similarly testified that teachings on the "sanctification gap" reshaped his understanding of spiritual growth. He realized, "No matter how hard I tried or pushed myself to fill the gap, I could not succeed without the help or guidance of the Holy Spirit. It is all about spiritual work, not my own hard-working." This insight, he said, deeply impacted his faith and ministry.

Emma recognized the Spirit's work even through academic practices, such as reading. She observed that "the reading materials for the classes were related to whatever God was doing in that season," and that reading itself became "a way of engaging with what the Holy Spirit was doing in my own life." Reflecting theologically, she explained,

> For me, I see the Holy Spirit as a dynamic in Philippians 2, where Paul says to "work out your salvation with fear and trembling, for it is God who is at work in you." I think our part is to work out our salvation, and the Holy Spirit works in these two processes. The Spirit comes alongside us in our working. He is at work inwardly as we seek growth outwardly through spiritual disciplines or even bodily health and wholeness. Without the Holy Spirit, nothing would have happened during these past five years. It would have been merely an intellectual attempt to grow. Without the Holy Spirit, transformation would not have happened—nothing would have happened.

Emma continued by emphasizing that even intellectual insight depends on the Spirit's work. She noted that growth in self-acceptance, integration of wounds, and healing of the "inner child" would not have been possible without the Holy Spirit's transforming presence.

Participants also described how the program helped them experience spiritual formation as an integrated whole rather than as fragmented practices. Jack reflected, "Spiritual direction, therapy—these things all played into it. They all blurred together." Olivia similarly observed that the program was intentionally designed to lead students toward God through multiple avenues, including spiritual disciplines, retreats, therapy, and soul-care training. "The different components of the program," she said, "were very intentional in that direction, and people acknowledge the value of that investment in their own growth."

Leo echoed this holistic understanding, noting that spiritual practices, spiritual direction, retreats, and counseling together reshaped his reliance on the Holy Spirit. He explained that these experiences not only deepened his relationship with God but also transformed his counseling paradigm, teaching him to "fully rely on the Holy Spirit in a different way" while processing his own inner life more deeply.

Through their study, participants became increasingly aware of the Holy Spirit's continual presence and active role, recognizing his transforming work across spiritual practices, intellectual formation, emotional healing, and daily life.

APPLYING SPIRITUAL FORMATION IN THE CHINESE CONTEXT

This section presents participants' experiences and perceptions of applying what they learned in the program to Chinese churches and ministry contexts. Participants consistently reported that efforts to introduce spiritual formation encountered resistance rooted in theological suspicion, cultural history, and ecclesial identity.

Bias Against Catholicism

Several participants reflected that in many Chinese evangelical churches, spiritual formation is viewed with suspicion because of its perceived association with Catholicism. Ethan explained, "Some people and some pastors have prejudice against spiritual formation. They may even become paranoid and suspicious about it because of its connection with Catholicism." When he taught meditation or contemplative prayer, he recalled that church leaders would reject these practices harshly, saying they originated with Catholic figures, such as the Dominicans or Henri Nouwen. Ethan added that similar attitudes existed within some Chinese seminaries, where professors held "bias against and misconception about spiritual formation" and repudiated disciplines such as silence, solitude, and retreat, sometimes labeling practitioners as "lazy."

Noah likewise observed that spiritual formation is often rejected because it is "connected with the Catholic church," which remains a taboo in many Chinese evangelical settings. He added that resistance is intensified by the program's emphasis on reliance on the Holy Spirit, which some churches associate with charismatic movements they strongly oppose. Lucas echoed this concern, noting that even when Chinese churches show curiosity about spiritual formation in theory, they are unlikely to practice it. "If they consider it heresy because it's Catholic," he said, "they will never touch it."

Leo, who has attempted to introduce spiritual formation practices in his church, described mixed responses. Some congregants were receptive, while others were wary or deeply skeptical. He explained that Protestant churches in China often lack familiarity with liturgical traditions and therefore react strongly against anything perceived as Catholic. Historically, Catholicism in China was widely regarded as occult, particularly before 2000. Leo explained that differences in the biblical canon, the presence of statues, and Marian devotion led many Protestants to conclude that Catholics worshiped "gods other than Jesus." As a result, many Christians adopted a simple posture of avoidance: "Catholic is occult. That's it." Although attitudes have softened somewhat in recent decades, Leo noted that Catholic associations remain "pretty touchy" when introducing practices rooted in Catholic or Eastern Orthodox traditions.

Leo concluded, "The number one reason that spiritual formation is hard to be accepted by many Chinese churches is because it is something related to Catholicism." Participants thus identified anti-Catholic bias as a primary obstacle to applying spiritual formation practices, shaping both institutional resistance and individual hesitation within Chinese evangelical contexts.

Not Relational

Some participants found that a major obstacle to applying spiritual formation in Chinese churches was a lack of relational capacity. Fred noted that spiritual formation was difficult to implement in church contexts where people were "not very relational," because "the common core of spiritual formation is the awareness of the inner life and the capacity to be present with another person—not necessarily God right from the start." He explained that many church cultures were shaped by busyness and task orientation: "Everyone is busy. It's all about getting things done." As a result, people were often reduced to tasks rather than treated as persons to be encountered. The prevailing mindset, he said, was, "Just tell me, and I'll do it," which he described as dehumanizing.

According to Fred, this efficiency-driven mentality was often transferred to one's relationship with God, who became "a giant list of commands that I need to obey and to keep him away." In such contexts, relational presence was largely absent. Fred argued that any meaningful application of spiritual formation in local churches requires "an awakening to the category of presence, the category of relationality," recognizing that not everything is about efficiency, productivity, or accomplishment.

Using prayer as an example, Fred explained that his earlier struggles with prayer stemmed from this performance orientation: "I always felt that I was failing at prayer because I wasn't getting anything done." Only later did he realize that "the point of prayer was not that you were supposed to walk away feeling I've accomplished something." Rather, prayer was meant to be a place of inner openness and transformation. He concluded that church ministries—whether evangelism, missions, or teaching—must be shaped not only by what is done but by how it is done. Without a relational way of being, ministry risks becoming problem-solving rather than presence.

Fred emphasized that genuine relational ministry emerges only when people have learned to experience themselves honestly before God and others. "That only comes," he said, "when the church has slowly been led down this path of experiencing themselves—so that they are able to really open their hearts and love another person."

Ethan likewise described significant difficulties when attempting to apply spiritual formation practices in Chinese church settings. He recalled leading a retreat where participants shared personal journeys and brokenness in small groups. Church leaders reacted strongly against this approach, asking, "Why were they crying?" and "Why did they share their own journey openly?" Ethan explained that such reactions were rooted in cultural taboos surrounding vulnerability: "For most Chinese, it is shameful to expose our weaknesses and struggles, especially for leaders. People want to save face."

Because of this deep shame dynamic, Ethan observed that although many Chinese believers acknowledged the need for spiritual formation in theory, they found it difficult to practice it in reality. He noted that fear of vulnerability often resulted in emotional distance and isolation within church communities. Having served as a pastor himself, Ethan understood these reactions and admitted that they were neither new nor surprising. Now teaching at a Chinese seminary, he tells his students, "Until the leaders themselves change, they cannot change the church." At the same time, he observed that some Charismatic churches were more open to spiritual formation practices than many Presbyterian or evangelical Chinese churches.

Overall, participants identified a lack of relational presence—shaped by performance orientation, efficiency, and shame surrounding vulnerability—as a significant barrier to applying spiritual formation in many Chinese church contexts.

Afraid of Changes

Another challenge participants faced in applying spiritual formation was resistance to change within some Chinese churches. Emma observed that many churches are "very conservative" and unlikely to "open themselves up to try it out." Even when younger members found spiritual formation helpful, she noted that hierarchical structures and generational divides created significant barriers. She explained that when she mentioned practices such as contemplation or meditative prayer, responses were often suspicious: "Oh, is that even Christian?"

Lucas similarly expressed discouragement after graduating from the program, observing that his church "doesn't care for spiritual formation." He clarified that it was not actively opposed as a controversial idea but was simply absent: "The concept of being in relationship with God beyond behavior management is not there."

In such contexts, participants found it difficult to apply spiritual formation when churches were reluctant to embrace unfamiliar spiritual practices or to move beyond established patterns of faith and ministry.

Lack of Introspection

Some participants identified another obstacle to applying spiritual formation in Chinese churches: many believers are reluctant, or not accustomed, to examining their inner lives. Emma expressed concern about translating the program's emphasis on self-reflection into this context. She explained,

> So much of what we were taught in the program was about looking at ourselves and our experiences, especially our family of origin, and how these shaped who we have become, including our insecurities, tendencies, wounds, desires, and life patterns.

> But I don't think Chinese people like to look at themselves. They really don't. They prefer to look at everything else rather than the self. They work really hard and tend to look constantly forward, whatever the next goal may be.

Emma observed that in a performance-oriented cultural context, inward examination and care for the soul are especially difficult. She explained,

> I feel like, as a culture, we are very driven and forward-thinking and do not really like to examine ourselves. I think this is also human nature. People do not like to look at themselves, especially at the painful and hurtful things they do not like. Many of the practices and teachings in the program involve looking at those painful areas and, in some ways, dwelling on them so that one can move through them. But that first step is very difficult, not only in Chinese churches but in many Christian contexts.

Without sustained inward reflection, participants suggested, it becomes difficult to apply spiritual formation practices or to foster deep and lasting spiritual growth.

Collectivist Culture

Several participants also noted that the collectivist nature of Chinese culture hindered the application of spiritual formation in their churches. Leo described this challenge by contrasting individual and collective orientations. He explained, "Spiritual formation is about relationship between me and God. It is about a one-on-one relationship with God. But in a collectivist culture, people do not think that way. They do not practice 'me with God'; they practice 'we with God.'" As a result, individual practices such as one-on-one spiritual direction often feel strange or suspicious. Leo observed, "If you do one-on-one direction, people wonder, 'What does that mean?' But if you do group direction, it is considered very good."

Leo further explained that collectivist norms complicate expectations around privacy and confidentiality. He noted that people are often hesitant to share deeply because confidentiality is understood differently. In his words, "In that culture, 'do not share with anybody' often means 'we only share this with people we know.' That is why people hesitate to open up, especially in counseling."

In a collectivist Chinese context where shame is emphasized and exposure of weakness is risky, participants reported that it is difficult to employ spiritual formation practices that require vulnerability for personal growth. Leo pointed out that Chinese and American understandings of confidentiality differ significantly. He explained,

> That is why when we do counseling, we tell people that when we say confidentiality, we really mean it. My wife and I are both counselors, but we never share cases with each other. If someone comes to her counseling and talks about their child, she will never mention it to me. That is how we practice confidentiality. But in China, this feels very strange. People say, "What? You do not even share with your family? You work together." That is one of the cultural challenges.

Amelia echoed this concern, noting that it is often unsafe to "share deep things" in Chinese culture because of gossip, even within Christian communities. She warned that she had seen spiritual authority abused, with some individuals using the role of spiritual director to manipulate or control others. Reflecting on the contrast between the program and local church contexts, she concluded, "The environment that the spiritual formation program provides is not the norm. I cannot expect all churches or people to be like that. The lack of safe, confidential spaces for open sharing in collectivist church culture makes it difficult to apply spiritual formation."

Together, these accounts suggest that collectivist norms, combined with shame dynamics and differing understandings of confidentiality, present significant barriers to the application of spiritual formation practices that depend on trust, privacy, and personal vulnerability.

Lack of Freedom to Try Out

Finally, some participants reported that they lacked freedom to experiment with spiritual formation practices in their Chinese churches. Emma implied that, although the program had been transformative for her personally, she had limited opportunity to apply what she learned in ministry. She explained,

> I'm still in full-time ministry right now. I find it difficult to apply what I have learned in the program in a very practical way in ministry. It was very useful for my personal growth and

> for personal relationships, but I don't really see it playing out at a professional level. As a female church leader in a Chinese church, it is very difficult to bring spiritual formation into the picture unless the leadership gives a lot of freedom to try things out.

Emma felt frustrated by hierarchical structures in which leadership approval was required before new practices could be introduced. As participants sought to apply spiritual formation in their churches, they often encountered resistance, not because the practices were rejected outright but because they were not granted the freedom to experiment or adapt them within existing church structures.

No Trusting Environment

Some participants also found that there was insufficient trust to support the practice of spiritual formation in Chinese church contexts. Amelia described feeling "very discouraged" after transitioning from the program's open and accepting environment to a Chinese Christian setting shaped by traditional norms. Having grown accustomed to a community where she felt "loved and accepted" and able to share from "the depth" of her heart, she struggled in a context marked by rigid expectations and gender roles. She reflected, "I was being open and loving, but very soon, I became discouraged. The church leaders did not appreciate that kind of openness. It was a different culture, and I had a really hard time there." She concluded that the spiritual formation program felt "somewhat like a vacation," noting that the "reality" of ministry in a Chinese context was far more restrictive.

Looking back, Amelia acknowledged that she had been overly optimistic when she first graduated. Although she was eager to apply what she had learned, she later realized that the program had not fully prepared her for working within a Chinese cultural environment shaped by shame dynamics, hierarchy, and limited trust. "The program prepared me to some extent," she said, "but it was very American and Western in its assumptions, and I was not really prepared for a Chinese setting. The first few years were very hard."

Similarly, Mason reflected that he lacked sufficient understanding of Chinese shame-based culture to apply spiritual formation effectively. He recognized that greater cultural awareness might have helped him understand both himself and others more deeply. As participants moved from a safe, trusting learning community into church contexts where vulnerability was risky, many experienced frustration and disillusionment in attempting to live out spiritual formation practices.

Psychology

Another factor that hindered the application of spiritual formation in many Chinese churches was their attitude toward psychology. Ethan noted, "It was very challenging to teach spiritual formation because many pastors do not believe in psychology or counseling." Some leaders regarded counseling as "a waste of time and energy," believing that the primary task of ministry was simply "to teach lessons from the pulpit."

Isabel encountered similar resistance when she attempted to introduce spiritual formation in her teaching at a Chinese seminary. She found that the school was "not there yet," explaining that it continued to prioritize head knowledge, preaching, and productivity over guiding students to experience God personally. Although the seminary affirmed the authority of Scripture, it tended to discount personal encounters with God. As Isabel observed, spiritual formation was viewed as optional: "They like spiritual formation, but it is OK not to have it."

Reflecting on the deeper reasons for this resistance, Isabel explained that cultural factors played a significant role:

> Chinese people don't talk about feelings. Period. That's why psychology has such a hard time surviving in the Chinese community. People usually only seek therapy when a marriage is about to collapse or when a child has already been expelled. There is little emphasis on prevention. Psychology is often dismissed as having no real value. Similarly, as long as people follow the principles and work harder, they believe everything will be fine. Struggle, darkness, and inner conflict are minimized. Cultural influence is the main factor behind this rejection, along with the general conservatism of many Chinese churches.

As a result, negative perceptions of psychology became a significant barrier to integrating spiritual formation principles.

Shameful to Seek Help

Emma likewise found it "super difficult" to apply spiritual formation in Chinese church contexts because seeking help itself was often viewed as shameful. She explained that unless people were fully convinced they needed help, they were unlikely to admit it. Therapy was commonly associated with personal failure, and those who sought counseling were often perceived as having something fundamentally wrong with them. Although Emma acknowledged that all people need help, she observed that shame prevented many from pursuing therapy or spiritual care.

Harry also encountered resistance rooted in suspicion and conservatism within his church context. While many people responded positively to spiritual formation, a few openly opposed it. After several conflicts that generated bitterness, Harry spoke with a pastor who later apologized for reacting strongly. Nevertheless, he noted, "We didn't talk about spiritual formation again."

Taken together, participants' experiences indicate that shame surrounding vulnerability and help-seeking, combined with skepticism toward psychology, significantly constrained the reception and practice of spiritual formation in many Chinese church settings.

Spiritual Formation Still Unknown

Some participants reported that spiritual formation remains largely unfamiliar to many Chinese churches and Christians. Harry noted that spiritual formation "is still largely unknown" in his church. Emma similarly observed, "I'm not sure that they know what that word means. I don't think they know what that word means at my church." Although she had seen "a number of churches creating spiritual formation directors and things like that," she did not believe that spiritual formation had become "anywhere near a central part yet."

Emma explained that spiritual formation was often offered as an optional ministry rather than a core dimension of Christian life. Churches tended to view it as a resource for those who were open to personal growth, rather than something essential for all believers. She noted that few churches believed that "everyone in our church should receive some version of this formation training or understanding or even direction." In her view, Chinese churches would likely be "the last in line" to embrace spiritual formation as a central practice.

Leo likewise asserted that most Chinese churches "have never heard about spiritual formation or know what that means." Because of this unfamiliarity, participants often found it necessary to adjust their language when introducing spiritual practices. Harry explained that he had to be "careful" with terminology, since phrases such as *spiritual formation* or *lectio divina* could create confusion or resistance. Instead, he reframed these practices using more familiar language, such as slowing down, reading Scripture attentively, and meditating on God's Word. As he noted, "We need to be careful with the language that we use."

Leo acknowledged that there was "a long way" between the program and its broader impact in China, yet he remained hopeful. While spiritual formation had not yet taken root widely, he believed that change remained possible. Overall, participants agreed that because spiritual formation is still unknown to many Chinese Christians and churches, sustained education and time are necessary for people to understand its meaning and significance.

Potentialities Through Contextualization

Despite these challenges, participants also identified significant potential for spiritual formation in Chinese contexts, particularly through careful contextualization. Several emphasized that meaningful application would require deep cultural change and transformative learning.

Ethan observed that Chinese Christians are often shaped by performance orientation, fear of failure, and shame surrounding weakness. He explained that many believers hide struggles and brokenness behind ministry success and productivity. Yet he argued that genuine spiritual formation requires openness to being loved by God in one's brokenness, rather than proving worth through achievement.

Bonnie similarly emphasized the liberating potential of spiritual formation. She described how the program helped her gain inner freedom from the heavy burdens of expectations, achievement, and responsibility toward family and community. For her, spiritual formation dismantled the assumption that identity is rooted in doing or performing and, instead, reoriented life toward being known and loved by God at the core of one's self.

Mia observed that many Chinese churches emphasize moral formation and diligent work, often equating faithfulness with effort. She argued that this emphasis on knowledge and behavior needed to be balanced with greater attention to experience, contemplation, and openness to God's presence.

Participants consistently stressed that spiritual formation cannot simply be transferred wholesale from a Western context into Chinese churches. Harry cautioned that practices learned in the program must be adapted thoughtfully rather than implemented directly. George likewise reflected on the need for cultural sensitivity, noting that while many aspects of the program resonate with Chinese moral seriousness, others may not translate easily due to cultural differences, including language, humor, and learning styles.

At the same time, George emphasized that the core dimensions of spiritual formation do translate well across cultures. Practices such as being present with others, attending to God's movements in daily life, and accompanying people through spiritual processes were, in his view, universally applicable and adaptable.

Lucas reflected that although the program itself felt like a "bubble," what endured beyond it was not a method but a deeper reliance on God. While the supportive environment of the program could not be replicated everywhere, he believed that learning to depend on God allowed him to carry what he had received into any context.

Several participants also raised the importance of developing culturally informed resources. Olivia noted that much of the psychology, literature, and spiritual disciplines used in the program reflected Western perspectives. While she found these resources valuable, she wondered how spiritual formation might look when interpreted through Asian and Asian American family systems, attachment patterns, and honor-and-shame dynamics. She expressed a desire for deeper exploration of how spiritual formation could support honoring parents, maintaining relationships, and establishing healthy boundaries within collectivist cultural frameworks.

Noah similarly believed that spiritual formation could flourish in Chinese churches if it were thoughtfully contextualized. He argued that while the entire program could not be transplanted intact, core biblical and spiritual formation principles could be adapted to meet the deep spiritual hunger he observed among Chinese Christians.

Bonnie reflected that returning to a culture shaped by performance and conformity was deeply challenging. Yet she believed that spiritual formation created space for hope and inner freedom, even if change occurred slowly and one person at a time. She concluded that the difficulty of contextualization ultimately deepened her dependence on God, reminding her that transformation cannot be manufactured but must be led by the Spirit.

Sophia observed that some Chinese churches and seminaries have already begun engaging in spiritual formation, including spiritual direction and various spiritual disciplines. She expressed excitement about these developments and believed that, over time, more Chinese Christians would recognize their need for spiritual formation and participate in this process of transformative learning.

Overall, while participants recognized that spiritual formation remains unfamiliar and difficult to implement in many Chinese church contexts, they also identified significant potential for growth through careful contextualization, cultural sensitivity, and sustained reliance on God's transforming work.

FINDINGS CONCLUSION

Across these three chapters, I presented data illuminating participants' perceptions of the impact of a Western Christian spiritual formation program on their lives. Chapter 4 examined participants' reflections on their upbringings and the cultural influences that shaped their spiritual and relational patterns. Chapter 5 explored both their prior meaning perspectives and the ways those perspectives were transformed in relation to self, God, and others. Chapter 6 focused on participants' recollections of how the program functioned as a catalyst for change by providing a safe and loving environment and by inviting them into sustained practice of spiritual disciplines.

In the next chapter, I interpret these findings and discuss their implications in light of the study's theoretical framework and research questions.

7

Discussion

THE CENTRAL INSIGHT EMERGING from this study is that a Western Christian spiritual formation program facilitated transformative learning among Chinese students by enabling them to critically reexamine their upbringing through a process that was both countercultural and challenging in light of their Confucian background. The program provided a safe and accepting environment in which participants could explore and disclose personal vulnerabilities—experiences that would typically be regarded as shameful within their native cultural context. In addition, the program offered a coherent integration of theological understanding of spirituality, the practice of spiritual disciplines, and experiential apprenticeship training.

As a result, participants experienced significant transformation in their meaning perspectives, particularly in their understanding of self, their relationship with God, and their relationships with others. Their autonomous and self-reliant orientation, shaped largely by Confucian values, gradually shifted toward a way of life marked by increased awareness of God's presence and a growing dependence on God.

To account for how this Western Christian spiritual formation program exerted such formative influence in the lives of these Chinese students, this study draws on transformative learning theory as the most fitting interpretive framework. While previous research has demonstrated the relevance of transformative learning theory within Western

Christian spiritual formation contexts,[1] the interaction between these two frameworks among Chinese students has remained largely unexplored. This study therefore contributes to the literature by examining how transformative learning unfolds when Western spiritual formation practices engage learners shaped by Confucian cultural assumptions.

Accordingly, this chapter begins with an overview of transformative learning theory, followed by a discussion of how the Western Christian spiritual formation program facilitated transformative learning among Chinese students, as evidenced in the findings presented in chapters 4, 5, and 6.

INTRODUCTION TO TRANSFORMATIVE LEARNING THEORY

Transformative learning theory, first introduced by Jack Mezirow,[2] has received considerable attention in the field of adult education. Since the rise of andragogy in the 1960s, theories of adult learning have developed rapidly in the United States, with transformative learning emerging as one of the most widely discussed and influential frameworks.[3]

Education enables changes in knowledge, skills, and attitudes,[4] and involves teaching and learning processes that can occur throughout one's lifetime. While pedagogy refers to the education of children, andragogy focuses on the distinctive characteristics of adult learning.[5] Unlike children, adult learners are typically voluntary, self-directed, and problem-solving-oriented, bringing extensive life experience and prior knowledge to the learning process.[6] In contemporary contexts shaped by globalization, technological advancement, and shifting demographics, learning now occurs across formal, non-formal, and informal settings.[7] This expansion has enabled increasing numbers of adults to return to education, participate in community-based learning, or pursue online studies.

1. Beard, "Connecting Spiritual Formation."
2. Mezirow, *Transformative Dimensions.*
3. Merriam and Bierema, *Adult Learning.*
4. Knowles et al., *Adult Learner.*
5. Knowles, *Modern Practice.*
6. Cranton, *Understanding and Promoting* (2nd ed.); Knowles, *Modern Practice.*
7. Merriam and Bierema, *Adult Learning.*

Through these learning experiences, adults not only acquire new knowledge but may also critically reassess their existing perspectives and alter how they understand themselves and the world.[8] As Cranton explains, "When people critically examine their habitual expectations, revise them, and act on the revised point of view, transformative learning occurs."[9] In this sense, adult learning is not merely about acquiring information but about personal transformation—what Cranton identified as a primary goal of adult education.[10] Consequently, adult educators have sought ways to facilitate this transformative process.[11]

Over the past four decades, transformative learning has become a central framework within adult education. Mezirow initially proposed the theory to explain adults' perspective transformation, drawing inspiration from what he described as his wife's "dramatically transformative experience" upon returning to college.[12] His subsequent research on women reentering higher education led to a broader theory of adult development that sought to explain how adults grow and change through critical reflection.[13]

In his seminal article "Perspective Transformation," published in *Adult Education Quarterly*, Mezirow articulated transformative learning as a process through which adults critically reassess their previously held assumptions and worldviews.[14] In 1985, he further linked perspective transformation with self-directed learning theory, integrating adult education with adult development.[15] Mezirow argued that education should be understood as a dialogical process in which adult learners reexamine and revise their meaning perspectives through interaction with others.[16]

At its core, transformative learning concerns the transformation of meaning perspectives, the frames of reference through which individuals interpret experience and understand themselves in relation to others and

8. Cranton, *Understanding and Promoting* (2nd ed.).

9. Cranton, *Understanding and Promoting* (2nd ed.), 19.

10. Cranton, *Understanding and Promoting* (2nd ed.).

11. Cranton, *Understanding and Promoting* (2nd ed.); Merriam and Bierema, *Adult Learning*; Mezirow, "Perspective Transformation."

12. Mezirow, "Perspective Transformation," xvii.

13. Mezirow, *Transformative Dimensions.*

14. Mezirow, "Perspective Transformation."

15. Mezirow, "Concept and Action."

16. Mezirow, "Critical Theory."

the world.[17] Mezirow's contribution shifted attention away from behavioral outcomes toward deeper changes in meaning-making. However, his early work was critiqued for privileging rationality and underemphasizing emotional, social, cultural, and power dimensions of adult learning.[18]

In response, Mezirow continued to refine his theory, acknowledging that emotions and affective experience play a crucial role in transformation alongside cognitive and rational processes.[19] He also recognized that transformative learning may occur either gradually or suddenly, but in both cases it results in new habits of mind—more inclusive, discriminating, and integrative ways of understanding experience.[20] His framework has provided educators with tools to help adult learners critically examine long-held assumptions and values, ultimately leading to significant changes in ways of living.[21]

As the theory evolved, other scholars, including Dirkx, Belenky, Tisdell, and Brookfield,[22] expanded and diversified transformative learning by examining its goals, processes, and contexts. Their contributions broadened the theory's applicability across educational, cultural, and spiritual settings.[23]

In her second edition of *Understanding and Promoting Transformative Learning*, Cranton approached transformative learning from the "learners' perspective,"[24] emphasizing "individual differences" in the transformative process.[25] She argued that individuation and authenticity are central to adult learning, noting that each learner brings a unique constellation of experiences.[26] Accordingly, transformative education must honor individuality and recognize diverse pathways of growth.[27] Cranton also offered practical guidance for educators, emphasizing

17. Mezirow, *Transformative Dimensions.*

18. Cranton, *Understanding and Promoting* (2nd ed.).

19. Mezirow, "Transformative Theory."

20. Mezirow, *Learning as Transformation.*

21. Cranton, *Understanding and Promoting* (2nd ed.); Mezirow, "Perspective Transformation."

22. Dirkx, "Transformative Learning Theory"; Dirkx, "Images, Transformative Learning"; Belenky et al., *Women's Ways of Knowing*; Tisdell, "Spirituality in Adult"; Tisdell, *Exploring Spirituality and Culture*; Brookfield, "Engaging Critical Reflection."

23. Gunnlaugson, "Metatheoretical Prospects."

24. Cranton, *Understanding and Promoting* (2nd ed.), xii.

25. Cranton, *Understanding and Promoting* (2nd ed.), vii.

26. Cranton, *Understanding and Promoting* (2nd ed.).

27. Cranton, *Understanding and Promoting* (2nd ed.).

reflective dialogue, experiential learning, and mutual trust, while reminding educators that they themselves are co-learners in the process.[28]

John Dirkx further expanded transformative theory by interpreting transformation through four lenses: consciousness-raising, critical reflection, psychological development, and individuation.[29] Drawing on Freire, Mezirow, Daloz, and Boyd, Dirkx proposed a holistic understanding of transformation that includes emotional and spiritual dimensions.[30] He emphasized the role of emotions,[31] what he termed "messengers of the soul,"[32] as guides toward deeper self-awareness.[33] When learners recognize, name, and engage their emotions, they move toward a "deeper, more conscious connection" with their inner life.[34] Dirkx also highlighted imagination and symbolic expression,[35] through art, image, poetry, and story,[36] as catalysts for transformation, since such "nonrational media" invite learners to encounter unconscious meanings and nurture the soul.[37]

Building on these insights, Merriam and Bierema affirmed the importance of both "critical reflection" and "noncognitive means," including emotional, intuitive, and embodied experiences, in facilitating transformation.[38] They further emphasized the role of "discourse and social interaction" in constructing new meaning within community.[39]

Scholars such as Edward Taylor and Patricia Cranton advanced the field through critique and synthesis.[40] Taylor, influenced by Paulo Freire, argued for a social-emancipatory perspective on transformative learning and emphasized the need for further research on the role of culture.[41]

28. Cranton, *Understanding and Promoting* (2nd ed.).
29. Dirkx, "Transformative Learning Theory."
30. Dirkx, "Transformative Learning Theory."
31. Dirkx, "Nurturing Soul Work."
32. Dirkx, "Power of Feelings," 66.
33. Dirkx, "Images, Transformative Learning."
34. Dirkx, "Power of Feelings," 69.
35. Dirkx, "Power of Feelings."
36. Dirkx, "Images, Transformative Learning."
37. Merriam and Bierema, *Adult Learning*, 95.
38. Merriam and Bierema, *Adult Learning*, 95.
39. Merriam and Bierema, *Adult Learning*, 95.
40. Cranton and Taylor, "Transformative Learning Theory"; Taylor, "Transformative Learning Theory."
41. Taylor, "Transformative Learning Theory."

Merriam and Bierema similarly noted that transformative learning can foster both individual and social change.[42] Mezirow and Cranton likewise acknowledged the need for greater attention to cultural context,[43] including intersections with gender, social status, and spirituality.[44]

By the late 1990s and early 2000s, scholars increasingly called for the recovery of spirituality and holism in education.[45] O'Sullivan argued that modern education had lost connection with the spiritual dimension of human life,[46] while Tisdell advocated a "spirituality-grounded, culturally relevant" pedagogy.[47] In *Exploring Spirituality and Culture in Adult and Higher Education*, Tisdell emphasized that genuine transformation must engage both spiritual depth and cultural particularity within multicultural learning environments.[48]

More recently, the spiritual dimension of transformative learning has gained broader recognition. English and Tisdell observed the growth of religious adult education programs that integrate spirituality and learning, such as lay ministry programs delivered in partial residential formats.[49] However, they noted a lack of systematic research evaluating their effectiveness and called for further study of cultural imagination and identity in higher education.[50] They emphasized that attentiveness to culture can stimulate spirituality and that learning communities should nurture the soul while pursuing justice together.[51]

In an effort to synthesize these diverse perspectives, Cranton and Roy proposed a holistic model integrating emotional, cognitive, spiritual, and social dimensions.[52] Critics, however, have questioned the feasibility

42. Merriam and Bierema, *Adult Learning*.

43. Mezirow, *Learning as Transformation*; Cranton, *Understanding and Promoting* (2nd ed.).

44. Cranton, *Understanding and Promoting* (2nd ed.); Merriam, *Non-Western Perspectives*; Mezirow, *Learning as Transformation*; Taylor, "Transformative Learning Theory.

45. Cranton, *Understanding and Promoting* (2nd ed.); Merriam, *Non-Western Perspectives*; Mezirow, *Learning as Transformation*; Taylor, "Transformative Learning Theory."

46. O'Sullivan, "Deep Transformation."

47. Tisdell, *Exploring Spirituality and Culture*, 184.

48. Tisdell, *Exploring Spirituality and Culture*.

49. English and Tisdell, "Spirituality and Adult Education."

50. English and Tisdell, "Spirituality and Adult Education."

51. English and Tisdell, "Spirituality and Adult Education."

52. Cranton and Roy, "When the Bottom Falls."

of unifying such divergent approaches[53] and raised concerns about the verifiability of transformation, noting that it can often be confirmed only by learners themselves.[54] Others have pointed out the difficulty of fostering transformative learning in practice, as few educators are trained to accompany learners through the emotional struggle and disorientation transformation often entails.[55] Despite these challenges, transformative learning theory continues to evolve, offering rich insight into adult growth in awareness, freedom, and relational capacity.[56]

In recent years, scholars have begun to explore transformative learning within Chinese cultural contexts.[57] Forrester et al. found that Chinese secondary-school teachers participating in learner-centered e-learning experienced shifts in beliefs, values, and perspectives.[58] However, participants also encountered barriers related to cultural tensions between Western pedagogical assumptions and Confucian norms, particularly around reflective questioning.[59] These findings suggest that transformative learning among Chinese learners can be both powerful and culturally dissonant.

Similarly, Stephen Gill's ethnographic study of Chinese postgraduate students in the United Kingdom demonstrated that intercultural exposure facilitated transformative learning through critical reflection and engagement with difference.[60] Gill found that participants developed new ways of thinking, greater openness to otherness, and reconstructed self-identity.[61] His study affirms that transformative learning occurs when Chinese learners encounter experiences that challenge and invite reconsideration of their habitual meaning perspectives.[62]

53. Gunnlaugson, "Metatheoretical Prospects."

54. Newman, "Calling Transformative Learning."

55. Merriam and Bierema, *Adult Learning.*

56. Cranton, *Understanding and Promoting* (2nd ed.).

57. Chen, "Empowering Identity Reconstruction"; Forrester et al., "Transforming Chinese Teachers' Thinking."

58. Forrester et al., "Transforming Chinese Teachers' Thinking."

59. Forrester et al., "Transforming Chinese Teachers' Thinking."

60. Gill, "Overseas Students' Intercultural Adaptation."

61. Gill, "Overseas Students' Intercultural Adaptation."

62. Gill, "Overseas Students' Intercultural Adaptation."

LINKING TRANSFORMATIVE LEARNING WITH CHRISTIAN SPIRITUAL FORMATION

Christian spiritual formation and transformative learning theory have increasingly converged within Western academic and ecclesial contexts.[63] In his study of the relationship between these two fields, Beard concluded that transformative learning theory significantly shapes participants' experiences of spiritual formation and that Mezirow's ten phases of perspective transformation can be identified within their spiritual narratives.[64] He observed that "the disorienting dilemma" central to transformative learning often functions as a catalyst for Christian spiritual growth.[65] When critical reflection and perspective transformation are situated within the context of spiritual formation, believers experience spiritual maturation and grow in Christlike character and discernment.[66]

Beard further argued that transformative learning and Christian spiritual formation intersect in three key domains: identity, process, and experience.[67] Both frameworks share a common aim of identity transformation, and the process of transformative learning closely aligns with the goals of spiritual formation. He described spiritual formation as emancipatory, in that it "liberates people from the hegemony of sin," which keeps them from "experiencing the full life that God intended for his people."[68]

Both approaches also emphasize the experiential and communal nature of transformation.[69] Change occurs not only through cognitive insight but through embodied participation, affective engagement, and relational interaction. Community plays a central role in both disciplines, as transformation deepens through shared stories, mutual reflection, and lived experience.[70] Practices such as mentoring and spiritual direction cultivate environments in which learners can safely explore their experiences and attend to God's presence and activity.[71] In such settings,

63. Beard, "Connecting Spiritual Formation."

64. Beard, "Missional Discipleship."

65. Beard, "Connecting Spiritual Formation," 257.

66. Beard, "Connecting Spiritual Formation."

67. Beard, "Connecting Spiritual Formation."

68. Beard, "Connecting Spiritual Formation," 260.

69. Beard, "Connecting Spiritual Formation."

70. Averbeck, "Spirit, Community, and Mission"; Cranton, *Understanding and Promoting* (2nd ed.)

71. Guenther and Jones, *Holy Listening.*

transformative educators and spiritual companions create spaces that are "safe, open, supportive, and . . . 'sacred,'" where participants listen to one another without judgment and engage in reflection and dialogue that draw upon their life experiences.[72] These communal practices foster transformation that is intellectual, emotional, spiritual, and relational.[73]

TRANSFORMATIVE LEARNING PHASES

In transformative learning theory, transformation begins when individuals critically examine their existing values and assumptions.[74] When confronted with alternative ways of thinking, learners may reassess and revise long-held beliefs and perspectives.[75] Through this process, transformative learning awakens adults to reflect critically on their way of life, leading to intentional and meaningful change. Mezirow proposed that transformation typically unfolds through ten interrelated phases, which may vary in sequence and intensity depending on the learner's experience:[76]

1. A disorienting dilemma
2. Self-examination with feelings of fear, anger, guilt, or shame
3. A critical assessment of assumptions
4. Recognition that one's discontent and the process of transformation are shared
5. Exploration of options form new roles, relationships, and actions
6. Planning a course of action
7. Acquiring knowledge and skills for implementing one's plans
8. Provisional trying of new roles
9. Building competence and self-confidence in new roles and relationships
10. A reintegration into one's life on the basis of conditions dictated by one's new perspective

72. Merriam and Bierema, *Adult Learning*, 96.
73. Merriam and Bierema, *Adult Learning*, 96.
74. Cranton, *Understanding and Promoting* (2nd ed.).
75. Cranton, *Understanding and Promoting* (2nd ed.).
76. Mezirow, *Learning as Transformation*, 22.

While some researchers employ all ten phases in their analyses, others focus on those most relevant to a particular context.[77] Charaniya emphasized that transformative learning is "not simply a linear progression of a ten-step process" but is instead recursive and spiralic, involving ongoing cycles of reflection and action.[78]

Not every learner experiences all ten phases, nor do the phases necessarily occur in sequence. Within a Christian spiritual formation context, educators and learners cooperate with the Holy Spirit, who initiates and completes the work of transformation. Consequently, transformative learning requires "humility and comfort with personal disclosure," as both educators and learners participate together in the process of change.[79]

Morrell and O'Connor described transformative learning as "a deep, structural shift in the basic premise of thought, feelings, and action," a change in consciousness that "dramatically and permanently alters our way of being in the world."[80] Cranton similarly affirmed that transformative learning results in "a changed self-perception."[81] While transformation occurs at the personal level, Merriam and Bierema reminded educators that its ultimate purpose is also to "effect change in the larger socio-political context."[82]

EXAMINING FINDINGS THROUGH TRANSFORMATIVE LEARNING THEORY

This section analyzes the study data to illustrate how participants experienced the phases of transformative learning and how the spiritual formation program facilitated these processes among Chinese students. Table 1 presents Mezirow's ten phases of transformative learning alongside the major themes that emerged from the data.

Among Mezirow's ten phases, participants most vividly described experiences corresponding to a disorienting dilemma, self-examination, recognition that transformation is shared, exploration of new roles and relationships, acquiring knowledge and skills, provisional trying of new

77. Glisczinski, "Transformative Higher Education."

78. Charaniya, "Cultural-Spiritual Perspective," 238.

79. Ettling, "Educator as Change Agent," 546.

80. Morrell and O'Connor, "Introduction," xvii.

81. Cranton, *Understanding and Promoting* (2nd ed.), 8.

82. Merriam and Bierema, *Adult Learning*, 94.

roles, building competence and self-confidence, and reintegration with new perspectives.[83] Overall, nine of the ten phases were clearly evident in participants' narratives.

Several phases appeared to occur concurrently rather than sequentially, while others were intentionally embedded within the design and structure of the spiritual formation program. One phase—phase 6 (planning a course of action)—was not explicitly articulated by participants. This absence does not suggest that the phase was entirely missing; rather, it appears to have been less self-directed in this context. Because the program followed a highly structured curriculum, planning may have been internalized, implicit, or integrated into adjacent phases, particularly the provisional trying of new roles.

The following sections examine each of the relevant phases in turn, demonstrating how the Western Christian spiritual formation program facilitated transformative learning among Chinese students.

Table 1. Phases Participants Experienced in Transformative Learning

Mezirow's Phase	Themes in the Study Data
1. A disorienting dilemma	Limitations in helping others; internal struggles; countercultural challenges
2. Self-examination with feelings of fear, anger, guilt, or shame	Hierarchical social culture; parenting; church culture
3. A critical assessment of assumptions	Assumptions about self; assumptions about God; assumptions about relationships
4. Recognition that transformation is shared	Humble and honest faculty; nonjudgmental cohort groups; loving spiritual directors
5. Exploration of options for new roles, relationships, and actions	New relationship with self; new relationship with God; new relationships with others
6. Planning a course of action	Not explicitly demonstrated by participants
7. Acquiring knowledge and skills for implementing one's plans	The "double knowledge"; theorization of spirituality; hands-on training in spiritual disciplines

83. Mezirow, *Learning as Transformation.*

Mezirow's Phase	Themes in the Study Data
8. Provisional trying of new roles	Challenging; Contextualization
9. Building competence and self-confidence in new roles and relationships	Phases 8, 9, and 10 were blended in participants' experiences.
10. Reintegration based on a new perspective	

Disorienting Dilemmas

Transformative learning typically begins with a disorienting dilemma, an experience that disrupts previously taken-for-granted meaning perspectives and compels individuals to question their assumptions.[84] In this study, participants encountered several forms of disorientation that initiated their transformative learning processes. Although the specific circumstances varied, most described reaching a point at which they recognized the limits of their ability to help others, confronted unresolved internal struggles in their spiritual lives, and encountered countercultural challenges within the spiritual formation program. Each of these dilemmas functioned as a catalytic moment that opened participants to transformation.

Limitations in Helping Others

Regardless of their initial motivations for entering the program, several participants arrived already immersed in a disorienting dilemma. Many had become acutely aware of the limits of their capacity to foster spiritual growth in others. While deeply attentive to the pain and struggles within their congregations, they felt ill-equipped to respond beyond offering biblical citations or surface-level encouragement. Some acknowledged that they had reached the end of their own resources and felt spiritually depleted themselves.

Most participants entered the program with altruistic intentions, hoping to become more sanctified individuals and more effective helpers. They aspired to grow personally in order to guide others toward maturity in Christ. Yet the recognition of their inadequacy in ministry became

84. Mezirow, *Transformative Dimensions.*

their first disorienting dilemma, prompting them to question long-held assumptions about spirituality, leadership, and spiritual formation. This realization destabilized their confidence in familiar approaches to ministry and laid the foundation for the deeper work of transformation that followed.

Internal Spiritual Struggles

Participants also spoke candidly about their personal struggles in their relationship with God. Some described burnout resulting from relentless ministry demands, while others wrestled with confusion over God's apparent silence amid ongoing battles with sin. Several expressed disillusionment with church politics or leadership conflict, and others felt stagnant in their spiritual growth, maintaining an outward appearance of strength in order to preserve "face." Beneath these experiences lay a profound longing to live with authenticity before God and others.

In both their narratives and emotional expressions, many participants echoed what John of the Cross described as the "dark night of the soul"[85] or what Demarest characterized as a "painful disorientation"[86] in the spiritual journey. Long-standing questions about faith, often left unaddressed within their home churches, resurfaced in this new learning environment. Participants expressed a desire for intimacy with God and a deeper understanding of prayer, seeking not merely theological knowledge but an experiential relationship with the Divine.

For these Chinese students, entry into the spiritual formation program was motivated by a desire to encounter God in a more integrated way—to move beyond intellectual mastery toward a spirituality that engaged the whole person. The program's integrated design—combining classroom instruction, reflective practice, and apprenticeship in spiritual disciplines—created a context in which these internal struggles became gateways to transformation. At the same time, this process introduced a new and complex form of disorientation: a countercultural tension arising from the interaction between their Confucian upbringing and the introspective ethos of Western spiritual formation.

85. Kavanaugh, *John of the Cross*, 162.

86. Demarest, *Seasons of the Soul*, 39.

Countercultural Challenges

In addition to ministerial and personal dilemmas, participants encountered significant countercultural challenges throughout the program. Entering a Western spiritual formation context exposed them to perspectives and practices that diverged sharply from their Chinese cultural assumptions. Many described the program's emphasis on deconstruction and intensive self-examination—particularly during retreats and guided reflective exercises—as painful, unsettling, and emotionally demanding.

Although such challenges are not unique to Chinese believers (see 2 Cor 4:7–12; 2 Cor 12:1–10; Jas 1:2–4; 1 Pet 1:6–7), cultural dissonance intensified the experience. The program invited participants to journey inward—an experience described as "difficult and intensely self-searching with fewer and fewer distractive props to lean on"[87]—yet this inward turn was unfamiliar for students shaped by a collectivist tradition that values harmony, restraint, and group-oriented identity.

Western spiritual formation emphasized self-awareness, emotional honesty, and reflection on formative influences such as family, church, and community life. For the Chinese participants, this process proved both disorienting and transformative. It required confronting deeply embedded cultural values, particularly Confucian ideals of filial piety, hierarchy, and moral performance, that had profoundly shaped their sense of self. Table 2 summarizes several of the major cultural tensions between Western spiritual formation practices and participants' Confucian upbringing.

For these students, the process was painful yet life-changing. As many testified, they had been taught from childhood that what mattered most was outward behavior and moral performance. In contrast, the spiritual formation program revealed that what mattered most was the transformation of the inner life—a renewed heart attuned to God's presence and grace.

87. Finch, *Intensive Therapy*, 3.

Table 2. Cultural Clashes Between Western Spiritual Formation and Chinese Confucian Upbringing

Category	Western Spiritual Formation Program	Chinese Cultural Upbringing
Parents	Examine upbringing and parental influence	Parents are not questioned; shortcomings are not discussed
Emotions	Recognize, feel, and express emotions	Emotions are controlled and rarely verbalized
Vulnerabilities	Openly acknowledge weakness	Vulnerability is shameful and concealed
Inner darkness	Bring hidden struggles into the light	Darkness is masked through performance
Relationship with parents	Differentiate from parents and depend on God	Obedience and lifelong dependence on parents
Self-identity	Discover identity and freedom in Christ	Identity shaped by parental expectations
Relationship with God	Awareness of the Spirit's work grounded in Scripture	Emphasis on Scripture, with limited pneumatology
Outcome	Increasing dependence on God	Dependence on parents, others, and self

The spiritual formation program invited students to examine their inner lives—a practice that stood in stark contrast to their cultural socialization. From childhood, many had been taught that outward behavior and moral performance were the primary indicators of virtue and maturity. In contrast, the program emphasized interior transformation—the renewal of the heart, character, and spiritual awareness.

This tension between external performance and internal authenticity constituted a major disorienting dilemma. Although participants rarely employed the language of "disorienting" or "dilemma," the data clearly indicate that the shift from an outward to an inward focus represented a profound transformation of their meaning perspectives. The following subsections explore how this countercultural process unfolded through three interrelated challenges: hierarchy, shame, and emotion.

Hierarchy

As part of the spiritual formation program, students were encouraged to reflect on past experiences, including painful or formative relationships with caregivers—most often their parents. This practice proved especially difficult for Chinese students raised within a Confucian hierarchical culture that prizes filial piety and unquestioning respect for elders. Many described feeling "forced" to revisit their upbringing, an act that directly challenged deeply ingrained values, such as "do not speak ill of your parents" and "parents are always right."

Because obedience to parental authority had long been internalized as a moral virtue, the invitation to critically examine family relationships initially felt dishonorable and culturally inappropriate. For some participants, revisiting childhood experiences meant confronting long-suppressed hurts and disappointments. Yet as they engaged in reflection within a safe and accepting learning environment, many came to recognize how these cultural norms had shaped their faith, relational patterns, and sense of self. Although painful, this process opened a pathway toward reinterpretation, healing, and spiritual growth.

Shame

The cultural emphasis on shame further complicated participants' engagement with spiritual formation. In many Chinese contexts, vulnerability is equated with weakness, and the public disclosure of personal struggles is considered deeply dishonorable. Participants reported that they were trained from childhood to conceal weaknesses and present a façade of strength and competence. By contrast, the spiritual formation program required honest self-revelation, emotional transparency, and exploration of identity, practices that brought participants face-to-face with inner struggles they had long hidden.

As one participant described, the process felt like "being peeled like an onion." Layers of self-protection were stripped away, revealing the inner darkness of the heart. Although this exposure was painful, it created space for authenticity, humility, and grace. The shift from concealing to confessing—from shame to acceptance—marked a crucial moment in participants' transformation. For these students, grace began to redefine shame not as a sign of failure but as an invitation to healing and deeper connection with God and others.

EMOTIONS

Another significant cultural clash concerned the expression and experience of emotion. In traditional Confucian thought, social harmony is valued, and emotional restraint is regarded as a moral ideal. Open confrontation is discouraged, and strong negative emotions, such as anger, grief, or frustration, are often viewed as shameful.[88] Historically, an emphasis on material survival and hard work, particularly among immigrant and post-war generations, further shaped family life, leading many parents to prioritize economic stability over emotional or psychological care.[89]

Several participants recalled that their parents, preoccupied with providing materially, neglected their emotional development. Feelings were rarely discussed at home, and children learned to suppress or ignore their inner experiences. As a result, many students entered the program feeling unseen, unknown, and emotionally unsupported. In spiritual direction and therapeutic settings, participants described feeling overwhelmed when asked to shift from a thinking-oriented posture to emotional awareness. Although exhausting, this process proved illuminating, as it required them to name emotions they had long disregarded.

Participants also reflected that their upbringing emphasized external behavior, comparison with others, and unquestioning obedience to authority, while emotions were implicitly or explicitly dismissed as unimportant. Although some childhood memories appeared harmonious on the surface, as participants revisited these experiences and allowed themselves to feel the associated emotions, their interpretations began to change. Many recognized that beneath the appearance of harmony, negative emotions had been consistently suppressed and subordinated to parental expectations. Emotional repression, they realized, had been internalized as obedience.

Several participants further observed that their parents' emotional neglect stemmed in part from the parents' own unresolved inner struggles. As they reflected on family dynamics, participants described patterns of anxiety, fear, and emotional instability—particularly among their mothers—that resembled what Janov termed "a disease of feeling."[90] Janov argued that neurosis originates in "the suppression of feeling and

88. Bond, "Emotions and Their Expression"; Chen, "Socio-Emotional Development"; Shin and Silzer, *Tapestry of Grace.*

89. Chen, "Socio-Emotional Development."

90. Janov, *Primal Scream*, 20.

its transmutation into a wide range of neurotic behavior."[91] Participants came to recognize similar patterns in themselves, manifesting as depression, anxiety, or burnout.

Participants also noted that emotional suppression shaped their relationship with God. Thompson observed that a person's "relationship with God is a direct reflection of the depth" of their relational experiences, particularly the experience of being known.[92] He argued that when "emotional life was either unattended to or overwhelmed by caregivers who were themselves burdened with the weight of their own emotional conflicts—their own lack of 'being known,'" intimacy with God was likewise constrained.[93]

As a Christian psychiatrist and neurologist, Thompson observed that "this form of generational sin inserts itself perniciously throughout the very fibers of" one's being.[94] He further argued that disdain toward emotion profoundly affects a believer's relationship with God. As he explained, "Emotion is the energy around which the brain organizes itself. Without emotion, life would come to a standstill. It is the means by which we experience and connect with God, others, and ourselves in the most basic way possible."[95] Because emotions communicate the meanings of the soul,[96] Thompson maintained that God often addresses his people through "the brain's medium of emotion,"[97] warning that to ignore emotion is, in effect, to "ignore the voice of God."[98]

Thompson further emphasized that hiding from emotions is equivalent to hiding from the truth, since emotion is an "authentic reflection of our subjective experience, one that is best served by attending to it."[99] He concluded that "if we do not attend to our emotional states, the Holy Spirit is restricted from engaging in this aspect of his work in our lives."[100] Moreover, when believers fail to engage with core emotions such as "joy, anger, and shame," their relationship with God becomes constrained, as

91. Janov, *Primal Scream*, 20.

92. Thompson, *Anatomy of the Soul*, 24.

93. Thompson, *Anatomy of the Soul*, 24.

94. Thompson, *Anatomy of the Soul*, 24.

95. Thompson, *Anatomy of the Soul*, 90.

96. Dirkx, "Power of Feelings."

97. Thompson, *Anatomy of the Soul*, 96.

98. Thompson, *Anatomy of the Soul*, 91.

99. Thompson, *Anatomy of the Soul*, 164.

100. Thompson, *Anatomy of the Soul*, 177.

these emotions play a crucial role in shaping intimacy with God and with others.[101]

Several participants further reflected on their parents' marriages, noting a lack of emotional connection and, in some cases, abuse or emotional distance. In families marked by authoritarian or absent fathers, mothers often exhibited symptoms of neurosis and became emotionally enmeshed with their children. These dynamics produced blurred emotional boundaries and reversed roles, forming patterns that profoundly shaped children's emotional and spiritual development. Finch observed that in such families,

> Some mothers will extend themselves to the ultimate limit of their powers to keep the umbilical cord intact. It serves their neurotic needs to have a son to lean on. Parenthetically, this leaning on a son or daughter too frequently intercepts Mothers' relation with her husband and reduces him to the role of servant, breadwinner and need-supplier for the children, while Mother's role becomes more children-focused. But these are not expressions of love from Mother, but expressions of her own neurotic needs. As a matter of fact, I would say that this interception of the husband-wife bond is the reason for 90 percent of family problems, of the father's decreasing interest in the family, and a highly significant reason for the large number of divorces. Husband-son, displaced and disaffected by surrogate mother, goes in search of another mother figure who will promise "to be good on his terms."[102]

In this way, the vicious cycle of unhealthy family relationships is perpetuated from one generation to the next.

Because emotional and psychological issues often remain unaddressed in many Chinese families, unhealthy parenting patterns persist. As several participants noted, Chinese traditions are frequently followed uncritically from one generation to the next, reinforcing recurring cycles of repression and dependency. Finch further explained this dynamic:

> When one's childhood experiences echo the Scriptural lament that "in sin did my mother conceive me" (Ps. 51:5), or "the [parents] have eaten sour grapes and the children's teeth are set on edge" (Ezek. 18:2), or again "the sins of the fathers are visited upon the children to the third and fourth generation"

101. Thompson, *Anatomy of the Soul*, 105.

102. Finch, *Intensive Therapy*, 61–62.

> (Num. 14:8), we are exposed to a deep, profound rift in human nature—a fault indeed as serious and dangerous as any fault in the earth's crust. And no super-imposition will remedy it. It is a radical flaw.[103]

This generational fracture was evident in many participants' reflections. They recognized that when parents raise their children according to inherited, unexamined patterns, emotional disconnection from God and others is inadvertently perpetuated. Spiritual formation, therefore, became a context in which participants could begin to name, grieve, and transform these generational patterns through the redemptive work of grace.

Reexamination of Confucian Upbringing

While Mezirow identified self-examination as the second phase of the transformative process,[104] this study considers it in conjunction with the critical assessment of assumptions (phase 3), since the two were closely intertwined in participants' experiences. The spiritual formation program facilitated Chinese students' reexamination of their upbringing in ways that deeply challenged assumptions formed in childhood and carried into adulthood. Participants described this process as unexpected, yet illuminating; painful, yet ultimately healing. The following discussion illustrates how participants critically reassessed their cultural and familial assumptions.

All participants in this study acknowledged their Chinese cultural heritage, regardless of their country of origin. As they reflected on their upbringing, most recognized the pervasive influence of Confucianism in their family, educational, and church contexts. Bond observed that "the historical record of the Middle Kingdom imparts a sense of continuity and identity to the myriad Chinese people scattered across the political and geographical spectrum of the globe."[105] Consequently, he noted, "people of this diaspora typically consider and present themselves as 'Chinese.'"[106] In a similar way, participants in this study recognized that they had been shaped by Chinese traditions characterized by hierarchy, shame, and performance orientation, regardless of where their families

103. Finch, *Intensive Therapy*, 28.

104. Mezirow, *Transformative Dimensions*.

105. Bond, *Psychology of the Chinese People*, 248.

106. Bond, *Psychology of the Chinese People*, 248.

had lived. Several observed that these traditions had been preserved and transmitted with little critical examination.

The following sections explore how participants reexamined their upbringing, particularly in relation to family and church culture.

Hierarchical Culture

Many participants indicated that from early childhood, they had been trained to obey and respect their parents and elders. Within Confucian society, filial piety is regarded as essential for maintaining "both family harmony and sociopolitical stability."[107] However, as participants revisited this virtue through reflective practices in the program, many came to recognize that obedience had often required the suppression of personal desires, questions, and opinions. Several acknowledged that their capacity for independent thought and decision-making had remained underdeveloped, as parenting practices were largely centered on parental will, expectations, and authority.

Participants further noted that these hierarchical expectations—reinforced by norms of emotional restraint—not only created internal pressure but also fostered a persistent fear of failure and inadequacy. This growing awareness prompted them to reconsider how deeply Confucian hierarchical values had shaped their identities, often at the expense of personal authenticity, emotional awareness, and spiritual freedom.

Parenting

Participants were also guided to reexamine their parents' approaches to parenting. Many perceived their fathers as distant or emotionally absent, while their mothers were often described as controlling or overly enmeshed. Several participants recognized that these patterns were closely tied to gender inequality embedded within Confucian patriarchy. Some female participants, upon reflection, acknowledged that they had been treated as less valuable than boys—both at home and within the church—though they had not recognized this bias earlier in life.

Nearly all participants described being raised in shame-based family systems in which vulnerability, such as sickness, emotional distress, or weakness, was regarded as shameful. In hierarchical households shaped

107. *Encyclopaedia Britannica*, "Xiao | Confucianism."

by shame, communication between parents and children tend to be one-directional and superficial with encouragement and affirmation notably absent. Many recalled being ordered, criticized, compared with others, and belittled by their parents—experiences that left lasting marks on their self-perception and spiritual lives.

Through the program's teachings and reflective practices, most participants eventually became aware of the pervasive influence of shame in their upbringing. One participant, however, did not fully recognize the depth of shame's impact until after graduation, describing the realization as an epiphany that reframed many of his struggles. Reflecting on this experience, he suggested that the program could benefit from more explicit teaching on the cultural dimensions of self-knowledge to help Chinese students more readily identify the intersection of culture and spirituality.

Shame, as Thompson noted, lies at the core of many relational ruptures.[108] He described shame as "the painfully acute awareness that something is wrong with me," a deeply embodied experience that shapes perception, behavior, and identity."[109] When left unaddressed, the "residue of shame that repeatedly coats the child's mind influences virtually all of his or her responses to life's circumstances."[110] Moreover, shame is "self-reinforcing"; as Thompson observed, people "tend to feel shame in response to feeling shame"[111] and often use "shame to cope with their shame."[112]

This cyclical pattern produces "a keen sense of painful isolation,"[113] not only from others but also within the self of the one "in the grip of shame."[114] Ironically, individuals trapped in shame may shame and judge others in arrogance, since "pride and shame are in fact two sides of the same coin."[115] Although collectivist Chinese culture idealizes social harmony, its accompanying emphasis on shame often makes genuine community difficult to achieve, for the essence of shame is fearful isolation rather than connection.[116]

108. Thompson, *Anatomy of the Soul*.
109. Thompson, *Anatomy of the Soul*, 192.
110. Thompson, *Anatomy of the Soul*, 194.
111. Thompson, *Anatomy of the Soul*, 192.
112. Thompson, *Anatomy of the Soul*, 225.
113. Thompson, *Anatomy of the Soul*, 195.
114. Thompson, *Anatomy of the Soul*, 195.
115. Thompson, *Anatomy of the Soul*, 241.
116. Thompson, *Anatomy of the Soul*.

Several participants recalled that their mothers lived with persistent anxiety and exercised control through fear. Jamieson argued that shame is invariably entangled with fear and anxiety, forming a triad that sustains emotional rigidity.[117] Participants' descriptions echoed this dynamic. Many noted that their mothers held exceptionally high expectations and continually reinformed performance-oriented values, a pattern popularly illustrated in Amy Chua's *Battle Hymn of the Tiger Mother*.[118] Although some parents modified these patterns after becoming Christians, others continued to reflect Confucian emphases on shame, self-improvement, performance, and reverence for authority.[119]

Participants further observed that shame was frequently intensified through fear—particularly the fear of disgracing the family. Fung found that shame is often employed as a tool for moral instruction in Chinese parenting, a practice consistent with the socialization of filial values.[120] Similarly, Lieber, Fung, and Leung observed that "training" in Chinese parenting entails both moral responsibility and "the development of pro-social behavioral characteristics," an effort that is "accompanied by 'shame' practices intended to heighten children's sensitivity to the emotional and behavioral cues in Chinese social contexts."[121]

Within such shame-based systems, participants reported limited emotional closeness between parents and children. Topics requiring vulnerability or intimacy—such as sexuality or emotional pain—were often taboo. Emotional problems were rarely acknowledged due to ignorance, neglect, or shame, a pattern reinforced by the stigma surrounding mental illness and emotional distress. As Koenig, McCullough, and Larson noted, such stigma discourages individuals from seeking professional or pastoral help, a tendency amplified in face-conscious cultures.[122]

Although shame is a universal human emotion,[123] Nichols argued that "populations in the Confucian diaspora have a unique shame profile compared to Western and non-Western populations."[124] He noted that "studies document correlations between shame and the basic emotion of

117. Jamieson, *Face of Forgiveness.*
118. Chua, *Battle Hymn.*
119. Ng et al., "Immigrant Chinese Mothers' Socialization."
120. Fung, "Becoming a Moral Child."
121. Lieber et al., "Chinese Child-Rearing Beliefs," 145.
122. Koenig et al., *Handbook of Religion and Health.*
123. Jamieson, *Face of Forgiveness*; Thompson, *Soul of Shame.*
124. Nichols, "Civilizing Humans with Shame," 254.

fear, especially as found in collectivist societies such as those constituting the Confucian diaspora, which includes China, Taiwan, Japan, Korea and Singapore."[125] In such cultures, Nichols explained, "individuals show greater awareness of what others are thinking, including what others are thinking about them. This awareness couples with the desire to avoid social devaluation prominent in collectivist cultures."[126]

Similarly, Fung observed that the "importance of shame in Chinese culture is reflected in its emphasis on face, criticism, and evaluation in interpersonal relationships," as well as "in its rich variety of lexical terms and labels for shame, humiliation, embarrassment, face, and related notions."[127] Nichols further elaborated that China's long-standing hierarchical social structure, collectivism and emphasis on social roles have "contributed to the formation of a social environment in which one can feel more varieties of shame as a result of a greater number of causes than anywhere in the world," noting that such "finely grained uses of the sense of shame must be produced through cultural learning."[128] Because the "development of senses of shame within a culture begins by encoding behaviorally and emotionally conditioned responses in children," Nichols concluded that "the encoding methods used in the Confucian diaspora have generated a distinctive shame profile for its children."[129]

Specifically, the Confucian shame profile is closely tied to outward performance and social evaluation. Research indicates that Chinese mothers often emphasize and employ shame to correct their children's misbehavior.[130] Fingarette explained that the Confucian concept of shame (Ch'ih, 恥) is a "moral concept" that designates "a moral condition or response," one defined by a person's status and role as prescribed by *li*.[131] He further elaborated that "violation of the moral order is thus of the essence in Confucian shame."[132] In other words, shame in Confucian thought is not primarily "a matter of the inward state" but is "oriented

125. Nichols, "Civilizing Humans with Shame," 257.
126. Nichols, "Civilizing Humans with Shame," 259.
127. Fung, "Becoming a Moral Child," 183.
128. Nichols, "Civilizing Humans with Shame," 275.
129. Nichols, "Civilizing Humans with Shame," 275.
130. Fung et al., "Parental Beliefs About Shame"; Miller et al., "Narrative Practices."
131. Fingarette, *Confucius*, 30.
132. Fingarette, *Confucius*, 30.

to morality as centering in *li*, traditionally ceremonially defined social comportment, rather than to an inner core of one's being, 'the self.'"[133]

Fingarette further noted that "shame is a matter of 'face,' of embarrassment, of social status. Shame says, 'change your ways; you have lost honor or dignity.'"[134] Thus, Confucian shame directs people to look outward rather than inward,"[135] and "savvy Confucians will avoid shame by cultivating respect and deference."[136] This outward orientation helps explain why many participants described relying on behavior modification and external performance to conceal inner struggles and counter feelings of shame. In the hierarchical Chinese culture, "characterized by large inequalities of discretionary power and by socialization for group responsibility," Bond observed that "careful self-presentation is especially important."[137]

Accordingly, participants noted that their parents primarily emphasized behavioral control rather than attending to children's inner emotional realities—their desires, fears, or pain. As long as children obeyed and behaved well, family harmony appeared preserved, order seemed intact, and no one dared to engage the deeper dimensions of the soul. Both at home and within church contexts, participants observed that Chinese Christians similarly strove to appear good, successful, healthy, and composed, fearing the loss of face that vulnerability might bring.

Thompson pointed out that hiding and covering constitute the "first fundamental behavioral outcome of sin."[138] While this tendency is universal to human nature, the Confucian system intensifies it by combining hierarchical collectivism, performance orientation, and a strong cultural emphasis on shame. Consequently, the Confucian moral order, though externally disciplined, often cultivates inner concealment and relational disconnection, precisely the dynamics that transformative spiritual formation seeks to heal and redeem.

133. Fingarette, *Confucius*, 30.
134. Fingarette, *Confucius*, 30.
135. Fingarette, *Confucius*, 30.
136. Nichols, "Civilizing Humans with Shame," 268.
137. Bond, "Emotions and Their Expression," 253.
138. Thompson, *Anatomy of the Soul*, 217.

Church Culture

Participants also examined the role of church culture in shaping their spiritual lives. As Yang concluded in his research on Chinese churches in the United States, Chinese churches often reinforce traditional cultural values in order to preserve cultural identity in contexts outside mainland China.[139] Most participants in this study were diaspora Chinese Christians who had attended Chinese churches abroad. They observed that church frequently mirrored traditional Chinese values—particularly with respect to hierarchy, shame, gender roles, and sexuality. In this senses, participants recognized that cultural assumptions were often carried into Christian communities with little critical reflection.

Several participants expressed frustration with church leadership structures and communication patterns. Some women reported feeling dismissed or ignored when attempting to share their perspectives in church settings. Others noted that leaders were expected to function as moral and spiritual exemplars, leaving little room for weakness, doubt, or transparency. As a result, participants described a pervasive fear of judgment and pressure to meet both internal and external expectations, which frequently resulted in burnout and emotional exhaustion in ministry.

Finch affirmed that "there is a distinct and determinative relation between upbringing and the Christian conversion experience,"[140] noting that unresolved "dependency needs" and projections often contaminate spiritual development.[141] He described a recurring problem in churches as "infant mortality," observing that new believers are often immersed in theological knowledge without being guided into experiential relationship with Christ.[142] As a result, believers may acquire the forms of godliness without its transforming power, carrying "a weight of knowledge that lacks any wisdom."[143] In a similar way, participants in this study recognized that although many Chinese Christians diligently confess sins, examine themselves, and serve zealously, they often carry into their spiritual lives deeply ingrained habits shaped by performance, shame, and

139. Yang, *Chinese Christians in America.*

140. Finch, *Intensive Therapy*, iv.

141. Finch, *Intensive Therapy*, iv.

142. Finch, *Intensive Therapy*, iv.

143. Finch, *Intensive Therapy*, iv.

fear. Beneath fervent religious activity, "unresolved childhood traumas and parental expectations" may continue to exert powerful influence.[144]

Participants further noted that church leaders often bear particularly heavy burdens, as they are expected to embody spiritual and moral perfection. Finch cautioned that such idealization overlooks the shared reality of human sinfulness and often leads to misplaced dependency on human authorities, which ultimately results in disappointment.[145] As he emphasized, "Only God—unadulterated by parental projections God as seen in the face of Jesus Christ—will suffice for our needs. He made us. He knows us. He accepts us. He welcomes us. He loves us *as we are*."[146]

Similarly, Thompson observed that "sometimes the most seemingly admirable people (as well as the rest of us) hide their own emotional brokenness behind a wall of altruism."[147] Participants recognized that many church leaders and their families were overburdened by unrealistic expectations, and that their churches often lacked safe and trusting spaces where struggles could be confessed and grace genuinely experienced without fear of judgment.

Taken together, these features of Chinese church culture—hierarchical authority, performance-based spirituality, and the absence of emotional safety—profoundly shaped participants' spiritual lives. As they reexamined their church experiences through the lens of transformative learning, many began to distinguish cultural expectations from biblical truth. They came to recognize that authentic transformation in Christ requires vulnerability, honesty, and dependence on grace rather than the pursuit of moral or spiritual perfection.

Critical Reflections of Assumptions

Critical reflection on one's assumptions, or meaning perspectives, is an essential component of transformative learning.[148] Transformative learning educators assist learners in becoming aware of their habitual assumptions, exploring their origins, examining their consequences, and

144. Finch, *Intensive Therapy*, 27.

145. Finch, *Intensive Therapy*.

146. Finch, *Intensive Therapy*, 81.

147. Thompson, *Anatomy of the Soul*, 245.

148. Cranton, *Understanding and Promoting* (2nd ed.); Mezirow, *Learning as Transformation*.

questioning their validity.[149] As Cranton noted, such awareness is difficult to achieve independently because "these things are a part of the fabric of who we are or who we perceive we are," and "we act on them without thought."[150] She further observed that "even when we suspect that something might be wrong with how we see ourselves or the world around us, it is hard to admit that, let alone bring it out into the open and turn it around and look at it from different angles."[151]

For this reason, educators, therapists, and spiritual directors play a vital role in the transformative process by listening attentively and posing reflective questions that enable learners to critically examine their assumptions.[152] The data indicate that the spiritual formation program effectively supported this phase of transformative learning by fostering critical reflection on participants' assumptions about themselves, God, and their relationships with others. The sections that follow examine each of these areas in detail.

Assessment of Assumptions About the Self

As participants reexamined their upbringing and families of origin, they also reassessed assumptions about selfhood that had been shaped by Chinese cultural norms and parenting patterns.

Loss of Self

Many participants recognized that within a hierarchical and collective culture, their individual sense of self had often been subordinated or suppressed during childhood. In order to survive emotionally, they learned to please caregivers—most often their parents—by being obedient, quiet, and compliant. Over time, they lost the capacity to express personal opinions or desires. As participants reflected on their experiences, many realized that they had stopped asking questions and refrained from challenging authority altogether. In families marked by distant or uninvolved fathers and anxious or controlling mothers, several participants came to see how their identities had become emotionally enmeshed with their

149. Cranton, *Understanding and Promoting* (2nd ed.).

150. Cranton, *Understanding and Promoting* (3rd ed.), 50.

151. Cranton, *Understanding and Promoting* (3rd ed.), 50.

152. Cranton, *Understanding and Promoting* (3rd ed.).

mothers, who—consciously or unconsciously—shaped their children to meet their own unmet emotional needs.

Because they were raised in shame-based family systems characterized by constant comparison and limited encouragement, participants discovered that they had developed low self-esteem and deep insecurity. Many felt compelled to work tirelessly to "appear good" in order to gain approval, particularly because parental affirmation was rare. Over time, they internalized the belief that they were not good enough and, in some cases, came to dislike themselves.

These experiences resonate with Bedford and Hwang's observation that "Chinese identity is defined in terms of the system of relationships in which a person is involved," and that "personal identity is dependent on continued relations with the group."[153] They explained that "close personal relations are treated as parts of the self and selfness is confirmed through interpersonal relationships."[154] Within this framework, shame plays a central role, for "shame is always linked to judgments about the self, and related to the sense of self and personal identity."[155]

Nichols likewise observed that a "keen sense of shame" often results in "conformist behavior, " as conformity is motivated by a desire to avoid shame and embarrassment, "the aversive emotions attending negative social appraisal."[156] In Confucian societies, "behavior is primarily evaluated according to how well it serves to enhance the interpersonal standards of society,"[157] and group-oriented-behavior—such as harmonious interaction—is valued more highly than individuality or personal freedom.[158] These cultural realities closely mirror participants' reflections that their individuality was rarely nurtured and that their sense of self had been absorbed into the collective expectations of family and society.

False Self

Further, when vulnerability is regarded as shameful and inner realities are suppressed, people learn to hide weakness beneath achievement

153. Bedford and Hwang, "Guilt and Shame," 130.
154. Bedford and Hwang, "Guilt and Shame," 130.
155. Bedford and Hwang, "Guilt and Shame," 128.
156. Nichols, "Civilizing Humans with Shame," 258.
157. Nichols, "Civilizing Humans with Shame," 278.
158. Bedford and Hwang, "Guilt and Shame," 130–31.

and performance. Participants reflected that they had constructed false selves—identities marked by fortitude, success, and moral goodness—to mask inner pain and insecurity. They became the "good" sons and daughters, "good" people, and "good" Christians who met external expectations while concealing their true emotions.

From a theological-psychological perspective, human beings after the fall are separated from God, the ultimate source of love and goodness.[159] As Janov observed, this separation gives rise to a universal search for love—"the search for the self that could never be"—a longing to find "that special someone who will let you be you."[160] Yet as a consequence of sin, people hide not only from God but also from themselves. "Since so many of us have had our feelings ignored or crushed," Janov noted, "we end up doing what we don't feel," constructing defenses to protect against emotional pain.[161]

Finch similarly described these defenses as false identifications that obscure the true self:

> Defenses are those tricks we use to identify ourselves which succeed only in hiding ourselves. They cannot adequately identify us because being made in the image of God, nothing but His image will truly identify us. Psychologists have been very wise in discerning that large numbers of people have an image problem. And no matter what we do to help them discover or improve their image, it will only be a Halloween mask if it does not portray the image of God. Unreal images need defenses to keep them in place. The image of God is our ontological reality.[162]

Because inward struggles were rarely addressed, participants noted that they had been trained to fix problems and modify behavior without attending to the heart. Emotional and spiritual exploration was discouraged; introspection was replaced by fortitude, discipline, and self-control. By contrast, the program's guided reflection practices invited participants to unmask these defenses and rediscover their true identity as beloved children of God, marking a crucial step in their transformative learning process.

159. Finch, *Intensive Therapy.*

160. Janov, *Primal Scream*, 279.

161. Janov, *Primal Scream*, 279.

162. Finch, *Intensive Therapy*, 94–95.

Assessment of Assumptions About God

The spiritual formation program also helped participants examine their perceptions of God, many of which had been unconsciously shaped by relationships with parents and other authority figures. As Finch argued, when "a child is implicitly taught that love is a demand for conformity, and that the way one returns 'love' is to repress and conform, the very notion of love is distorted."[163] He further explained that "if this kind of parenting becomes a model for God, our authority problems can only become infinitely worse."[164] When parental expectations are "projected on to God," Finch noted, "it infinitizes the gap and becomes an all but impossible hurdle to overcome."[165] Consequently, misconceptions about God's character, rooted in early relational experiences, often create emotional and spiritual distance between believers and God.[166]

Although many participants affirmed cognitively that God is loving and caring, they acknowledged that their lived, experiential perception of God was distant, demanding, and controlling—a mirror image of their parental relationships. Some described God as abstract, "a bunch of facts," rather than a personal presence. They recognized that they had projected images of Chinese authority figures onto their understanding of God. Just as they had sought to please their parents through obedience and performance, they approached God with the same striving posture: working, serving, and praying diligently in order to sustain the relationship. Participants noted that they tended to credit themselves when they sensed God's presence and blame themselves when God felt absent.

Participants also reconsidered their understanding of prayer. Having grown up in families where emotional expression was discouraged and honest self-disclosure felt unsafe, many struggled to come before God authentically. They hid their true selves from God just as they had hidden from their parents. Prayer became ritualized and mechanical—a duty to perform rather than a relationship to enjoy. Words such as "boring," "dry," and "obligatory" recurred in their descriptions. Some reported feeling guilty when they did not want to pray or read Scripture. When prayers were answered, they felt affirmed; when they were not, they experienced confusion, disappointment, or shame. Participants recognized

163. Finch, *Intensive Therapy*, 28.

164. Finch, *Intensive Therapy*, 28.

165. Finch, *Intensive Therapy*, 29.

166. Reed et al., *Spiritual Companioning*.

that their discomfort with God's silence revealed deeper misconceptions about God's nature and significantly hindered intimacy.

Through the spiritual formation program, participants began to recognize and reframe these projections, learning to perceive God not as a demanding taskmaster but as a loving Father who desires authentic relationship. This reframing marked a crucial movement in their transformative learning process, corresponding to Mezirow's third phase—the critical assessment of assumptions—and signaled a profound theological realignment in their inner image of God.

Assessment of Assumptions About Others

Participants also reexamined their relationships with others, acknowledging that many of their relational patterns were unhealthy and shaped by cultural conditioning. They identified tendencies toward codependency, people-pleasing, judgmentalism, and a savior complex—patterns they traced to the interplay of shame, hierarchy, and collectivism in their upbringing.

As Nichols noted, "When a culture modifies evolutionary norms having to do with shaming and being shamed, its social communities are led to endorse some behaviors and condemn others."[167] Raised within such a shame-based culture, participants admitted that they had internalized habits of judgment and comparison. Finch similarly argued that unless individuals "release significant others" from their childhood, they inevitably project their unmet needs and expectations onto "significant others in the here and now."[168] Thus, participants recognized that patterns formed under parental expectations were often repeated in adulthood relationships.

Finch further observed that all people "need freeing, liberation—from the unconscious dependence that blames the world for not being good on our terms and thus evades the responsibility for being a whole person."[169] This cycle of projection and dependency closely reflected participants' experiences. Many came to see that their judgmental attitudes toward others stemmed from unresolved parental expectations and internalized shame. In relationships, they often prioritized behavioral

167. Nichols, "Civilizing Humans with Shame," 270.

168. Finch, *Intensive Therapy*, 11.

169. Finch, *Intensive Therapy*, 14.

correction over emotional connection, responding with fact-oriented or solution-driven approaches rather than empathy. Even in ministry or counseling contexts, participants acknowledged that their care could lack authentic compassion because it remained driven by performance and duty rather than love.

Through guided reflection and spiritual direction, the program helped participants reevaluate these relational assumptions in light of grace. They came to recognize that genuine care for others arises not from control or perfectionism but from humility, shared vulnerability, and dependence on God's transforming love. This shift represented both personal healing and relational reorientation, deepening their capacity to engage others with authenticity and compassion—an essential outcome of transformative learning.

Transformed in Community

Mezirow emphasized that transformative learning often occurs within community, as individuals come to recognize that others share similar struggles and are undergoing parallel processes of change.[170] Findings from this study revealed that the Western spiritual formation program provided a trusting and caring community in which Chinese students felt safe and encouraged to share their weaknesses and even their sins. Although many participants described the process of transformation as painful, they consistently testified that it was also life-changing.

As students learned to acknowledge their emotions and relinquish long-held defenses, their trust in God and dependence on him deepened. In Finch's words, they became progressively "immunized or insulated against fear—even of destruction."[171] Despite its challenges, participants affirmed that the program was ultimately liberating, helping them shift their focus from external performance toward attentiveness to God's presence and their inner lives. The following sections examine how the program's communal structure—through humble faculty, unjudging cohort groups, and loving spiritual directors—facilitated this transformation.

170. Mezirow, *Transformative Dimensions.*

171. Finch, *Intensive Therapy*, 9.

Humble and Honest Faculty

Participants frequently noted that the faculty modeled a form of community markedly different from that of traditional Chinese seminary professors. Faculty members demonstrated humility and courage by openly sharing their own weaknesses and struggles. Having themselves journeyed through various stages of spiritual formation, they were unafraid to confront students' inner darkness or sin. Rather than responding with judgment, they offered acceptance and care, enabling students to experience God's love and grace through relational presence.

Students felt respected and valued as faculty members invested time in listening and accompanying them on their spiritual journeys. Faculty members' integration of character, wisdom, and theological knowledge provided living examples of transformed lives. For many participants, these professors embodied the kind of person they aspired to become. At the same time, some participants struggled to form close relationships with faculty, perceiving them as authoritative figures—an echo of hierarchical dynamics shaped by their cultural background.

Unjudging Cohort Groups

Participants also emphasized the importance of cohort groups—intentionally designed spaces where students could share struggles and experiences in an atmosphere of trust and vulnerability. Within these small communities, students journeyed together, learning to speak truthfully, listen without judgment, and support one another in love. Through this shared process, participants found freedom from fear and pretense; they no long needed to wear the mask of fortitude or appear as though they "have it all together."

Recognizing that others faced similar struggles normalized their pain and deepened mutual empathy. Many described the cohort environment as healing and liberating, a space where authenticity replaced shame and isolation. Participants discovered that transformation was not a solitary endeavor but a shared pilgrimage of grace.

Loving Spiritual Directors

Nearly all participants identified spiritual direction as central to their transformation. Although a few initially felt "forced" to confront their emotions, most described their spiritual directors as the first persons who genuinely attended to their souls by listening without judgment, caring deeply for their hearts, and guiding them to discern God's presence in their lives. Despite cultural differences, participants consistently testified that they felt understood, affirmed, and loved by their directors, who embodied Christlike compassion and attentiveness to the Holy Spirit.

Spiritual direction, a practice rooted in centuries of Christian tradition,[172] "helps people pay attention to God's presence and call in their everyday lives" and rests within "a paradigm of prayer and discernment."[173] While "all Christians are called to the ministry of listening," spiritual directors "see themselves as specially called to this ministry, by the grace of the One who is the true spiritual director."[174] As conduits of divine love, they listen "in a way that invites others to speak the truth about themselves, including areas of vulnerability and brokenness,"[175] opening pathways to healing and transformation.

Van Dragt described healing as occurring "in a reality in which temporal-spatial, physical, and personal boundaries, as well as barriers to the transcendent, become permeable," allowing restoration to take place through compassionate presence.[176] Similarly, Thompson affirmed from a neuropsychological perspective that transformation requires "substantial interaction with an outside brain relationship or a change in circumstances."[177] When people experience being "felt" and "known" by another, God often uses these relational encounters as instruments of healing and renewal.[178]

Raised in shame-based cultural contexts, many participants were unfamiliar with emotional awareness and found it difficult to remain present with their pain. Some described therapy as emotionally exhausting, though ultimately redemptive. In this process, spiritual directors

172. Reed et al., *Spiritual Companioning.*
173. Greenman and Kalantzis, *Life in the Spirit*, 167.
174. Greenman and Kalantzis, *Life in the Spirit*, 163.
175. Reed et al., *Spiritual Companioning*, 45.
176. Van Dragt, "Paranormal Healing," 309.
177. Thompson, *Anatomy of the Soul*, 133.
178. Thompson, *Anatomy of the Soul.*

served as embodied expressions of Christ's empathy, offering safe and sacred companionship. With a deep awareness of God's sovereignty and love, directors helped participants shift from self-centered striving toward God-centered trust, enabling them to recognize God's redemptive work even within painful memories.

Clinton and Ohlschlager defined empathy as "the ability to get inside a client's world and develop a sense of what that world looks like from her point of view."[179] For participants, the directors' capacity to enter their inner world—to reflect their emotions and affirm their worth—proved profoundly transformative. This relational attunement functioned as a sacramental space in which human compassion and divine grace converged, leading to deep spiritual and emotional renewal.

Acquiring Knowledge and Skills

Mezirow emphasized that transformative learning involves the acquisition of new knowledge and skills, which serve to "bring valuable new contents into the existing form of our way of knowing."[180] In this study, participants testified that they acquired both conceptual understanding and practical skills through teaching, lived experience, and hands-on training. These learning experiences differed markedly from anything they had previously encountered and became catalysts for deep reflection and transformation.

The Double Knowledge

Participants reported that the program's faculty consistently emphasized what John Calvin described as "the double knowledge."[181] Calvin wrote, "Nearly all the wisdom we possess, that is to say, true and sound wisdom consists of two parts: the knowledge of God and of ourselves."[182] An essential implication of this claim is that genuine self-knowledge—as the recognition that one has "nothing but subsistence in the one God"—does not detract from knowledge of God but rather leads into and deepens it.[183]

179. Clinton and Ohlschlager, *Competent Christian Counseling*, 206.

180. Mezirow, *Learning as Transformation*, 49.

181. Calvin, *Institutes of the Christian Religion*, 35.

182. Calvin, *Institutes of the Christian Religion*, 35.

183. Calvin, *Institutes of the Christian Religion*, 35.

According to participants, the spiritual formation program was intentionally structured around cultivating this double knowledge through theological instruction, guided self-reflection, and embodied practice. This integrated approach fostered greater awareness of both their inner lives and their relationship with God, enabling participants to hold self-knowledge and God-knowledge together rather than treating them as competing domains.

Integration of Psychology

Participants also reflected that the program's integration of psychology significantly enriched their understanding of both self and God. Although some initially felt "forced" to revisit their past and examine their families of origin, many later recognized this process as essential for uncovering their authentic selves. By revisiting and re-feeling repressed pain and unresolved wounds, participants encountered long-silenced emotions and reclaimed voices muted by their cultural upbringing. Beneath outward displays of competence and fortitude, they discovered vulnerability and a deep need for grace.

Because this work took place within a safe and caring environment—through classes, cohort groups, retreats, therapy, and spiritual direction—participants experienced how knowledge of self naturally led to deeper knowledge of God. In their weakness, they encountered the embodied Christ, whose love and acceptance affirmed their identity as fully forgiven and beloved children of God. As a result, their way of life was transformed; they became increasingly aware of God's presence and more secure in their identity in Christ.

Scholars have likewise emphasized the importance of integrating psychology and theology within spiritual formation.[184] Coe argued that spiritual theology's distinctive task is "to integrate a theology of sanctification with a broadly empirical study of what is relevant to understanding spiritual growth in the real world."[185] Psychology, he explained, offers "extrabiblical wisdom" that is valuable "for understanding and participating in the process of spiritual growth."[186] Building on this conviction, Coe

184. Barry and Connolly, *Practice of Spiritual Direction*; Coe, "Theological-Experiential Methodology"; McGrath, *Psychology of Christian Character Formation.*

185. Coe, "When Psychology and Theology," 23.

186. Coe, "When Psychology and Theology," 24.

and Hall developed "transformational psychology," a model that unites scientific inquiry and faith within a "single, unified act of studying all reality in the Spirit."[187]

In this framework, transformational psychology serves as a means of formation for both those who practice it and those who are helped through it.[188] Because human growth often involves fragmentation and inner division, healing occurs only "by union with God and filling the human spirit with God's Spirit on the basis of the work of Christ on the cross,"[189] resulting in "conformity to the image of Christ" and love for God and neighbor.[190] Coe and Hall further emphasized that Christian discipleship is inherently holistic: "to live Christianly is to allow Jesus Christ to be Lord of every aspect" of one's life, leaving no room for a sacred-secular divide.[191]

Psychology, therefore, can illuminate how spiritual disciplines are practiced—whether openly or defensively, authentically or performatively.[192] As Coe and Hall illustrated, insight into childhood relationships with domineering or overly critical parents can reveal how such dynamics shape a prayer life marked by performance and fear, preempting honest self-disclosure before God.[193]

Many participants recognized this dynamic in their own spiritual lives. They came to see how demanding parental relationships had shaped their understanding of prayer and their image of God. Through the program's integration of psychology and theology, and through practices such as honest self-presentation before God and recollection of their identity in Christ, participants learned to relate to God not through fear or performance but through intimacy and authenticity.[194] In this way, spiritual formation informed by transformational psychology provided them with a new way of life, characterized by growing attentiveness to God's presence and a deepening awareness of Jesus' holistic lordship over every aspect of existence.

187. Coe and Hall, "Transformational Psychology View," 207.
188. Coe and Hall, "Transformational Psychology View."
189. Coe and Hall, "Transformational Psychology View," 111.
190. Coe and Hall, "Transformational Psychology View," 211.
191. Coe and Hall, *Psychology in the Spirit*, 13.
192. Coe and Hall, "Transformational Psychology View," 219.
193. Coe and Hall, "Transformational Psychology View," 219.
194. Coe and Hall, *Psychology in the Spirit*, 117.

Theorization of Spirituality

Participants reported that the program's teachings on spirituality dramatically reshaped their understanding of the Christian life. A central theme was the indwelling of the Holy Spirit and his transformative work within believers. Prior to entering the program, many participants had pursued sanctification primarily through self-effort and fortitude, attempting to bridge the perceived gap between themselves and God through sheer willpower, discipline, and obedience. Through the program's presentation of spiritual theology and its accompanying practices, participants learned to experience God's presence and follow the guidance of the indwelling Spirit rather than striving in their own strength.

Participants further noted that the program's teachings provided a theological framework that helped them interpret their lived experiences of disorientation, struggle, and spiritual dryness. In many Chinese church contexts, such experiences had been viewed as signs of weakness or spiritual failure. Hearing faculty normalize and contextualize these painful seasons as integral to God's transforming work was deeply relieving and liberating. Through this reframing, participants gained new perspectives on their spiritual journeys, recognizing that seasons of confusion, silence, and suffering could be understood not as divine abandonment but as invitations into deeper trust and intimacy with God.

Spiritual Disciplines

Participants also reported that practicing spiritual disciplines—such as prayer projects, journaling, *lectio divina*, contemplative prayer, spiritual direction, and retreats—provided concrete opportunities to embody the concepts and theories they were learning. These practices facilitated the movement of their "double knowledge" from head to heart, allowing intellectual understanding to become lived experience.

The spiritual formation program integrated intensive therapy and the Ignatian exercises in a synergistic manner, helping participants encounter their true selves and experience God's love and acceptance amid brokenness. For those who attended the inward journey retreat, this process often reached a climax as they confronted the depths of darkness and helplessness within their hearts while simultaneously encountering God's redemptive presence. In this way, all components of the program worked together toward a shared goal: a progressively deepened knowledge of God and of self.

In addition, the apprentice training model for spiritual directors equipped participants to listen attentively and care for others' souls by discerning and following the guidance of the Holy Spirit. Through this multifaceted engagement with spiritual disciplines, participants became increasingly aware of God's presence and the work of the Holy Spirit in their own lives and in the lives of others. As a result, most participants testified that they developed sustainable habits of spiritual practice during the program—habits they continued to cultivate long after graduation.

Through these integrated practices of theology, psychology, and spiritual discipline, participants not only acquired new knowledge and skills but also embodied Mezirow's seventh phase of transformative learning: acquiring the competence needed to live out a renewed perspective. Their transformation thus prepared them to move into the next phase—exploring new relationships with themselves, God, and others.

Exploring New Relationships

Mezirow observed that once transformation occurs, learners can "never return to an old perspective," even though "the process is seldom one of consistent forward movement."[195] The data from this study revealed that participants' engagement with spiritual knowledge and disciplined practice led to new perspectives on self, God, and others. This stage corresponds most closely to Mezirow's fifth phase—the exploration of new roles, relationships, and actions—while remaining grounded in critical reflection on assumptions.

Although the process was often painful and disorienting, participants encountered God's love and acceptance in the midst of weakness and inner darkness. These encounters produced significant shifts in how they understood themselves, their relationship with God, and their relationships with others. Table 3 summarizes the major changes in participants' views of self before and after their participation in the program.

195. Mezirow, "Perspective Transformation," 16.

New Relationships with Self

One of the most profound transformations participants experienced was learning to accept themselves and attend to their emotions. Through revisiting their upbringing, reexperiencing formative memories, and allowing themselves to feel long-repressed emotions, participants reconnected with their inner lives—the dimension of self that had long been silenced by cultural and familial expectations.

Finch emphasized that maturity requires every person to "release" or "exorcise" parental influences that bind the mind.[196] He explained,

> This does not mean that he has nothing ever again to do with a living parent, but that all the former ways of relating with him are no longer viable. They are dead. Bit by bit he has stripped off all the introjected images so he is now free to be his own man, his own person. While this is a very freeing experience, it is no less frightening. Having been "lived by another," to take reins of his own life and be responsible for himself has often been described as a new birth, with all the accompanying hazards, uncertainty, unfamiliarity, and just plain newness.[197]

Table 3. Participants' Transformed Views of Self

Before Studying in the Program	**After Studying in the Program**
Self lost or repressed	Awareness of emotions and movements of the heart
Low self-esteem; dislike of self	Liking oneself; freedom to be authentic
Performance-oriented; wearing masks	Knowing God's love as unconditional; extending grace to oneself and embracing growth as a process
False self-identity	Discovery of the true self; identity rooted in God
Self-dependent or codependent	Dependence on God
"I am the center of the world."	"God is the center of the world."

Because negative emotions had been suppressed and deemed unacceptable in childhood, participants confessed that they had seldom felt known, accepted, or loved prior to entering the program. While some initially blamed their parents, who had consciously or unconsciously

196. Finch, *Intensive Therapy*, 14.
197. Finch, *Intensive Therapy*, 10.

shaped them according to expectations other than the image of God, many eventually recognized their own responsibility and freedom. As Finch further noted,

> Each of us is given our own two feet to stand on, no matter how cruelly we have knocked to the ground. Moreover, to remain in our childish fear and dependence, projecting our resentment on other authority figures, is to live in a world of illusion. You're blaming the wrong guy! In any case, "blame is no blame good." If blame were a viable option, the world would be a wonderful place. If dependence were the way to go and if it worked, we would be more effective. But life *doesn't* work that way. There is no way that dependence is going to work. Indeed it is at the *root* of all our problems, from the womb to tomb. Whether it be personally or in the family or society or with the nation, we must each pull our own weight![198]

Through this process, participants learned to stand on their own "two feet" before God, secure in divine love, responsible for their own growth, and increasingly free from the controlling influence of shame and dependency.

Deep experiential knowledge of self not only led participants into fuller dependence on God but also empowered them to take responsibility for their own lives. As a result, their former dependence on parents was gradually transformed into dependence on God. Willard affirmed that because human beings are "spiritual beings . . ., it is for our good, individually and collectively, to live our lives in interactive dependence upon God and under his kingdom rule."[199]

Through transformative learning, participants learned to distinguish their parents' voices from God's voice, gaining freedom to live authentically as their true selves. Several female participants, in particular, described a renewed sense of dignity and personal worth, along with the courage to express voices long silenced by cultural expectations.

New Relationships with God

Participants' relationships with God also underwent profound change. God was no longer perceived as distant, fearful, or demanding, nor

198. Finch, *Intensive Therapy*, 21–22.

199. Willard, *Divine Conspiracy*, 82.

merely as "a bunch of facts" or theological concepts. Instead, participants came to know God as a loving and personal presence intimately involved in their daily lives. They learned that they could approach God without first attempting to purify or perfect themselves.

Many discovered the joy of slowing down and simply being with God rather than striving to please him through performance. Secure in their identity as beloved children of God, they learned to speak honestly with God about sin, weakness, frustration, and fear. Table 4 summarizes these changes.

Table 4. Participants' Transformed Relationships with God

Before Studying in the Program	After Studying in the Program
Unhealthy images of God	Distinguishing God's voice from parental voices
Duty-bound spirituality	Trust in God's sovereignty
Inability to be honest with God	Honest self-disclosure before God
Self-blame for God's absence	Awareness of God's presence in all things

New Relationships with Others

Participants also adopted new ways of relating to others. Having experienced God's acceptance in their own vulnerability, they became more capable of empathizing with others' pain. Rather than fixing or correcting, they learned to listen, accompany, and be present with people in their life struggles.

Because they discovered their identity in Christ, participants developed healthier boundaries, stepped away from codependent patterns, and ceased seeking approval through performance. While some continued to struggle—particularly with shame and confrontation—most recognized transformation as an ongoing process rather than a completed state. Table 5 illustrates these changes.

Table 5. Participants' Transformed Relationships with Others

Before Studying in the Program	*After Studying in the Program*
Unhealthy relationships (e.g., savior complex, codependence, people-pleasing)	Healthier boundaries
Judgmental attitudes	Increased grace
Shallow connections	Deeper, authentic relationships
Helping out of obligation	Compassion rooted in love

The spiritual formation program facilitated these changes by helping participants confront their true selves—sinful, vulnerable, and yet beloved—within a safe and trusting community. During the intensive inward retreat, participants were invited to revisit their emotions repeatedly until they were able to face their true identities before God. This "inside view" offered them what Finch described as "a deeply humbling awareness of the vagaries and varieties" of their own hearts.[200]

As participants expressed long-repressed emotions and deep longings, many came to realize that they had continued to seek parental approval and depended on others' affirmation. Recognizing this dependency became a breakthrough moment. They began to see how reliance on parents and, more broadly, on human approval had hindered their spiritual growth and freedom in God.

This painful yet necessary process echoes Finch's assertion that "one cannot be without this humbling awareness" of one's sinful condition.[201] Such awareness, he argued, "precludes judgmental attitudes," "enables patience," and "uncovers the fact that he is no better than the one he works with."[202] Participants found that as they allowed their defenses to fall and acknowledged their own darkness, pretenses of righteousness and perfection dissolved. They no longer felt compelled to appear good because they encountered God's love precisely in the midst of their brokenness.

The transcendent encounter initiated and completed by God led to a profound awareness of divine acceptance amid human frailty—a transformation both internal and external. Having experienced God's love in vulnerability, participants came to recognize themselves as God's

200. Finch, *Intensive Therapy*, 8.
201. Finch, *Intensive Therapy*, 8.
202. Finch, *Intensive Therapy*, 8.

creation, relinquish control, and embrace their true selves. Empowered by grace, they were freed to love themselves and others more deeply.

When participants confronted the depth of sin and weakness within their hearts, they, like the apostle Paul, could only confess: "Christ Jesus came into the world to save sinners, among whom I am foremost of all" (1 Tim 1:15). Through this realization, they acknowledged that apart from God, they could do nothing, and they rested anew in dependence on him, rejoicing in their unique identity as God's beloved creation.

With this renewed awareness, participants' judgmental attitudes toward others began to shift. They were no longer surprised or threatened by brokenness in others, knowing that Jesus is present even in the mess. Acceptance of self naturally gave rise to deeper acceptance of others. Having received God's unconditional love, participants became increasingly able to empathize with others' pain and to embody that same love in relationships and ministry.

This transformation also reshaped participants' approach to evangelism and discipleship. Many had entered the program hoping to become more effective evangelists or disciple-makers. Through the process of spiritual formation, however, they discovered that authentic ministry flows not from effort or technique but from the overflow of a transformed heart. As the kingdom of God grew within them, they began to embody divine love in their daily lives, becoming what Finch (1974) described as "ever cleaner conduits for the love of God to flow" through them.[203]

Finch further affirmed, "Hitherto we have been possessed by alien forces. Now, we are becoming one with God. That is what God-like means. His image appears in us. This is how we incarnate the Word."[204] In this way, participants' transformation was not only personal but also incarnational—a visible manifestation of God's redemptive work in and through human lives.

Trying Out New Roles

Mezirow observed that as transformative learners critically reflect on their assumptions, explore alternative meaning perspectives, and acquire new knowledge and skills, they begin to experiment with newly formed

203. Finch, *Intensive Therapy*, 93.

204. Finch, *Intensive Therapy*, 93.

habits of mind.[205] Within Mezirow's framework, phase 8 (provisional trying of new roles), phase 9 (building competence and self-confidence in new roles and relationships), and phase 10 (a reintegration into one's life based on new perspectives) are distinct yet closely related stages.[206] Collectively, these phases often culminate in a crucial benchmark of the transformative process: a deepened awareness of self, others, and one's place in the world.

In this study, participants described these stages as concurrent and interwoven rather than sequential. Their experimentation with new roles occurred primarily within their families and Chinese church communities, where long-standing cultural expectations intersected with newly formed spiritual insights.

Challenging

According to the data, many participants gained renewed confidence and expressed readiness to serve the Lord in a variety of contexts as a result of their transformative learning experiences. Several had already begun to engage in ministry, applying what they had learned and inviting others into similar journeys of transformation. They experimented with new roles within their families, as spouses, parents, and adult children, adopting more open, grace-filled approaches. Some began parenting in nontraditional ways that emphasized emotional presence and honesty rather than control or performance.

However, not all participants felt equally integrated upon graduation. A few described themselves as "deconstructed but not yet rebuilt," while others struggled to translate the program's intensive focus on inner transformation into outward ministry practice. Although most affirmed the value of spiritual formation, some offered critical cautions. One participant warned against overinflating the importance of spiritual formation, while another noted the risk that achievement-oriented Chinese Christians might misunderstand it, turning vulnerability into a new form of competition or spiritual performance. Still others questioned whether the process was equally effective for everybody.

Most participants also encountered resistance when attempting to apply what they had learned within their churches or seminaries. They

205. Mezirow, "Perspective Transformation."

206. Mezirow, *Learning as Transformation*.

faced obstacles rooted in the "cultural DNA" of many Chinese congregations, including hierarchical leadership structures, resistance to change, discomfort with emotional vulnerability, suspicion toward psychology, and lingering bias against practices perceived as "Catholic." Yet paradoxically, participants also recognized that these very challenges underscored the urgent need for spiritual formation within Chinese Christian communities.

Moreover, several participants reflected that the program could have offered more explicit guidance in cultural contextualization. Shin and Silzer, drawing on their years of teaching Asian American seminary students, observed that many experienced frustration and disillusionment due to "a lack of cultural self-knowledge," particularly an unawareness of how Confucian hierarchy and collectivism shape ministry identity and differ from both American individualism and biblical truth.[207] Echoing this insight, participants in the present study suggested that cultural knowledge should be more intentionally integrated into processes of self-knowledge and spiritual formation.

Contextualization

Despite these challenges, participants overwhelmingly affirmed the necessity of spiritual formation for Chinese Christians. They observed that many believers in Chinese churches are deeply thirsty for intimacy with God and long for authentic spiritual growth. At the same time, participants recognized that spiritual formation must be thoughtfully contextualized for Chinese and other non-Western settings. Several expressed ongoing efforts to translate and adapt spiritual formation principles in ways that resonate with Chinese cultural values while remaining faithful to biblical truth.

CHAPTER 7 CONCLUSION

In summary, participants in this study clearly demonstrated nine of the ten phases of transformative learning described by Mezirow.[208] They encountered personal and ministerial dilemmas before entering the program and experienced significant cultural disorientation during their

207. Shin and Silzer, *Tapestry of Grace*, xiii.

208. Mezirow, *Learning as Transformation.*

studies. The Western spiritual formation curriculum guided them to re-examine their Chinese upbringing and critically assess their assumptions about self, God, and others.

Within a loving and trusting community, where faculty and peers modeled vulnerability and authenticity, participants explored alternative ways of understanding life and faith. The acquisition of theoretical and experiential spiritual knowledge, along with training in spiritual direction, equipped them to try out new roles in family, church, and workplace contexts. Although some encountered difficulty reintegrating their newly formed meaning perspectives into daily life, participants nonetheless grew in competence, confidence, and cultural awareness, and many sought to contextualize spiritual formation for Chinese settings.

Ultimately, transformative learning emerged not as a completed event but as a lifelong journey.[209] Through this process, the Western spiritual formation program led Chinese students into a deeper awareness of God's presence, a greater dependence on the Holy Spirit, and a renewed capacity to live and minister from the indwelling life of Christ.

209. Mezirow, *Learning as Transformation.*

8

Conclusions and Implications

In this chapter, I examine how this research contributes to both the academic and practical fields of transformative learning and Christian spiritual formation.

THEORETICAL CONTRIBUTIONS

This grounded theory research demonstrates that a Western Christian spiritual formation program successfully facilitated transformative learning among Chinese students, despite the cultural distance between members of the Confucian Chinese diaspora and a Western educational framework. The study thus contributes to both transformative learning theory and spiritual formation scholarship by expanding academic understanding of how these two disciplines intersect in intercultural contexts.

Contributions to Transformative Learning Theory

This study found that the Chinese students experienced nine of Mezirow's ten phases of transformative learning.[1]

First, the findings reveal that Chinese seminary students encountered disorienting dilemmas that motivated them to pursue adult education within a Western spiritual formation program. Although participants

1. Mezirow, *Learning as Transformation*.

did not explicitly use the term *dilemma*, their descriptions of burnout, depression, disillusionment, and spiritual stagnation clearly indicate encounters with such life challenges. Many had been Christians and active in ministry for more than a decade. Some longed to escape the pressures of service, others sought a deeper understating of spirituality that their churches could not provide, and still others wished to become better equipped to help others. In various ways, all expressed dissatisfaction with their current spiritual condition and a desire for transformation.

While Mezirow's second phase involves "self-examination with feelings of fear, anger, guilt, or shame,"[2] this phase in the present study was closely intertwined with the first. The data indicate that Chinese students faced a distinctly cultural dilemma within their transformative experience. Because the program's reflective and dialogical components required participants to reexamine their upbringing and disclose personal vulnerabilities, these processes were experienced as countercultural and emotionally challenging in light of their Confucian background. This cultural tension was especially evident in the conflict between hierarchical family values and filial piety on the one hand, and the program's emphasis on honest self-reflection and emotional transparency on the other. The findings suggest that shame and performance orientation, deeply ingrained in the Chinese psyche, rendered this phase particularly painful, yet ultimately liberating.

Moreover, this phase of self-examination was inseparable from critical reflection on assumptions, as both were mediated through culturally shaped meaning systems. The Confucian worldview that had formed participants' early development and self-understanding was brought under scrutiny as the program prompted them to reconsider its formative influence. This stage proved crucial to transformation, as it enabled participants to transcend cultural constraints that traditionally discourage introspection and critical self-examination. Thus, although Mezirow conceptualized these as three distinct phases,[3] my findings of this study suggest that disorienting dilemmas, self-examination, and critical reflection occurred simultaneously and recursively among Chinese learners.

Mezirow's fourth phase—recognizing that one's transformative experience is shared by others[4]—appears vividly in the section "Transformed in Community." Because participants came from shame-based

2. Mezirow, *Learning as Transformation*, 22.

3. Mezirow, *Learning as Transformation*.

4. Mezirow, *Learning as Transformation*.

cultural contexts, community was indispensable to their transformation. The data reveal that a safe and trusting learning environment, though unfamiliar, became essential to growth. The humility of faculty members, the empathy of spiritual directors, and the mutual acceptance within cohort groups created a space in which participants could share their struggles without fear of judgment. For these Chinese students, community was not supplementary but essential: without it, transformative learning would likely have failed. This finding highlights the vital role of authentic community for learners shaped in Confucian contexts—a dimension underemphasized in many Western formulations of transformative learning theory.

Mezirow's fifth phase, the exploration of new roles and relationships,[5] corresponds with the section "Exploring New Relationships." This ongoing process reflected participants' emerging identity in Christ and their reoriented understanding of self, God, and others, each standing in sharp contrast to earlier Confucian-influenced perspectives.

The seventh phase, acquiring knowledge and skills,[6] also emerged clearly in this study and carried significant cultural implications. Participants not only learned new theological and psychological frameworks but also began to unlearn cultural patterns, such as shame-based motivation, self-reliance, and perfectionism, that had hindered spiritual growth. At the same time, the findings suggest that insufficient attention to cultural awareness, particularly in relation to shame sensitivity and performance orientation, occasionally limited the effectiveness of transformative learning within spiritual direction training.

The final three phases—provisional trying of new roles, building competence and self-confidence, and reintegration,[7]—appeared interwoven in participants' attempts to apply new insights within family, ministry, and church contexts. Although participants actively sought to embody their new perspectives, many noted the difficulty of contextualizing what they had learned upon returning to Chinese settings, due in part to limited cultural engagement within the program.

Although Mezirow's sixth phase—planning a course of action[8]—did not emerge as a discrete stage in this study, the data suggests that it

5. Mezirow, *Learning as Transformation.*

6. Mezirow, *Learning as Transformation.*

7. Mezirow, *Learning as Transformation.*

8. Mezirow, *Learning as Transformation.*

was implicitly integrated with other phases as participants continued to enact transformation throughout the program.

In sum, this research contributes a Confucian cultural dimension to Mezirow's transformative learning theory. As Mezirow observes, "culture can impede or facilitate the development of self-consciousness and the ability to make symbolic representations."[9] This study confirms that cultural frameworks profoundly shape each phase of transformative learning. Awareness of Confucian values, particularly hierarchy, shame, and performance orientation, is therefore essential for educators and practitioners seeking effective transformation among Chinese students.

Finally, this study highlights two components as especially critical for Chinese students: the reexamination of upbringing and the creation of a safe learning community. Participants' reflections reveal how deeply formative family and cultural influences shaped their spiritual development and how necessary it was to revisit those experiences within a supportive environment. While psychological safety and openness are important for learners across cultures, they are indispensable for those formed within contexts where emotional restraint and face-saving are normative.

Contributions to Spiritual Formation

This study also highlights the spiritual dimension of transformative learning and connects it to the discipline of spiritual formation. Educators engaged in spiritual formation may look to this research as an example of how transformative learning theory can be integrated into the process of spiritual growth. In this study, the Chinese adult learners entered the program after encountering significant life dilemmas that left them spiritually fatigued or disoriented. Through the program, transformation was facilitated by reexamining their upbringing, critically reflecting on assumptions, and exploring alternative perspectives. The effectiveness of this Western spiritual formation program among Chinese students offers valuable insight for educators seeking to incorporate transformative learning principles into spiritual formation curricula.

This research contributes a cultural lens to the study of spiritual formation by illuminating how Chinese believers experience spiritual growth. The findings indicate that many Chinese seminary students felt

9. Mezirow, *Transformative Dimensions*, 147.

spiritually stagnant and longed for a deeper knowledge of God prior to entering the program. Although most had been Christians and active church workers for more than a decade, they struggled with inner disorientation and shame related to their perceived lack of spiritual progress. Their shame-based cultural formation, which emphasizes the concealment of weakness through moral performance, played a major role in this struggle.

The Western spiritual formation program—integrating psychology, reflection on family of origin, emotional awareness, communal vulnerability, and spiritual disciplines—proved effective even for students shaped by Confucian values. Although cultural clashes rendered the process painful, the integration of these elements enabled participants to experience breakthroughs in spiritual growth. As traditional Chinese ideals and defense mechanisms were challenged, participants began to experience greater freedom as children of God. In this way, spiritual formation allowed them to look beneath cultural conditioning and attend more fully to the deeper work of the Holy Spirit in their inner lives.

A central contribution of this study is its illumination of how shame, moral perfectionism, and performance orientation shape the spiritual lives of Chinese Christians. Many participants testified that shame had permeated their sense of identity, rooted in early family and cultural conditioning. Thompson observed that "one measure of the abundance of his life was the degree to which he was liberated from his experience of shame. And for Paul, to be present with Christ meant to be absent from shame completely."[10] In this study, although participants expressed a desire for more explicit cultural teaching, the program's safe, trusting, and loving community proved to be the most powerful context for liberation from shame, an experience that can only be healed through honest exposure in the presence of grace.

In many Confucian-influenced families characterized by distant fathers and controlling mothers, children's authentic selves are often suppressed in order to conform to parental expectations. To survive within a hierarchical, collectivist culture that elevates moral exemplars, minimizes individual worth, and masks shame through performance, many Chinese individuals construct defensive façades—defining themselves by moral rectitude rather than relational authenticity. Yet as the findings reveal, the true self, created in the image of God, cannot remain buried

10. Thompson, *Anatomy of the Soul*, 195.

indefinitely. When fear, anxiety, and frustration are repressed, they frequently reemerge later as depression, anxiety, or burnout, even among church leaders.[11]

The study also demonstrates how upbringing within a shame-based culture profoundly influences Chinese Christians' perception of God. Many participants had internalized parental images of authority—strict, punitive, and conditional—and projected these onto God. As a result, they perceived God as distant or displeased and felt fundamentally unworthy of love. Shame thus permeated both their theology and their psychology. Because shame is self-reinforcing, it can only be dismantled within a safe, grace-filled community. The spiritual formation program's climate of acceptance played a decisive role in helping participants reimagine God as loving and present, transforming their spirituality from performance-driven striving to grace-grounded intimacy.

This insight is particularly valuable for Western educators and missionaries who serve among Chinese believers and may underestimate the cultural power of shame. It may also assist Chinese Christians themselves in recognizing the destructive mechanisms of shame operating within their own faith experience.

The research further contributes to understanding how emotional repression affects the spiritual lives of Chinese Christians. Because many have not been trained to recognize or express their emotions, they often struggle to integrate their feelings into their relationship with God. Since emotions communicate the movements of the soul, this disconnection can impede the transformative work of the Holy Spirit. The program helped students rediscover emotional awareness by guiding them to revisit and reexperience past wounds within a loving, Spirit-led environment.

Although some participants initially felt uncomfortable or "forced" to engage their emotions, they later recognized that this process enabled them to present their true selves honestly before God. This new congruence between emotion and faith fostered self-acceptance, deeper communion with God, and more authentic relationships with others. Spiritual formation thus emerges as a vital pathway for Chinese Christians, including pastors, missionaries, and lay leaders, to transcend cultural defenses and rediscover their true identity in Christ.

11. Williamson, "Stress or Burnout."

Finch observed that "you only become real if you go back and start where your real feelings are,"[12] emphasizing that authentic healing requires confronting childhood wounds, projections, defenses, and substitutionary realities "at an emotional level."[13] For Chinese believers, this recovery of genuine emotional awareness is indispensable for becoming the persons God created them to be. As Finch further argued, "unless this is done, there remains a heavy, unseen but felt pall that curtains us from all we attempt to do."[14] The findings of this research confirm that spiritual formation must engage this emotional depth if genuine transformation is to occur.

Finally, this study underscores the necessity of contextualizing spiritual formation for Chinese believers and theological institutions. Although the program examined here was situated within a Western conservative evangelical seminary offering robust theological training, the findings suggest that contextual adaptation is essential for spiritual formation to take root in Chinese contexts. Theology alone, without culturally sensitive formation practices, may fail to address the emotional and relational dimensions of faith most deeply shaped by Confucian cultural values.

PRACTICAL CONTRIBUTIONS

This section discusses the practical implications of the study for educators, seminaries, churches, and individuals.

For Transformative Learning Educators

This research offers insights to help Western educators better understand Chinese students shaped by Confucianism, particularly their heightened sensitivity to shame and fear of authority. The findings demonstrate that transformative learning, grounded in critical reflection and supported by a safe, trusting community, can effectively facilitate changes in meaning perspectives and foster holistic human development—the central aim of adult education. Accordingly, cultivating a safe and caring learning environment is essential when teaching Chinese learners.

12. Finch, *Intensive Therapy*, 32.
13. Finch, *Intensive Therapy*, 36.
14. Finch, *Intensive Therapy*, 32.

Although some Chinese students' creativity and critical reflection may appear underdeveloped due to their cultural formation, these capacities are not absent; rather, they remain latent, awaiting discovery within a nurturing context. Rather than interpreting silence as passivity, educators can attend to students' inner lives and provide space for thoughtful expression. Such an environment strengthens confidence and allows competence to emerge organically. While this process requires patience, it also embodies the heart of transformative learning: the mutual transformation of both educators and learners through increasingly empathetic and inclusive perspectives.

In addition, transformative learning educators must pursue cultural literacy. In an increasingly globalized educational landscape, classrooms are multicultural. Educators therefore benefit from developing familiarity with cultures beyond their own. Such awareness enriches not only Western transformative learning instructors but also Western spiritual formation educators and Chinese church leaders, who can learn from one another's strengths. Cross-cultural dialogue enhances mutual understanding and deepens the transformative learning process.

Finally, because learners shaped by Confucian traditions tend to flourish in collective settings, educators may prioritize communal classroom practices. Building community through group activities and shared reflection enables students from collectivist backgrounds to engage more fully. Viewing the classroom not merely as a gathering of individuals but as a learning community allows Confucian-background students to experience deeper and more sustainable transformation.

For Chinese Seminaries

Chinese seminaries are encouraged to integrate spiritual formation throughout the entirety of theological education, ensuring that knowledge moves from head to heart. Finch observed that seminary students often construct "defenses" within theological education, seeking approval from their "professorial authority figures."[15] He warned that, rather than encountering God "in the abyss," students may become preoccupied with grades and academic achievement, growing "weary of well-being and

15. Finch, *Intensive Therapy*, 38.

substitute for it more tangible ways of doing-well."[16] This study identified similar patterns within some Chinese seminaries.

Accordingly, integrating spiritual formation with theological study is vital for leading students toward dependence on God rather than reliance on academic performance. A holistic curriculum that intentionally balances theology, formation, and self-reflection can help prevent students from replacing spiritual vitality with intellectual accomplishment.

For Spiritual Formation Ministers

Spiritual formation may be practiced corporately and individually within the church. Corporately, it is important to appoint trained spiritual formation ministers or spiritual directors who can guide communities in spiritual disciplines and in sharing life struggles. Attentive to the Holy Spirit, these leaders should cultivate environments of trust, safety, and love in which believers may disclose vulnerabilities without fear of gossip or judgment.

Particular care should be taken to help Chinese believers grow in emotional awareness. In spiritual direction and mentoring relationships, ministers can assist believers in recognizing and naming emotions as an essential dimension of discernment and healing.

For Chinese Christians

Individual believers, including pastors and lay leaders, can be encouraged to practice a range of spiritual disciplines beyond Bible study. Disciplines such as silence, solitude, and rest, though countercultural and unfamiliar to many Chinese Christians, are especially beneficial. For example, church leaders might schedule one-day retreats free from ministry responsibilities, simply to pray, share meals, or enjoy creation without pressure to produce or perform.

Such practices help believers experience God's grace apart from achievement, cultivating receptivity rather than striving. While disciplines such as *lectio divina* and contemplative prayer can be practiced individually, spiritual direction or mentoring is strongly recommended, as many Chinese believers benefit from companionship and guidance in processing emotions and discerning God's presence.

16. Finch, *Intensive Therapy*, 38–39.

Ultimately, Chinese believers must recognize that spiritual formation is a lifelong journey, completed only when they meet God face to face. It is an ongoing process of "re-centering" and "re-focusing."[17] Conversion marks the beginning of life in Christ, not its culmination (Phil 1:6). Christians are not called to moral superiority or perfection but to continual transformation into Christ's likeness—humble, undefended, and free.[18] Though often painful, this process yields healing and freedom, leading believers toward the "double knowledge" of God and self.

For Chinese Parents

Traditional Confucian parenting frequently employs shame as a means of control. In light of this study's findings, parents are encouraged to attend not only to children's behavior but also to their emotional lives. As contemporary Chinese families experience increasingly enjoy material security, parents may invest greater time listening to their children without criticism or comparison, allowing them to express themselves honestly without fear of judgment.

Avoiding comparison mitigates shaming, while encouragement nurtures confidence and emotional health. When parents replace rigid expectations with unconditional acceptance, children experience a form of love that reflects God's own. To cultivate such parenting, however, parents must also confront their personal experiences of shame and rediscover their identity in Christ. In this way, parenting itself becomes a journey of spiritual growth for both parents and children.

FURTHER RESEARCH

This study examined Chinese students participating in a Western spiritual formation program. Future research may extend this inquiry in several directions. Scholars could explore how culturally sensitive components might be intentionally integrated into formation and training programs, particularly given that both transformative learning theory and spiritual formation have largely emerged from Western contexts. Comparative studies could also examine how spiritual formation functions in

17. Finch, *Intensive Therapy*, 39.

18. Finch, *Intensive Therapy*.

other non-Western settings, especially across Asian cultures influenced by Confucianism.

Researchers in psychology may investigate the psychological dimensions of spiritual formation among Chinese Christians. Several participants described enmeshment with maternal figures and noted how the program helped them develop emotional differentiation and personal voice. Future studies might explore how spiritual formation supports healthy attachment and emotional regulation within Chinese families.

Gender differences also warrant further investigation. Given persistent gender hierarchies within Chinese society, comparative studies of men's and women's experiences of spiritual formation may yield important insights. One participant additionally highlighted the role of spiritual warfare in his formation, suggesting a need for further exploration of how spiritual conflict intersects with transformation among Chinese believers. Because participants in this study were diaspora Chinese from diverse regions, future research could include regional or comparative studies among different Chinese populations, including those in mainland China. Age-related differences also merit examination, as participants ranged from twenty-five to fifty-five years old.

Finally, some participants observed that although the program was designed primarily for Western audiences and lacked explicit cultural sensitivity, it nevertheless proved transformative. Future studies might explore how non-Western learners navigate the tension between cultural dissonance and personal transformation. Are such learners able to sustain this tension due to graduate-level maturity, communal resilience, or other factors? Investigating this paradox may yield valuable insights into cross-cultural spiritual formation.

CONCLUSION

This study has contributed cultural and spiritual depth to the field of transformative learning and has introduced heightened awareness of Confucian values into the discipline of spiritual formation. With respect to transformative learning, the findings demonstrate that integrating cultural and spiritual awareness enables educators to guide learners more effectively by recognizing how Confucian traditions may inhibit critical self-reflection.

Within the domain of spiritual formation, the study identifies Confucianism as a central influence shaping Chinese self-understanding and spiritual experience. The Chinese students in this research shared openly about their transformative journeys within a Western program that invited them to reexamine their upbringing, confront deeply ingrained assumptions, and form new relationships with God, self, and others.

Through a loving community, guidance from expert professors, and experiential spiritual disciplines, participants who had entered the program burdened by spiritual exhaustion and life dilemmas experienced renewal. Over time, Confucian patterns of striving and performance gave way to lives increasingly guided by the Holy Spirit. Accordingly, this research makes both theoretical and practical contributions to transformative learning and spiritual formation by demonstrating how cultural awareness and divine grace together create the conditions for genuine, holistic transformation.

Appendix

Interview Protocol

Before beginning each interview, I briefly introduced myself, explained the purpose of the study, and reviewed confidentiality and consent. I then invited participants to share their experiences through the following questions:

1. Could you please tell me something about yourself and your family?
2. What led you to study in the spiritual formation program?
3. What were your expectations before you came to study in this program?
4. How would you describe your experience of studying in this program?
5. Looking back on your studies, how do you think this program affected you?
6. How has this program influenced your relationship with God (including God's image, love, grace, forgiveness, and awareness of God's presence in daily life)?
7. How has this program influenced your relationship with yourself (including self-identity, self-love, self-acceptance, and self-image)?
8. How has this program influenced your relationship with others (including family members, parents, siblings, relatives, friends, colleagues, pastors, church leaders, laypeople, and strangers)?
9. How do you think about ministry now that you have finished this program?

10. What do you think about your upbringing? What about Confucianism? (If the participant raised the topic, I invited them to elaborate.)
11. What are the components of this program? Which ones did you appreciate? Which ones did you dislike or struggle with? What made you struggle?
12. What would you tell another Chinese student who was considering this program?

Bibliography

Ames, Roger T. "Zhu Xi." *Encyclopaedia Britannica*, 2019. https://www.britannica.com/biography/Zhu-Xi.

Anderson, Neil, et al., eds. *Handbook of Industrial, Work, and Organizational Psychology*. Vol. 1. Personnel Psychology. Thousand Oaks, CA: Sage, 2002.

Augsburger, David W. *Pastoral Counseling Across Cultures*. Philadelphia: Westminster John Knox, 1986.

Averbeck, Richard E. "Spirit, Community, and Mission: A Biblical Theology for Spiritual Formation." *Journal of Spiritual Formation & Soul Care* 1 (2008) 27–53.

Barber, Betsy, and Chris Baker. "Soul Care and Spiritual Formation: An Old Call in Need of New Voices." *Journal of Spiritual Formation & Soul Care* 7 (2014) 270–83.

Barry, William A., and William J. Connolly. *The Practice of Spiritual Direction*. New York: HarperOne, 2009.

Beard, Christopher B. "Connecting Spiritual Formation and Adult Learning Theory: An Examination of Common Principles." *Christian Education Journal: Research on Education Ministry* 14 (2017) 247–69.

———. "Missional Discipleship and Adult Learning Theory: A Study of Missional Spiritual Formation Experiences and Their Connection to Adult Learning Principles." PhD diss., Northern Seminary, 2015. ProQuest Dissertations & Theses Global (10149234).

Beck, Sanderson. *Confucius and Socrates: Teaching Wisdom*. Goleta, CA: World Peace Communications, 2006. http://www.san.beck.org/C%26S-Contents.html.

Bedford, Olwen, and Kwang-Kuo Hwang. "Guilt and Shame in Chinese Culture: A Cross-Cultural Framework from the Perspective of Morality and Identity." *Journal for the Theory of Social Behaviour* 33 (2003) 127–44. https://doi.org/10.1111/1468-5914.00210.

Belenky, Mary Field, et al. *Women's Ways of Knowing: The Development of Self, Voice, and Mind*. New York: Basic, 1986.

Berthrong, John, and Evelyn N. Berthrong. *Confucianism: A Short Introduction*. London: Oneworld, 2000.

Bloesch, Donald G. *Spirituality Old and New: Recovering Authentic Spiritual Life*. Downers Grove, IL: IVP Academic, 2007.

Bond, Michael H. "Emotions and Their Expression in Chinese Culture." *Cognition and Emotion* 17 (1993) 245–62. https://doi.org/10.1007/BF00987240.

———. *The Psychology of the Chinese People*. Hong Kong: Oxford University Press, 1986.

Brock, Sabra E. "Measuring the Importance of Precursor Steps to Transformative Learning." *Adult Education Quarterly* 60 (2010) 122–42. https://doi.org/10.1177/0741713609333084.

Brookfield, Stephen D. "Engaging Critical Reflection in Corporate America." In *Transformative Learning in Practice*, edited by Jack Mezirow et al., 125–35. San Francisco: Jossey-Bass, 2009.

Calhoun, Adele Ahlberg. *Spiritual Disciplines Handbook: Practices That Transform Us*. Downers Grove, IL: InterVarsity, 2005.

Calvin, John. *Institutes of the Christian Religion*. Edited by John T. McNeill. Translated by Ford Lewis Battles. Louisville: Westminster John Knox, 2006.

Cha, Peter, and Grace May. "Gender Relations in Healthy Households." In *Growing Healthy Asian American Churches*, edited by Peter Cha et al., 164–82. Downers Grove, IL: InterVarsity, 2006.

Cha, Peter, et al., eds. *Growing Healthy Asian American Churches*. Downers Grove, IL: InterVarsity, 2006.

Chandler, Diane J. "African American Spirituality: Through Another Lens." *Journal of Spiritual Formation & Soul Care* 10 (2017) 159–81.

Charaniya, Nadira K. "Cultural-Spiritual Perspective of Transformative Learning." In *The Handbook of Transformative Learning: Theory, Research, and Practice*, edited by Edward W. Taylor and Patricia Cranton, 231–44. San Francisco: Jossey-Bass, 2012.

Charmaz, Kathy. *Constructing Grounded Theory*. 2nd ed. Thousand Oaks, CA: Sage, 2014.

———. "Grounded Theory: Objectivist and Constructivist Methods." In *The Handbook of Qualitative Research*, 2nd ed., edited by Norman K. Denzin and Yvonna S. Lincoln, 509–35. Thousand Oaks, CA: Sage, 2000. http://qualquant.org/wp-content/uploads/text/Charmaz%202000.pdf.

Chen, Peiying. "Empowering Identity Reconstruction of Indigenous College Students Through Transformative Learning." *Educational Review* 64 (2012) 161–80. https://doi.org/10.1080/00131911.2011.592574.

Chen, Xinyin. "Socio-Emotional Development in Chinese Children." In *The Oxford Handbook of Chinese Psychology*, edited by Michael H. Bond, 37–52. New York: Oxford University Press, 2010.

China Mike. "Confucius 101: Key to Understanding the Chinese Mind." May 1, 2024. http://www.china-mike.com/chinese-culture/understanding-chinese-mind/confucius/.

Ching, Jackson Chi Shun. "Helping English Pastors to Be More Culturally Sensitive in Canadian Chinese Churches." PhD diss., Tyndale University, 2017. ProQuest Dissertations & Theses Global (10274039).

Chittister, Joan. *The Rule of Benedict: Insights for the Ages*. New York: Crossroad, 1992.

Chua, Amy. *Battle Hymn of the Tiger Mother*. New York: Penguin, 2011.

Clark, Kenneth E., and Miriam B. Clark. *Choosing to Lead*. Greensboro, NC: Center for Creative Leadership, 1996.

Clinton, Timothy, and George Ohlschlager, eds. *Competent Christian Counseling*. Colorado Springs: WaterBrook, 2002.

Coe, John H. "The Call and Task of This Journal." *Journal of Spiritual Formation & Soul Care* 10 (2017) 138–40.

———. "Resisting the Temptation of Moral Formation: Opening to Spiritual Formation in the Cross of the Spirit." *Journal of Spiritual Formation & Soul Care* 1 (2008) 54–78.

———. "The Seven Deadly Disconnects of Seminary Training: Theological and Spiritual Formation Reflections on a Transformation Model." Unpublished manuscript, Biola University, 2005.

———. "Spiritual Disciplines and Retreat Musings." Class handout, Institute for Spiritual Formation, Biola University, 2000.

———. "Spiritual Theology: A Theological-Experiential Methodology for Bridging the Sanctification Gap." *Journal of Spiritual Formation & Soul Care* 2 (2009) 4–43.

———. "Spiritual Theology: When Psychology and Theology in the Spirit Service Faith." In *Psychology and Spiritual Formation in Dialogue*, edited by Thomas Crisp et al., 17–36. Downers Grove, IL: InterVarsity, 2019.

Coe, John H., and Todd W. Hall. *Psychology in the Spirit: Contours of a Transformational Psychology*. Downers Grove, IL: IVP Academic, 2010.

———. "A Transformational Psychology View." In *Psychology and Christianity: Five Views*, edited by Eric L. Johnson and David G. Myers, 199–244. Downers Grove, IL: IVP Academic, 2010.

Confucius. *Analects*. Translated by David Hinton. Berkeley, CA: Counterpoint, 2014.

———. *Analects of Confucius* [Lunyu]. Translated by A. Charles Muller, Dec. 1, 2021. http://www.acmuller.net/con-dao/analects.html#div-4.

———. *Understanding the Analects of Confucius: A New Translation of Lunyu with Annotations*. Translated by Peimin Ni. Albany: State University of New York Press, 2017.

Corbin, Juliet, and Anselm Strauss. *Basics of Qualitative Research: Techniques and Procedures for Developing Grounded Theory*. 3rd ed. Los Angeles: Sage, 2007.

Cranton, Patricia. *Understanding and Promoting Transformative Learning: A Guide for Educators of Adults*. 2nd ed. San Francisco: Jossey-Bass, 2006.

———. *Understanding and Promoting Transformative Learning: A Guide to Theory and Practice*. 3rd ed. Sterling, VA: Stylus, 2016.

Cranton, Patricia, and Edward W. Taylor. "Transformative Learning Theory: Seeking a More Unified Theory." In *The Handbook of Transformative Learning*, edited by Edward W. Taylor and Patricia Cranton, 3–20. San Francisco: Jossey-Bass, 2012.

Cranton, Patricia, and Merv Roy. "When the Bottom Falls Out of the Bucket: Toward A Holistic Perspective on Transformative Learning." *Journal of Transformative Education* 1 (2003) 86–98.

Creswell, John W. *Research Design: Qualitative, Quantitative, and Mixed Methods Approaches*. 4th ed. Thousand Oaks, CA: Sage, 2014.

Demarest, Bruce A. *Seasons of the Soul: Stages of Spiritual Development*. Downers Grove, IL: InterVarsity, 2009.

Dirkx, John M. "Images, Transformative Learning and the Work of Soul." *Adult Learning* 12 (2001) 15–16.

———. "Nurturing Soul Work: A Jungian Approach to Transformative Learning." In *The Handbook of Transformative Learning*, edited by Edward W. Taylor and Patricia Cranton, 116–30. San Francisco: Jossey-Bass, 2012.

———. "The Power of Feelings: Emotion, Imagination and the Construction of Meaning in Adult Learning." *New Directions for Adult and Continuing Education* 89 (Spring 2001) 63–72.

———. "Transformative Learning Theory in the Practice of Adult Education: An Overview." *PAACE Journal of Lifelong Learning* 7 (1998) 1–14.

Dzubinski, Leanne M. "Distance Interviews in Qualitative Research: Some Reflections on Technology-Assisted Qualitative Data Collection (TAQDAC)." In *Technology and Christian Faithfulness*, edited by Ruth Langer and Michael Jenson, 59–76. North Charleston, SC: CreateSpace Independent Publishing Platform, 2018.

Edwards, Jonathan, and James M. Houston. *Religious Affections: A Christian's Character before God*. Vancouver, BC: Regent College, 2003.

Encyclopaedia Britannica. "Xiao | Confucianism." https://www.britannica.com/topic/xiao-Confucianism.

English, Leona M., and Elizabeth J. Tisdell. "Spirituality and Adult Education." In *Handbook of Adult and Continuing Education*, edited by Carol E. Kasworm, Amy D. Rose, and Jovita M. Ross-Gordon, 285–94. Los Angeles: Sage, 2010.

Ettling, Dorothy. "Educator as Change Agent: Ethics of Transformative Learning." In *The Handbook of Transformative Learning*, edited by Edward W. Taylor and Patricia Cranton, 536–51. San Francisco: Jossey-Bass, 2012.

Finch, John G. *Intensive Therapy and the Three Ways*. Pasadena, CA: Integration, 1989.

Fingarette, Herbert. *Confucius: The Secular as Sacred*. Long Grove, IL: Waveland, 1998.

Forrester, Gillian, et al. "Transforming Chinese Teachers' Thinking, Learning and Understanding via E-Learning." *Journal of Education for Teaching* 32 (2006) 197–212. https://doi.org/10.1080/02607470600655276.

Foster, Richard J. *Celebration of Discipline: The Path to Spiritual Growth*. San Francisco: HarperSanFrancisco, 1998.

Freeburg, Karen Walker. "Nurturing Spiritual Formation Among American Baptist Churches USA Students at Northern Baptist Seminary Through Small Group Process." Dissertation, Northern Baptist Theological Seminary, 2002. https://www.worldcat.org/title/nurturing-spiritual-formation-among-american-baptist-churches-usa-students-at-northern-baptist-seminary-through-small-group-process/oclc/61356973.

Fung, Heidi. "Becoming a Moral Child: The Socialization of Shame Among Young Chinese Children." *Ethos* 27 (1999) 180–209. https://doi.org/10.1525/eth.1999.27.2.180.

Fung, Heidi, et al. "Parental Beliefs About Shame and Moral Socialization in Taiwan, Hong Kong, and the United States." In *Progress in Asian Social Psychology: Conceptual and Empirical Contributions*, edited by Kuo-Shu Yang et al., 83–109. Westport, CT: Praeger/Greenwood, 2003.

Gill, Scherto. "Overseas Students' Intercultural Adaptation as Intercultural Learning: A Transformative Framework." *Compare: A Journal of Comparative Education* 37 (2007) 167–83. https://doi.org/10.1080/03057920601165512.

Glisczinski, Daniel J. "Transformative Higher Education: A Meaningful Degree of Understanding." *Journal of Transformative Education* 5 (2007) 317–38. https://doi.org/10.1177/1541344607312838.

Goldin, Paul R. *Confucianism*. New York: Routledge, 2014.

Greenman, Jeffrey P., and George Kalantzis, eds. *Life in the Spirit: Spiritual Formation in Theological Perspective*. Downers Grove, IL: IVP Academic, 2010.

Grudem, Wayne A. *Systematic Theology: An Introduction to Biblical Doctrine*. Grand Rapids: Zondervan, 1994.

Guenther, Margaret, and Alan Jones. *Holy Listening: The Art of Spiritual Direction.* Cambridge, MA: Cowley, 1992.

Gunnlaugson, Olen. "Metatheoretical Prospects for the Field of Transformative Learning." *Journal of Transformative Education* 6 (2008) 124–35.

Hall, Christopher A. "Historical Theology and Spiritual Formation: A Response." *Journal of Spiritual Formation & Soul Care* 7 (2014) 210–19.

———. *Learning Theology with the Church Fathers.* Downers Grove, IL: IVP Academic, 2002.

Hindmarsh, D. Bruce. "Contours of Evangelical Spirituality." *Journal of Spiritual Formation & Soul Care* 10 (2017) 195–206.

Hofstede, Geert. *Culture's Consequences: Comparing Values, Behaviors, Institutions, and Organizations Across Nations.* Thousand Oaks, CA: Sage, 2001.

———. *Culture's Consequences: International Differences in Work-Related Values.* Newbury Park, CA: Sage, 1984.

Hofstede, Geert, and Gert Jan Hofstede. *Cultures and Organizations: Software of the Mind—Intercultural Cooperation and Its Importance for Survival.* London: McGraw-Hill, 2004.

Holm, Neil. "Identity Formation Through Classroom Conversations and Collaboration with the Spirit." *Journal of Christian Education* 50 (2007) 45–54. https://doi.org/10.1177/002196570705000206.

Horney, Karen. *Neurosis and Human Growth: The Struggle Toward Self-Realization.* New York: Norton, 1991.

Houston, James M. "Living Through a Decade of Fluidity: The Future of 'Soul Care.'" *Journal of Spiritual Formation & Soul Care* 10 (2017) 141–46.

Howard, Evan B. "Advancing the Discussion: Reflections on the Study of Christian Spiritual Life." *Journal of Spiritual Formation & Soul Care* 1 (2008) 8–26.

Hu, Wenzhong, et al. *Encountering the Chinese: A Modern Country, an Ancient Culture.* 3rd ed. Boston: Intercultural, 2010.

Huang, Yenlan Sarah. "Evaluating the Effectiveness of the Spiritual Formation Curriculum for Seminary Students in Central Taiwan Theological Seminary." PhD diss., Central Taiwan Theological Seminary, 2012. Theological Research Exchange Network (TREN) Theses & Dissertations (97196040).

Jackson, Jane. *Introducing Language and Intercultural Communication.* London: Routledge, 2014.

Jamieson, Philip D. *The Face of Forgiveness: A Pastoral Theology of Shame and Redemption.* Downers Grove, IL: InterVarsity, 2016.

Janov, Arthur. *The Primal Scream: Primal Therapy—the Cure for Neurosis.* New York: G. P. Putnam's Sons, 1980.

Jao, Greg. "Relating to Others—Understanding Yourself." In *Following Jesus Without Dishonoring Your Parents*, edited by Jeanette Yep et al., 17–30. Downers Grove, IL: InterVarsity, 1998.

Jiang, Dengxing. "Zhongguo Jiaohui de Zhuanzhizhuyi Weiji [The crisis of despotism in Chinese churches]." *Church China* 2 (Nov. 2006). https://churchchina.org/archives/061101.html.

Kang, S. Steve. "Truth-Embodying Households." In *Growing Healthy Asian American Churches*, edited by Peter Cha et al., 39–57. Downers Grove, IL: IVP, 2006.

Kavanaugh, Kieran. *John of the Cross: Selected Writings.* New York: Paulist, 1987.

Keely, Barbara A. "Spiritual Formation for Ordained Ministry: An Ecumenical Approach." *Teaching Theology & Religion* 6 (2003) 202–10. https://doi.org/10.1111/1467-9647.00176.

Knowles, Malcolm S. *The Modern Practice of Adult Education: From Pedagogy to Andragogy*. New York: Cambridge, 1980.

Knowles, Malcolm S., et al. *The Adult Learner: The Definitive Classic in Adult Education and Human Resource Development*. 6th ed. Burlington, MA: Elsevier, 2005.

Koenig, Harold G., et al. *Handbook of Religion and Health*. Oxford: Oxford University Press, 2001.

Küng, Hans, and Julia Ching. *Christianity and Chinese Religions*. New York: Doubleday, 1989.

Langer, Rick C. "Points of Unease with the Spiritual Formation Movement." *Journal of Spiritual Formation & Soul Care* 5 (2012) 182–206.

Lee, Helen. "Healthy Leaders, Healthy Households, Part 1: Challenges and Models." In *Growing Healthy Asian American Churches*, edited by Peter Cha et al., 58–76. Downers Grove, IL: InterVarsity, 2006.

Lee, Haesung. "Neo-Confucianism of Joseon Dynasty—Its Theoretical Foundation and Main Issues." *Asian Studies* 4 (2016) 165–94. https://doi.org/10.4312/as.2016.4.1.165-194.

Lee, KangHack. *Christian Spiritual Direction for a Confucian Culture: A Korean Perspective*. PhD diss., Graduate Theological Union, 2009. https://www.proquest.com/docview/304889666.

Levi, Nicolas. "Confucianism in South Korea and Japan: Similarities and Differences." *Acta Asiatica Varsoviensia* 26 (2013) 185–93.

Lewis, John. "Redefining Qualitative Methods: Believability in the Fifth Moment." *International Journal of Qualitative Methods* 8 (2009) 1–14.

Liao, Yiwu. *God Is Red: The Secret Story of How Christianity Survived and Flourished in Communist China*. New York: HarperOne, 2011.

Lieber, Eli, et al. "Chinese Child-Rearing Beliefs: Key Dimensions and Contributions to the Development of Culture-Appropriate Assessment." *Asian Journal of Social Psychology* 9 (2006) 140–47. https://doi.org/10.1111/j.1467-839X.2006.00191.x.

Liefeld, Walter, and Linda M. Cannel. "Spiritual Formation and Theological Education." In *Alive to God: Studies in Spirituality*, edited by J. I. Packer et al., 239–52. Downers Grove, IL: InterVarsity, 1992.

Liu, Qingping. "May One Murder the Innocent for the Sake of Faith in God or Filial Piety to Parents?: A Comparative Study of Abraham's and Guo's Stories." *Asian Philosophy* 27 (2017) 43–58.

Livermore, David A. *Cultural Intelligence: Improving Your CQ to Engage Our Multicultural World*. Grand Rapids: Baker Academic, 2009.

MacEwen, Lisa Grace. "The Impact of a Contextualized Spiritual Formation Strategy for Korean Christians." PhD diss., Regent University, 2015. ProQuest Dissertations Publishing (bio.b2179435).

Mason, Mary Elizabeth. *Active Life and Contemplative: A Study of the Concepts from Plato to the Present*. Milwaukee, WI: Marquette University Press, 1961.

McCombe, Leonard, et al. *Navaho Means People*. Cambridge, MA: Harvard University Press, 1952.

McDonald, Paul. "Confucian Foundations to Leadership: A Study of Chinese Business Leaders Across Greater China and South-East Asia." *Asia Pacific Business Review* 18 (2012) 465–82. https://doi.org/10.1080/13602381.2012.693770.

McGrath, Joanna C. *The Psychology of Christian Character Formation*. London: SCM, 2015.

McGreal, Ian P., and John K. Roth. "I Ching." Salem Press Biographical Encyclopedia, 2019. https://searchworks.stanford.edu/articles/ers__89876436.

McMinn, Lisa G. "Perceiving the Cultural Sea That Is Our Home—Spiritual Formation and Western Twenty-First-Century Culture." *Journal of Spiritual Formation & Soul Care* 10 (2017) 147–58.

Merriam, Sharan B. *Non-Western Perspectives on Learning and Knowing*. Malabar, FL: Krieger, 2007.

Merriam, Sharan B., and Elizabeth J. Tisdell. *Qualitative Research: A Guide to Design and Implementation*. 4th ed. San Francisco: Jossey-Bass, 2016.

Merriam, Sharan B., and Laura L. Bierema. *Adult Learning: Linking Theory and Practice*. San Francisco: Jossey-Bass, 2014.

Merriam, Sharan B., et al. "Power and Positionality: Negotiating Insider/Outsider Status Within and Across Cultures." *International Journal of Lifelong Education* 20 (2001) 405–16. https://doi.org/10.1080/02601370120490.

Mezirow, Jack. "Concept and Action in Adult Education." *Adult Education Quarterly* 35 (1985) 142–51. https://doi.org/10.1177/0001848185035003003.

———. "A Critical Theory of Self-Directed Learning." In *Self-Directed Learning: From Theory to Practice*, edited by Stephen Brookfield, 17–30. New Directions for Continuing Education 25. San Francisco: Jossey-Bass, 1985.

———. *Learning as Transformation: Critical Perspectives on a Theory in Progress*. San Francisco: Jossey-Bass, 2000.

———. "Perspective Transformation." *Adult Education* 28 (1978) 100–110.

———. *Transformative Dimensions of Adult Learning*. San Francisco: Jossey-Bass, 1991.

———. "Transformative Theory Out of Context." *Adult Education Quarterly* 48 (1997) 60–62.

———. "Understanding Transformation Theory." *Adult Education Quarterly* 44 (1994) 222–32.

Mezirow, Jack, and Edward W. Taylor, eds. *Transformative Learning in Practice: Insights from Community, Workplace, and Higher Education*. San Francisco: Jossey-Bass, 2009.

Miller, Kara. "Keeping the Faith in Seminary." *Christianity Today* 60 (2016) 87–104.

Miller, Peggy J., et al. "Narrative Practices and the Social Construction of Self in Childhood." *American Ethnologist* 17 (1990) 292–311. http://www.jstor.org/stable/645081.

Morrell, Amish, and Mary O'Connor. "Introduction." In *Expanding the Boundaries of Transformative Learning*, edited by Edmund V. O'Sullivan et al., xv–xx. New York: Palgrave, 2002.

Newman, Michael. "Calling Transformative Learning into Question: Some Mutinous Thoughts." *Adult Education Quarterly* 62 (2012) 36–55.

Ng, Annie Yi Jung Pan. "Ignatius' Spiritual Exercises and Chinese Women's Spiritual Formation in the Hong Kong Protestant Evangelical Context." *Spiritus* 14 (2014) 187–207.

Ng, Florrie Fei-Yin, et al. "Immigrant Chinese Mothers' Socialization of Achievement in Children: A Strategic Adaptation to the Host Society." *Child Development* 88 (2017) 979–95.

Nichols, Ryan. "Civilizing Humans with Shame: How Early Confucians Altered Inherited Evolutionary Norms Through Cultural Programming to Increase Social Harmony." *Journal of Cognition and Culture* 15 (2015) 254–84. https://doi.org/10.1163/15685373-12342150.

Nisbett, Richard E. *The Geography of Thought: How Asians and Westerners Think Differently . . . and Why*. New York: Free Press, 2004.

Nouwen, Henri J. M. *In the Name of Jesus: Reflections on Christian Leadership*. New York: Crossroad, 1992.

Onsman, Andrys. "Recognizing the Ordinances of Heaven: The Role of Confucianism in Higher Education Management in the People's Republic of China." *Journal of Higher Education Policy & Management* 34 (2012) 169–84. https://doi.org/10.1080/1360080X.2012.662741.

O'Sullivan, Edmund. "Deep Transformation: Forging a Planetary Worldview." In *The Handbook of Transformative Learning*, edited by Edward W. Taylor and Patricia Cranton, 162–77. San Francisco: Jossey-Bass, 2012.

Pennington, James M. "The Dynamics of Contextualized Spiritual Formation for the Educated Urban Chinese Christian of Yunnan: A Case Study." PhD diss., Regent University, 2009. ProQuest Dissertations Publishing (UMI 3388396).

Pocock, Michael, et al. *The Changing Face of World Missions: Engaging Contemporary Issues and Trends*. Grand Rapids: Baker Academic, 2005.

Porter, Steve L. "Sanctification in a New Key: Relieving Evangelical Anxieties over Spiritual Formation." *Journal of Spiritual Formation & Soul Care* 1 (2008) 129–48.

Poston, Dudley L., and Juyin H. Wong. "The Chinese Diaspora: The Current Distribution of the Overseas Chinese Population." *Chinese Journal of Sociology* 2 (2016) 348–73. https://doi.org/10.1177/2057150X16655077.

Quen, Stephen. "Reaching and Retaining American-Born Asian Millennials at Bay Area Chinese Bible Church." PhD diss., Western Seminary, 2018. ProQuest Dissertations & Theses Global (13420724).

Ralston, David A., et al. "Doing Business in the Twenty-First Century with the New Generation of Chinese Managers: A Study of Generational Shifts in Work Values in China." *Journal of International Business Studies* 30 (1999) 415–27.

Reagan, Timothy. *Non-Western Educational Traditions: Indigenous Approaches to Educational Thought and Practice*. 3rd ed. Mahwah, NJ: Routledge, 2004.

Reed, Angela H., et al. *Spiritual Companioning: A Guide to Protestant Theology and Practice*. Grand Rapids: Baker Academic, 2015.

Ritchlin, Sheri. "The Oneness (and One-ing) of the Way Using Both Hemispheres of the Global Mind." *ReVision* 31 (2010) 22–28.

Ro, Jonathan Calvin. "Globalization's Impact on the Urban Church in China: A Multiple Case-Study of Four Churches in a Major Urban Center." PhD diss., Trinity International University, 2013. ProQuest Dissertations Publishing (UMI 3590556).

Roberts, J. J. M. "Seminaries, 'Spirituality,' and 'Spiritual Formation.'" *Christian Studies Journal* 20 (2004) 43–50.

Russell, Patricia, et al. "Making Disciples of All Nations: Spiritual Formation Education and Training Experience for Chinese Women Leaders." *Journal of Spiritual Formation & Soul Care* 11 (2018) 182–200. https://doi.org/10.1177/1939790918796835.

Scorgie, Glen. "Overview of Christian Spirituality." In *Dictionary of Christian Spirituality*, edited by Glen Scorgie et al., 27–33. Grand Rapids: Zondervan, 2011.

Sheard, Reed A. "The Role of Spiritual Formation in the Development of Religious Leaders at George Fox Evangelical Seminary." PhD diss., George Fox Evangelical Seminary, 2004. ProQuest Dissertations Publishing (UMI 3159531).

Sheldrake, Philip. "Christian Spirituality and Social Transformation." *Oxford Research Encyclopedia of Religion*, 2016. https://doi.org/10.1093/acrefore/9780199340378.013.231.

Shin, Benjamin C., and Sheryl T. Silzer. *Tapestry of Grace: Untangling the Cultural Complexities in Asian American Life and Ministry*. Eugene, OR: Wipf & Stock, 2016.

Silver, Anne W. *Trustworthy Connections: Interpersonal Issues in Spiritual Direction*. Cambridge, MA: Cowley, 2004.

Sittser, Gerald L., and Eugene H. Peterson. *Water from a Deep Well: Christian Spirituality from Early Martyrs to Modern Missionaries*. Downers Grove, IL: InterVarsity, 2007.

Smith, Gordon T. "Generation to Generation: Inter-Generationality and Spiritual Formation in Christian Community." *Journal of Spiritual Formation & Soul Care* 10 (2017) 182–93.

Spiritual Directors International. "About Us." http://www.sdiworld.org/about-us.

Stark, Rodney, et al. "Counting China's Christians: There Are as Many Christians in China as There Are Members of the Communist Party." *First Things: A Monthly Journal of Religion and Public Life* 213 (2011) 14–16.

Sugikawa, Nancy, and Steve Wong. "Grace-Filled Households." In *Growing Healthy Asian American Churches*, edited by Peter Cha et al., 19–38. Downers Grove, IL: InterVarsity, 2006.

Taylor, Edward W. "Transformative Learning Theory." In *Third Update on Adult Learning Theory*, edited by Sharan B. Merriam, 5–16. New Directions for Adult and Continuing Education 119. San Francisco: Jossey-Bass, 2008.

Taylor, Rodney L. *The Religious Dimensions of Confucianism*. Albany: State University of New York Press, 1990.

TenElshof, Judith K., and James L. Furrow. "The Role of Secure Attachment in Predicting Spiritual Maturity of Students at a Conservative Seminary." *Journal of Psychology & Theology* 28 (2000) 99–108.

Thompson, Curt. *Anatomy of the Soul: Surprising Connections Between Neuroscience and Spiritual Practices That Can Transform Your Life and Relationships*. Carol Stream, IL: Salt River, 2010.

———. *The Soul of Shame: Retelling the Stories We Believe About Ourselves*. Downers Grove, IL: IVP, 2015.

Thong, Chan-Kei, and Charlene L. Fu. *Finding God in Ancient China*. Grand Rapids: Zondervan, 2009.

Tisdell, Elizabeth J. *Exploring Spirituality and Culture in Adult and Higher Education*. San Francisco: Jossey-Bass, 2003.

———. "Spirituality in Adult and Higher Education." ERIC Digest, identifier ED459370. Columbus, OH: ERIC Clearinghouse on Adult, Career, and Vocational Education, 2001.

Tokunaga, Paul. "Pressure, Perfectionism and Performance." In *Following Jesus Without Dishonoring Your Parents*, edited by Jeanette Yep et al., 17–30. Downers Grove, IL: InterVarsity, 1998.

Van Dragt, Bryan. "Paranormal Healing: A Phenomenology of the Healer's Experience." PhD diss., Fuller Theological Seminary, 1980. ProQuest Dissertations Publishing (UMI 8107422).

Wang, Robin. "Dong Zhongshu's Transformation of 'Yin-Yang' Theory and Contesting of Gender Identity." *Philosophy East and West* 55 (2005) 209–31.

Warner, Larry. *Journey with Jesus: Discovering the Spiritual Exercises of Saint Ignatius.* Downers Grove, IL: InterVarsity, 2010.

Wilhelm, Hellmut, and Cary F. Baynes. *The I Ching; or Book of Changes*. Princeton, NJ: Princeton University Press, 1976.

Willard, Dallas. *The Divine Conspiracy: Rediscovering Our Hidden Life in God.* San Francisco: HarperSanFrancisco, 1998.

Williamson, Natalie. "A Quantitative Research Study Analyzing Responses or Reactions of Personal and Professional Stress-Related Factors That Can Lead to Ministry Stress or Burnout in Chinese Pastors." PhD diss., University of the Rockies, 2011. ProQuest Dissertations Publishing (UMI 3459848).

Worldometers. "China Population (2018)—Worldometers." http://www.worldometers.info/world-population/china-population/.

Wright, Arthur F., and Denis C. Twitchett. *Confucian Personalities.* Stanford, CA: Stanford University Press, 1962.

Wu, Zhen. "Service to Heaven and Reverence for Heaven: Religious Concerns of Four Marginal Confucians in the Late Ming and Early Qing Dynasties." *Tsing Hua Journal of Chinese Studies* 39 (2009) 125–63.

Xu, Xiaoqun. "The Dilemma of Accommodation: Reconciling Christianity and Chinese Culture in the 1920s." *Historian* 60 (1997) 21–33.

Yang, Fenggang. *Chinese Christians in America: Conversion, Assimilation, and Adhesive Identities.* University Park, PA: Pennsylvania State University Press, 1999.

Yep, Jeanette, et al. *Following Jesus Without Dishonoring Your Parents.* Downers Grove, IL: InterVarsity, 1998.

Zhang, Maoze. "Confucius' Transformation of Traditional Religious Ideas." *Frontiers of Philosophy in China* 6 (2011) 20–40.

Zhao, Yanxia. *Father and Son in Confucianism and Christianity: A Comparative Study of Xunzi and Paul.* Brighton, UK: Sussex Academic, 2007.

www.ingramcontent.com/pod-product-compliance
Lightning Source LLC
LaVergne TN
LVHW050616100826
845148LV00011B/1614

* 9 7 9 8 3 8 5 2 6 6 1 9 7 *